D0204391

Understanding Violence

SECOND EDITION

Understanding Violence

SECOND EDITION

Elizabeth Kandel Englander
Bridgewater State College

LEA LAWRENCE ERLBAUM ASSOCIATES, PUBLISHERS
2003   Mahwah, New Jersey   London

Lawrence Erlbaum Associates, Inc., Publishers
10 Industrial Avenue
Mahwah, NJ 07430

LIBRARY OF CONGRESS CATALOGING-IN-PUBLICATION DATA

Englander, Elizabeth Kandel.
    Understanding violence / by Elizabeth Kandel Englander.—2nd ed.
      p.   cm.
    Includes bibliographical references and index.
    ISBN 0–8058–3629–2 (cloth) — ISBN 0–8058–3630–6 (pbk.)
    1. Violent crimes—United States. 2. Violent crimes—United States—Psychological aspects. 3. Criminal psychology—United States. 4. Violence—United States. I. Title.
HV6789 .E54 2002
364.1'5'0973—dc21   2002022514

For Michael and my own Little Men—
And all the Little Men in the world

Contents

Preface

This book was conceived of in a simpler era—B.S.E. (Before September Eleventh). Then, in 1993 B.S.E., the worst problems our nation faced were a spate of violent crimes. I did not know then, as I do now, that the violent crime rate in the United States would peak and begin to decline after 1994.

Since that time, however, new years have brought new problems. School shootings, a crime inconceivable in 1993, were all too common by 1998. And although the menace of terrorism existed abroad in 1993, here at home it was still a distant bell.

The first edition of this book dealt with the causes of crime across a broad range of fields. My good fortune, and a good deal of dumb luck, enabled me to study the causes of violence in such diverse areas as biology, sociology, and psychiatry. Having worked with professionals from all those fields, I was struck by their lack of coordination and the limited understanding many professionals bring to the wide range of knowledge about what causes violence. In 1993 I was teaching a course called the Psychology of Criminal Behavior (a course I still teach) with no text available that spanned the breadth of the fields that contributed to our knowledge about crime, violent crime in particular. On a walk with me, my husband could have let me gripe. Instead he pointed out this niche and sensibly suggested that I fill it.

More than 8 years after I first put pen to paper for the first edition, the second edition is now completed and spans the breadth of different fields even more effectively, I think, than before. My goals remain unchanged. I am convinced that violence is a relentlessly self-destructive human behavior that may be justifiable at the individual level, but makes no sense from the standpoint of human society in general. The causes of violence, however, are endlessly complex—everything makes sense, as I think you will find when you read this book, but nothing is as simple as it appears at first. What causes one man to be violent is like a house of cards: His problems must be stacked up just so, in a particular order, with great complexity and great simplicity. Students who used the first edition often tell me how deceptive understanding violence really is: Listen to the explanation of a theory and it seems straightforward—until you apply it to a case, or until you try to mesh it with another theory. Then the complexity reveals itself.

Despite this, the solutions are not difficult or obtuse. Human beings *can* make a difference. We do not *need* to be violent. We need to learn to help each other live with as much dignity and comfort as possible. Why we have such a difficult time achieving what should be a simple goal is perhaps the most complex lesson of all. In any case, my hope is that by making as many people as possible begin to understand what causes this behavior in human beings, we may be able to eradicate it.

ACKNOWLEDGMENTS

Many of the people I would like to thank for making this book possible are predictable. My graduate school advisor, Dr. Sarnoff Mednick, was especially valuable to me during my doctoral training. Dr. David Finkelhor was, and still is, an inspiration to me through his diligence and hard work to end human suffering through productive research. My editor, Susan Milmoe, always works hard with me and has helped my writing tremendously. I could not have accomplished these books without her help. My father, Stephen Kandel, has always offered up a good argument and is a very real source of intellectual light.

However, as with my first edition, the lion's share of the credit must go to my husband Michael, who proves the adage that marrying the right person can make you the better human being you were meant to be. The keenness of his intellect, his enduring patience, his wry sense of humor, and his utter confidence in my abilities have kept me going more than once. Plus, he even goes to the market.

Finally, this book is for my Little Men—my three sons, Joshua, Nicholas, and Max—who rattle happily and noisily through life, and who have taught me that the only perfect love in this life is little arms around your neck. I hope that one day they do not even understand why such a book needed to be written.

—Elizabeth Kandel Englander

Chapter 1

Introduction:
The Problem of Violence

Good evening. Add Conyers, Georgia, to the list of high schools where a young gunman has caused chaos. Another school, another shooting. Six people wounded this time.

—Peter Jennings, ABC News, *World News Tonight With Peter Jennings*, May 20, 1999

In Texas, a young woman is shot to death outside the elementary school where she taught. Her killer was her former boyfriend, who was able to commit the homicide because he was freed on bail earlier in the month, after he had put a gun to her head and tried to kill her once before.

—Associated Press (1995, May 25)

In 1651, English philosopher Thomas Hobbes wrote with despair that most human beings had "... No arts, no letters, no society, and which is worst of all, continual fear and danger of violent death, and the life of man solitary, poor, nasty, brutish, and short" (p. 2). A grim view of life, and not one that most of us in the First World at the turn of the 21st century share. Modern life holds many pleasures, and today the 17th-century world of Hobbes is as foreign to us as living on the moon. However, for all our progress, some social problems remain intractable. One in particular affects all human beings. *Violence* is a behavior that has little or no equal. Present in the caves, tens of thousands of years ago, it has survived every human society's attempt to eradicate it. Despite its burdensome costs and its almost unique ability to promote acute human misery, violence persists, and we have not been able to solve this most basic of human problems.

Of course, not all violence is the same. In general, *violence* is aggressive behavior with the intent to cause harm (physical or psychological). The word *intent* is central; physical or psychological harm that occurs by accident, in the absence of intent, is not violence. Even our legal system recognizes the critical role that *intent* plays. If you deliberately plot to kill someone, and succeed, you will be charged with *murder;* conviction can imprison you for life or even sentence you to execution. On the other hand, if you kill someone by accident, you typically would be charged with *manslaughter,* a less serious offense that, in some cases, does not even warrant imprisonment.

The understanding that all violence is not the same encompasses the issue of motivation, not just intent. Certainly, human beings are not the only animals who are violent—almost any animal, including an insect, can deliberately inflict harm. The difference between human aggression and the aggression of other animals seems to lie in motivation. Although any animal can engage in *instrumental aggression* (aggression that has as its purpose the achievement of a separate goal), only humans engage in *hostile aggression* (aggression performed for the purpose of harming the victim). For example, hitting a woman over the head in order to steal her purse is instrumental aggression. The motive is not ultimately to harm, but to gain the purse. The extent of her injuries may affect what the offender is ultimately charged with, but psychologically it does not affect the motivation for the violence. Of course, one always hopes for no, or at most minor, injuries, but even if a victim is ultimately killed for the purpose of getting her purse, the motivation remains instrumental.

This distinction may seem heartless, but in terms of understanding what causes violence it is important. An instrumental motive should not and does not imply that it is insignificant if the consequences of violence are damaging or lethal. It is always horrible if a purse-snatching victim dies. Nevertheless, it is important to understand whether the motive was instrumental or hostile, because *hostile aggression* appears to involve significantly different causes and risk factors. In general, hostile aggression more closely fits our definition of *violence:* It is performed for the purpose of harming (physically or psychologically) another person. Human beings and other animals differ in their use of *hostile* versus *instrumental* aggression. Whereas human beings engage in both types of aggression, other animals primarily, if not exclusively, engage in instrumental aggression. They may use threats of violence to psychologically intimidate a competitor, but these threats are made for an instrumental purpose: to gain what the competitor is also seeking (as in competition for a mate; Bandura, 1989).

Mawson (1999) proposed a new, third type of violence that might be called *impulsive* or *stimulus-seeking* violence. He pointed out that a violent offender does not always wish, or intend, to harm his victim. Rather, much violence is impulsive and/or the offender may be seeking intense sensory stimulation (Mawson, 1999). This theory is consistent with findings emerging from two major areas of research. First, that some violent offenders are indeed impulsive stimulus-seekers, that is, individuals who constantly crave dangerous and risky situations because of chronic nervous system underarousal (Raine, 1997a), and second, that many violent crimes are committed while under the influence of drugs or alcohol, which are behaviors also common among those who are impulsively seeking intense stimulation (Mueller, Wilczynski, Moore, Fusilier, & Trahant, 2001). A new study (Houston & Stanford, 2001) did indeed find that some violent offenders do appear to be impulsive people with extremely quick, hot tempers who become violent in response to minor problems that would not provoke most people.

Family violence is hostile aggression between people who are intimately involved with each other. By traditional definition, this has meant those who are married or related to one another; in current practice, the term refers to all those who are intimately involved, including, for examples, couples who are cohabiting or dating (Straus & Gelles, 1990; Straus, Gelles, & Steinmetz, 1980). There is no universal agreement about what the term *family violence* means. For example, the terms *family violence* and *domestic violence* are sometimes seen as synonymous with wife-beating, although spouse abuse is only one type of family violence. Other types are child abuse, incest or child sexual abuse, marital and date rape, and elder abuse.

Until the end of the 20th century, the causes of violent behavior were not widely studied. Shared social values constrained aggressive behavior in public; domestic abuse was concealed as a private family problem. Today, however, violence is among the most pressing problems with which behavioral experts must cope. It is clear that violence is neither so rare nor so private as it once was, or was popularly supposed to be. One survey of children in a Boston-area health clinic, for example, found that 1 in 10 had, by age 6, witnessed a knifing or a shooting; half of these shootings and three quarters of the knifings had been witnessed by the children in their own homes (Cohen, 1992). In addition, whereas violence was once seen as a problem exclusively found in poor, inner-city regions of the United States, during the latter half of the 1990s it has emerged in a large variety of middle-class, suburban areas, particularly in the case of school shootings (Associated Press & Seattle Times Staff, 1998).

The increasing significance of violence can be seen in a cost analysis of the problem. Even when one ignores the cost to the victim in suffering and pain, and the emotional cost to family relationships, substantial financial costs can be identified as follows:

1. Medical expenses to victims.
2. Lost productivity due to injuries.
3. Expenditures for mental health services.
4. Expenditures for police, social services, and investigations.

5. Financial support of victims (e.g., through public assistance, battered women's shelters, etc.)
6. Expenditures for prosecution and/or incarceration of the offenders.

It is very difficult, if not impossible, to estimate all these costs exactly. However, the figures we do know precisely are staggering enough. For example, in 1990 the U.S. federal and state prison systems alone spent $11.5 billion—an average of about $15,603 per inmate (Greenfeld, 1992). Whereas Americans spent $22 billion a year in 1994 on maintaining and building prisons, that figure jumped to $29 billion by 1998 (Koppel, 1998).

Popular media have estimated that crime in the United States costs hundreds of billions of dollars every year. The Bureau of Justice Statistics, an arm of the United States Department of Justice, estimates that in 1992, $94 billion was spent for civil and criminal justice by federal, state, and local governments put together. The report pointed out that this constitutes a staggering 59% increase over 1987 (U.S. Dept. of Justice, 1992a). For every resident, the three levels of government together spent $368.

The National Crime Victimization Survey of 1992 found that crime victims lost a staggering $17.6 billion, which included property and cash losses, wage losses, and medical expenses (Klaus, 1994). More than two thirds of personal crimes involve an economic loss to the victim, as do almost one in four violent crimes (Klaus, 1994). Rape, robbery, and assault alone cost victims almost $1.5 billion in 1992 (Klaus, 1994). Approximately 8% of all victims counted in 1992 lost time from work as the result of a violent crime (Klaus, 1994). Statistics such as these do not typically include costs such as long-term medical costs, psychological counseling, decreased productivity at work, higher insurance premiums, or moving costs. Additionally, as large as these numbers are, they do not represent the total cost of violent crime because not all violent crime is detected.

The secrecy that surrounds most cases of family violence makes them particularly difficult to detect, which means that most of the statistics cited here probably do not include domestic violence and are thus likely to be underestimates. It is, in fact, probable that most violence is domestic in nature. Although we suspect that most violence does occur between intimates, such as spouses, this hypothesis does not make it any easier to estimate the hidden costs of such abuse. For example, it is not known how many women stay home from work each day to hide, or recover from, injuries caused by abusive spouses. Because most cases of family violence are never reported to the authorities, we have no way of knowing how many women call in sick to work when in fact they have been injured by a spouse or partner. Similarly, how can we estimate the costs of mental health services? Presumably, some violence and abuse is revealed to mental health service workers and not to law enforcement authorities, but we cannot tell what proportion of these services goes to victims and/or abusive families. However, some estimates do help to clarify the costs of family violence.

For example, the cost of family homicide in 1984 alone was estimated to be $1.7 billion (Straus & Gelles, 1986). We also know that severely battered women average almost twice as many days in bed as other women (Straus & Gelles, 1990). Three times as many battered women as nonbattered women reported being in "poor" health during a 1985 survey of Americans (Straus & Gelles, 1990). Battered women appear to have higher rates of all types of illnesses, including depression, headaches, and suicidal thoughts. Interestingly, abusers may also suffer from higher rates of psychosomatic illnesses, depression, and other problems requiring costly medical intervention (see chapter 13). And of course, none of these problems takes into account the additional cost of psychological intervention aimed at eliminating the violent behavior to begin with (for example, marriage counseling). Finally, there is another cost to domestic violence that is frequently overlooked: that is, there appears to be a relationship between being abused and reliance on taxpayer-supported welfare for financial support. Generally, "past and current victims of domestic violence are over-represented in the welfare population. The majority of welfare recipients have experienced domestic abuse in their adult lives, and a high percentage are currently abused" (Raphael & Tolman, 1997).

Abused children have higher rates of all types of social and medical problems, such as difficulty in making friends, learning problems, or aggressive behavior (Straus & Gelles, 1990). How can we possibly estimate the costs associated with a child who might have succeeded in school but failed because of victimization? Finally, it is well known that abused children are more likely to be arrested (Spatz Widom, 1989a), which costs police, judicial, prison, and social services resources. Although each of these costs are ultimately borne by taxpayers, most of us have only recently become aware of the scope and seriousness of violent behavior in society. However, experts in a variety of fields have been trying for years to understand why human beings become, on occasion, violent with each other. Psychologists, sociologists, biologists, and criminologists have all been studying human violence from different perspectives, and each group has a valuable contribution to make.

Sometimes a multiperspective approach seems tiresome and irrelevant to readers who can often "see" the causes of violence quite easily. Gain seems to be the motive in cases of instrumental aggression; there are other obvious motives in cases of hostile aggression. For example, when you read in the newspaper about a young man who kills another man in a gunfight for "no apparent reason," the story often describes the perpetrator as having been the victim of abuse, a broken family, or poverty. What else do you need to know? The answer to the question of why this young man is violent seems self-evident—all the reader has to do is consider his early deprivation. If he had been born into wealth and privilege, if he had been raised in a loving, nurturing, nonviolent environment, we all feel sure that he would not have so easily committed murder. In fact, our analysis may be correct.

But consider, for a moment, the possibility that this perpetrator has a brother. Perhaps this brother is not violent; perhaps there are other siblings who are not violent. Yet all the offspring in this family shared a psychosocially impoverished and troubled childhood. Why was this one man so vulnerable, when his siblings managed to stay out of trouble? Many individuals are exposed to early stress or neglect, even to violent abuse, yet most of them do not grow up to become violent themselves (Spatz Widom, 1989b). There are individual differences in vulnerability; in other words, factors other than the young man's environment must be at work. To the student who asks why, when a history of victimization is so clearly important as a precursor of violence, it is necessary even to study other factors, I reply that no one factor, no matter how compelling, can completely explain why some individuals are violent and others are not. It is clear that a person's situation is vitally important in understanding his or her violent behavior, but there are always reasons why one individual was influenced by a situation when others were not.[1] In chapter 6, I develop a model of violent behavior that attempts to account for a variety of influences in assessing the potential of an individual for violence.

The first step in understanding risk for violence must be understanding where and when violence occurs. We are beginning to realize that by far the most common type of violent behavior may occur not on the street, but in the family (Cervi, 1991; Hotaling, Straus, & Lincoln, 1989; Kandel-Englander, 1992; Pittman & Handy, 1964; Shields, McCall, & Hanneke, 1988; Straus, 1992). Historically, family violence has been seen as fundamentally "different" from "traditional" criminal violence. But in the second half of the 20th century, the U.S. judicial and criminal justice systems began to undergo a significant change of attitude: Attacks on family members began to be viewed as violent crimes, and victims of family violence began to be recognized by law enforcement authorities as being in need of protection. Thus, family violence became located squarely within the jurisdiction of the criminal justice system. One survey found that by 1986, most police officers considered violence between spouses to be "criminal and unacceptable" (Saunders & Size, 1986).

Even so, new ideas and beliefs gain wide acceptance at a very slow pace. Thus, criminal justice authorities have very uneven knowledge of, sophistication about, and training in the recognition of the seriousness of family violence. Even today some do not see it as the expensive and potentially lethal threat that it is, despite its prevalence in Western nations (discussed in detail in subsequent chapters). It is startling that a crime of such widespread proportions could have escaped public concern for so long.

---

[1]No matter how many factors one takes into account, it is impossible to predict with complete precision who will act violently and who will not. Nevertheless, a multidisciplinary approach enhances understanding of why some people become violent and others do not in a way that no single-discipline approach can.

When domestic violence is detected, most societies are reluctant to take action against it. In the United States, we have abhorred child abuse and the beating of women, but many have also been reluctant to label incidences as crimes. It is as though cultural blinders were in place. To be murdered by a burglar breaking into your house is terrible, but to be murdered by your own husband, although shocking, is not so clearly a heinous crime.

Some of the reluctance to criminalize family abuse can be traced to the roots of the U.S. legal system. Under *English Common Law* (the basis for much of the U.S. legal system), a man could not be punished for beating his wife or children. In fact, the legal system operated specifically to protect a man's right to chastise his wife and children by physical means (Paterson, 1979). However, there were limits: The law stipulated that a man should not, when beating his wife, use a rod thicker than his own thumb (Paterson, 1979). It is from this centuries-old law that we get our modern saying "by rule of thumb." Although it was illegal for a man to beat his wife with a rod thicker than his thumb, fewer, if any, limits were placed on how severely parents could beat their children. Children could be starved, tortured, abandoned; children were property and parents had the right to do with them as they pleased (Paterson, 1979). The first time the U.S. public rallied to the defense of an abused child was around the turn of the 20th century, when a horribly abused little girl was rescued by the American Society for the Prevention of Cruelty to Animals—because although Americans had begun to object to the abuse of animals, they had not yet begun to object to the abuse of children! (The American Society for the Prevention of Cruelty to Children was subsequently formed and remains in existence today.)

Until recently, our personal behavior was guided by two conflicting principles: first, the right of privacy to decide how to treat family members—abusively or kindly; second, the right to protection by the government from physically violent criminals. Many U.S. scholars (and others) recognized that these two principles were in conflict. In theory, a government cannot tell its citizens that they have the right not to be assaulted while telling certain citizens that they have the right to assault others without interference. An example of this conflict can be seen in a session of the Washington State legislature in the mid-1980s, where, while attempting to assure children that they would be protected from assault by their parents, the Legislature simply could not agree if it should ban "kicking" or "punching" as abusive (Berliner, 1988).

To the U.S. public, the right to treat family members as they pleased, without interference, often outweighed the right of spouses and children not to be abused. Americans did not believe that it was acceptable for a man to strike his wife or for a parent to assault a child, but were nevertheless squeamish about interfering in family affairs, including a man's or woman's right to treat his or her family as he or she wishes without interference. In Boston as late as 1986, for example, when a woman named Pamela Dunn sought protection from her abusive husband, she was told by a judge that she was just taking up the court's time when it had many more serious crimes to cope with. Ms. Dunn was refused police escort and told to "act as an adult"; approximately 5 months later, her body was found in a dumpster and her husband, who had abducted her, was charged with first-degree murder. Many similar cases have occurred in the United States.

Despite tragedies such as these, some Americans still believe that family violence is not a serious enough offense to warrant official interference. Nonfamily violence is frequently perceived as more serious, more potentially lethal, and more common. However, many others no longer believe that family violence is insignificant enough to simply tolerate. Legally, no state in the Union now permits a husband to hit his wife (Browne, 1987). Although states began changing their laws as early as the end of the last century, U.S. social beliefs did not begin to really change until much more recently. It was only a few decades ago that a profound shift in public attitude began to change the criminal justice systems of the Western world. People in many countries now recognize that private relationships do not give a person the right to victimize family members and other intimate acquaintances and that such violence should be regarded as criminal. We have begun to fundamentally change our willingness to tolerate assault, regardless of the presence or absence of a relationship between perpetrator and victim.

Although almost all Americans would agree that family violence is a tragedy, not everyone agrees that the criminal justice system is the correct agency for dealing with it. Criminalizing family violence has been controversial for at least the following four reasons:

1. All families have conflicts, and we all sympathize when families fight. Violence between a husband and wife, however unjustified, is undoubtedly one type of family fight.

2. Members of a family may feel humiliated or embarrassed by the existence of violence within their family. Most of us would like to keep our family problems private and may feel we can best help those in conflict by pretending that we do not notice the violence. Designating family fighting as a *crime* means bringing in outsiders (e.g., police officers, attorneys, judges, psychological and psychiatric experts), and potential witnesses may feel that such legal scrutiny would only be an embarrassing invasion of an already troubled family.

3. Some aggression between family members is clearly legal and (to many) acceptable. Two examples of legal aggression are parent-to-child physical punishment for discipline purposes and physical fighting between siblings (which is generally regarded as naughty but not a case for the criminal justice system). The fact that some types of illegal violence (e.g., child abuse) are legal in milder forms (spanking) may make it difficult for both experts and the general public to know where to draw the line. Is hitting a child with a leather belt discipline or abuse? Many Americans are confused about what constitutes child abuse or

child discipline. As recently as 1988, a pastor whose daughter was beaten to death said that the beatings were nothing more than "tough discipline" (United Press, 1988), despite the fact that they were ultimately lethal.

These three factors—the common fact that families fight, the natural urge to respect the privacy of family problems, and the fact that some degree of family aggression is clearly legal—all work together to make some members of society fearful of labeling family violence a crime.

4. The fourth factor affecting our attitudes toward family violence is that most publicized cases have dealt with male perpetrators and female and child victims. As future chapters discuss, men are the primary, but not the only, perpetrators of violence (Ageton, 1983; Shanok & Lewis, 1981; Stets & Straus, 1990a; Straus & Gelles, 1990; Wolfgang, 1983). Many societies are struggling to redefine their conceptions of male and female roles. In past generations, men essentially owned their families and therefore were permitted relative freedom of behavior with wives, parents, and children. Under the influence of the feminist movement, women and children have ceased to be considered possessions; they have increasingly fought for the legal right not to be violently victimized by family members. As support for women's rights grows, some men may feel that their rights are shrinking—including their "right" to treat their families however they wish.

Criminalization of street violence has not presented the same psychological barriers. However, other issues have presented themselves as obstacles to an accurate understanding of this problem. U.S. prisons and jails currently overflow with offenders, yet the public perception is that violent crime is constantly and alarmingly increasing. Governments have responded to this concern by increasing spending on crime; in fact, between 1985 and 1990, spending on the criminal justice system increased twice as much as spending on all other government expenditures (Lindgren, 1990). Despite public concern, or in part because of it, the fact is that the overcrowded conditions in U.S. prisons are primarily due to the enormous increase in drug offenders, rather than to the violent convict population (U.S. Department of Justice, 1992; Lesnik-Oberstein, Koers, & Cohen, 1995; Snell, 1992). In addition, there is no longer any doubt that rates of violent crimes are actually decreasing overall, rather than increasing (Lesnik-Oberstein et al., 1995). Despite these facts, Americans perceive violent street crime to be the threat of the century (Arends, 1996; DeFrances & Smith, 1994). It may be that the quality of violent street crime is changing even more than its quantity. For example, youth violence is without a doubt dramatically increasing (Freeh, 1995). In Portland, Oregon, a 9-year-old boy shot and killed his 5-year-old sister, allegedly because she refused to go to her room (Reuters, 1995, Nov. 21). Despite the boy's youth, he faced homicide charges and if convicted could have been held until his 25th birthday. In many states, such young children are traditionally conceived of as incapable of comprehending the meaning of death and thus unable to form homicidal intent—in fact, Brandon Roses is the youngest child to ever face homicide charges in Oregon. The fact that this child is being formally charged demonstrates society's decreasing tolerance of youth violence. It may be this changing tolerance, rather than a change in the level of violent crime per se, that feeds our impression that America's streets, as well as her homes, are becoming more dangerous all the time.

Violent behavior is a serious problem with many social costs. As such, it provokes many questions. What constitutes a violent crime? What should we, as a society, do with violent offenders? How should victims best cope with the trauma? How do we prevent children from growing up to become violent? All of these questions are important and are dealt with in subsequent chapters. Until we understand violence, we cannot hope to eradicate it.

Part **I**

GENERAL ISSUES

Chapter 2

The Numbers: How Common Is Violent Behavior Today?

METHODOLOGICAL ISSUES IN COUNTING VIOLENCE

On January 10th, 1995, a young man brought his bleeding girlfriend to an emergency room in Massachusetts. The young woman explicitly denied that her boyfriend had stabbed her in the chest, and died 20 minutes later. In earlier decades of the 20th century, that might have been the end of this case. But in 1996, a prosecutor vehemently contended that despite the victim's declaration, there was evidence that her boyfriend had in fact been the perpetrator of this murder. On June 26th, a jury agreed and found John McIntyre guilty of first-degree murder.

There is little doubt that "domestic" murders, once routinely given little or no attention, are now considered to be legitimate cases for the criminal justice system. However, despite the mass media's increasing recognition of the toll (and frequency) of domestic violence, most Americans still believe that the violence that we are most likely to encounter (i.e., the majority of U.S. violence) occurs on our streets. Women are often taught to defend themselves against street crime; for example, a woman may attend a self-defense class, or may carefully check her car before getting into it at night. When she thinks of being attacked, raped, or beaten, she may imagine that the city streets hold the greatest threat.

Actually, a typical U.S. woman is much more likely to be assaulted in her own home than in the streets of her neighborhood. In fact, the leading cause of injury to U.S. women is domestic, not street, violence (Jones, 1990). Nearly 2 in 3 female victims of violence in 1994 were attacked by relations or someone they knew (Bachman, 1994). The National Family Violence Survey (NFVS) estimates that 1.8 million women are beaten domestically each year, compared to the National Crime Survey's most recent (1992–1993) estimate of 660,000 women assaulted by strangers on the street—numbers that suggest that women may be three times more likely to be assaulted in their homes than on the street (National Archive of Criminal Justice Data, 1991; Straus & Gelles, 1990). People are often unaware of these facts, although the public's knowledge about domestic violence is increasing every day.

Our perceptions about the sources of danger around us are based largely on what we "count" as *violent crime*. "How much child abuse is there in America?" I was recently asked. As is seen here, the answer depends on who does the counting, and how.

SOURCES OF CRIME STATISTICS

We glean most of our knowledge about crime from government and the mass media (e.g., newspapers and television). Thus, most of the misconceptions about the frequency of domestic violence can be traced to the way in which government authorities compile and release statistics about violent crime. Although official statistics about domestic violence are not a deliberate attempt to mislead the public, they can be easily misinterpreted. How does this happen?

There are three sources of statistics on crime:

1. Official statistics based on police reports of arrests and convictions.
2. Statistics based on government surveys of victims of crime.
3. Self-report surveys, in which people are asked to report on their own criminal activity.

At first glance, many make the error of assuming that "official statistics" are the only reliable, valid, and legitimate measures of crime. Many people, when questioning the value of self-report surveys, ask, "Why would any violent person voluntarily report his own criminal activities to anyone?" However, the job of gathering statistics on crime is not as simple as it may seem.

The Uniform Crime Reports. The "official" source of crime statistics in the United States are the Uniform Crime Reports (UCR), which are compiled by the FBI and are based on local police reports. The FBI uses the UCR to form estimates on the frequency of a variety of crimes in the United States. In theory, local police detect all crime in their jurisdiction, record that crime, and send these records to the FBI, who compiles them into the UCR. However, in reality, we know that the UCR is only an estimate because there are several steps in this process that may fail. First, the local police are rarely able to detect all crime that occurs in their jurisdiction, and second, for a variety of reasons, local police probably fail to record all the crime that they do detect.

Why Don't Police Record All Crime?

At first, it may seem shocking that police do not record, and send on to the FBI, all the crime that they encounter in their district. It is easy to understand that police simply do not detect all crime, but it is more difficult to understand why they would fail to report crime that they do detect.

However, there are several logical and understandable reasons why local police might not record all the crime they encounter on their job. First, the officer(s) may be unable to identify the offender, which may make recording the crime irrelevant. For example, if a minor vandalism is reported to the police but there are no clues as to the identity of the offender, both the victim and the officer may see no good reason to record the crime officially.

In other cases, crime may not be officially recorded because it is not possible to prosecute the case. For example, all records of a crime may be discarded if there is no evidence that is strong enough to support the prosecution of a suspect. Third, sometimes the victims themselves urge the court to drop all charges in a case, thus dismissing the case. In some cases, the court will go along with the victim's wishes in these matters. For example, one reason that official statistics are a poor reflection of domestic violence is that victims of battering husbands, fearing retaliation or other consequences, may choose to drop charges rather than pursue them.

Finally, police see a great deal of crime in the United States today. They are aware that their time is best spent on the most serious crimes. Therefore, if a case appears to be "not serious," then police may choose not to bother recording that crime. There is no doubt that this is illegal, but psychologically, it is understandable.

At best, the UCR fails to reflect only the crime undetected by police. At worst, it omits both the undetected crime and the unrecorded crime. It is important to remember, however, that the UCR has significant advantages; for example, the information it contains tends to be very reliable and accurate. For some types of crime, the UCR is the best statistic available. However, for two major reasons, its weaknesses make it a poor choice for understanding the incidence of domestic violence. First, domestic violence often occurs in the privacy of the family home. As a "hidden" crime, police may detect it only in relatively extreme cases. In contrast, street crime occurs in public and is thus much more easily detectable. (Remember that the UCR only reflects detected and recorded crime.) Second, police are often reluctant to take official action, such as arresting the offender, for a variety of concerns. Even if the police do arrest the offender, the victim may refuse to press charges, thus dropping the case from official statistics.

National Crime Survey.   Fortunately, the UCR is not the only source of statistics on crime. The federal government, recognizing that the UCR reflects only detected and recorded crime, provides a different source for some statistics, called the National Crime Survey (NCS). Rather than counting the criminals, as the UCR does, the NCS counts the victims. The NCS is a large-scale survey that asks Americans about their criminal victimization experiences; by counting the victims instead of the criminals, it avoids restricting itself to detected and reported crime. The presumption is that victims will report their criminal victimization experiences, even if the crime was never reported to the police or the criminal never caught.

However, the NCS (and other victimization surveys) are also, unfortunately, less than ideal in the case of domestic violence. For victimization surveys to be successful in accounting for all criminal behaviors, several factors must be present:

1. The victim must be able fully and accurately to recall the crime.
2. The victim must be aware that the behavior of the offender constituted a criminal offense.
3. The victim must be willing to disclose the crime (i.e., the victim must not be motivated to protect the offender and/or must not be ashamed of the crime).

In the case of domestic violence, all three factors may not be present in many cases. The accuracy of human recall is frequently poor (Bartol, 1991; Reiss, 1975), and may be especially so for traumatic events such as violent encounters. Furthermore, it is not uncommon for female victims of domestic violence to believe that their male partners were not committing any crime (Finkelhor & Yllo, 1985); many Americans believe that it is legal for a man to hit his wife. In addition, the NCS asks about assault in general, rather than assault specifically at the hands of a partner; many victims may be unaware that being beaten by one's partner constitutes the crime of assault. Finally, intense fear of repercussions and shame over domestic violence increases the probability that victims of domestic violence may fail to admit their own victimization. Female victims of domestic violence often believe that they are at fault for the failure of the relationship (Langhinrichsen-Rohling, Neidig, & Thorn, 1995) and, as such, they may be motivated to conceal the crime. Their dependence on their partners (including financial dependence) may also motivate them to remain silent, even in the face of what may be brutal violence (Saunders & Size, 1986; Straus, 1992b).

National Family Violence Surveys.   Self-report surveys share some of the problems of victimization surveys, especially those of fallible memory and reluctance to report on account of shame. However, some self-report surveys use improved methods of interviewing that are much more likely to elicit frank information about family violence from an otherwise reluctant respondent. In the area of domestic violence, these surveys stand out above the rest and have provided the nation with the most accurate statistics on domestic violence to date. These surveys are called the National Family Violence Surveys of 1975 and 1985, conducted by researchers from the Family Research Laboratory at the University of New Hampshire.

These surveys include thousands of American households, and they address the problems of estimating the frequency of domestic violence in a unique manner. Rather than speaking to either perpetrators or victims only, the researcher surveyed husbands half of the time and wives half of the time. For each household, either the husband or the wife was chosen at random and asked to report the frequency of violence in the household. However, because the researchers were interested in gaining as much information as possible, they did not ask respondents questions like, "Are you criminally violent with your wife?" Rather, the interviewers pointed out that all families had conflicts, and then gave each individual a list of specific behaviors and asked him or her if that behavior was engaged in during conflicts. The list included benign items such as "discussions," but also violent items such as "shoving," "pushing," and "punching."

Because no one was interviewed using legal terms such as assault, a respondent did not need to know that punching a spouse is a crime in order to report it to the interviewer. Both respondents who thought the violence was legal and those who knew it was criminal could equally report violence. In addition, the way in which the question was asked tended to minimize any feelings of shame that might have prevented someone from admitting to the violence. The violent items were presented in a list of possible responses and were not emphasized by the researchers. In addition, the researchers reminded respondents that "all" families fight; therefore, conflict was not made to seem deviant.

STREET VIOLENCE

Most of what we know today about the types and frequencies of U.S. domestic violence is the result of studies such as those conducted at the University of New Hampshire. The UCR and the NCS may be better estimates of street violence. What are the different types of street and domestic violence, and how common are they?

Assault

Probably the most striking characteristic of assault toward the end of the 20th century is its decrease. During 1998, assault, as with all violent crimes, continued a decline that began in 1994—the rates of violent crime in the United States today are the lowest since 1974 (Rennison, 1999). However, violent crimes still occur much too frequently, and the sources of violence in the United States today are not always clear.

The Bureau of Justice Statistics at the National Institute of Justice releases crime statistics gathered by the UCR and the NCS. For example, in 1998 there were more than 1.6 million cases of assault reported in the NCS (this number includes simple assaults). How many of these occurred between strangers? Of the aggravated assaults, approximately half of the victims reported that they did not know the perpetrator. Encouragingly, every area of violent victimization dropped in the United States between 1993 and 1998 (Rennsion, 1999). Despite these numbers, most criminologists believe, on the basis of the majority of victimization research, that most assaults occur between people who know each other (Cervi, 1991; Kandel-Englander, 1992). The NCS numbers suggest that many victims of domestic assault are either unwilling or unable to report it to interviewers from the National Institute of Justice, or do not conceptualize their domestic victimization as a case of assault (Kandel-Englander, 1992).

Stranger assault seems to occur to both men and women, in roughly equal numbers; simple assault is approximately 1.5 times more common than aggravated assault on the streets.

Assault using firearms is becoming increasingly common, including the use of automatic and semiautomatic weapons (Associated Press, 1995, July 10). Almost all victims of perpetrators carrying a gun reported that the weapon was a handgun. Approximately 70% of all murders in 1997 were committed using firearms (Rennsion, 1999). Despite these numbers, Americans remain ambivalent about gun control. They are more in agreement about the seemingly increasingly bizarre nature of assault in the United States. For example, a magazine salesman in Texas assaulted an 88-year-old woman because she refused to buy a subscription (Associated Press, 1995, Dec. 10). In an assault that allegedly mimicked a movie scene, two robbers set a New York subway clerk on fire by squirting flammable liquid into his booth (Reuters, 1995, Nov. 27). Finally, two sisters in Stratford, Connecticut, assaulted a woman with a jar of sauce when she moved their grocery cart without asking (Associated Press, 1995, Nov. 11). Although rates of assault are increasing, it seems to be these type of attacks—provoked by seemingly trivial issues—that frighten Americans most, in addition to the perception that when assault is not punished, it escalates to more serious violent crimes. A case in point is that of Gerald Craffey, a 29-year-old cleaning man, who had assaulted women in 1989, 1991, and 1992 without significant punishment before he was ultimately arraigned for murder in 1995 (Ellement, 1995).

Homicide

Homicide is counted only by the UCR because the NCS is a victim survey and, obviously, homicide victims are unavailable for interviewing. In 1998, authori ties recorded 16,910 murders. Of these, approximately 4% of male victims were killed by people known to them intimately; in contrast, 32% of female victims were killed by intimates (Fox & Zawitz, 1999). The proportion of homicides committed by intimates is decreasing in the United States, however, especially among male victims and especially since 1993 (Fox & Zawitz, 1999). Although these numbers imply that most homicides occur between strangers, it is possible that a somewhat higher proportion did actually occur between intimates because many homicides had no information recorded on the relationship or lack of relationship between perpetrator and victim. In any case, other data has suggested that most violence, including homicide, occurs intrafamily (Cervi, 1991; Kandel-Englander, 1992). The conflicting evidence in the case of homicide makes it difficult to be certain which poses a greater risk: homicide from strangers or homicide from intimates.

In general, homicide rates in the United States declined dramatically during the 1990s (Fox & Zawitz, 1999). In 1993, there were more than 24,000 homicides in the United States; by 1998, this number was less than 17,000. Homicide declines also occurred in cities of more than 1 million citizens. Despite such decreases, however, Americans remained concerned about stranger homicide, for three major reasons. First, although homicide by juveniles peaked in 1993 and has been decreasing since then, it is only very recently that killings by 14- to 17-year-olds have dipped to pre-1988 levels (Fox & Zawitz, 1999; Freeh, 1995); second, homicides seem to be increasingly gruesome and unnecessarily violent (Briggs, Martin, & Cuza, 2000); and third, killings appear to happen, at times, in response to trivial provocations. One example of the latter is the case of Donald Graham, a 56-year-old Rhode Island man. Graham, who has been described as a "self-appointed highway vigilante," was driving at night on a highway when another car's headlights flashed him. When both cars pulled over and the other driver approached Graham's car, Graham shot and killed the man with a crossbow. Although he later maintained that he was "threatened" by the victim's approaching him, Graham was convicted of murder (Associated Press, 1995, Oct. 17).

Gruesome murders have always existed, but their scope and intensity appear to have increased. One of the most shocking cases happened in Illinois, where a woman and two men killed a pregnant woman and sliced open her body to retrieve a baby the killer wanted; the murderers also killed the pregnant victim's two other children. The killing was described as "unimaginable" by local authorities and was publicized around the country (Associated Press, 1995, Nov. 21). Such publications probably serve to increase the public's fear of stranger homicide.

Sexual Assault

Apart from assault and homicide, one of the most commonly perpetrated violent crimes is sexual assault. Before 1992, the NCS did not ask subjects directly if they had been sexually assaulted. Rather, they asked respondents if they had been physically assaulted or assaulted in "some other way." During the 1992 survey, the NCS retained this traditional wording for half of the sample. Not surprisingly, very few respondents volunteered the information that they had been sexually assaulted, and the numbers from this half of the sample yielded the estimate that "only" 140,930 sexual assaults had occurred in the United States in 1992. Of these, approximately half of the victims reported that they did not know their perpetrator. These numbers suggested that 68,140 rapes took place between strangers in 1992.

However, the second half of the respondents were given a newer version of the NCS, and the numbers obtained here show how misleading the traditional version of the NCS was when estimating rates of sexual assault. These respondents were asked directly about sexual assault: "Incidents involving forced or unwanted sexual acts are often difficult to talk about. Have you ever been forced or coerced to engage in unwanted sexual activity by (a) someone you didn't know before; (b) a casual acquaintance; or (c) someone you know well." This newer version yielded a much higher estimate of sexual assault incidence: It suggested that fully 607,000 sexual assaults had occurred in the United States in 1992.

By 1993, 100% of the sample was interviewed using the new wording, and this yielded an estimate of 485,000 sexual assaults for that year. This was a significant drop from the estimate of 607,000 for 1992, suggesting that the incidence of sexual assault decreased between 1992 and 1993. This significant downward trend, evident in other violent crimes as well, continued through the 1990s. By 1998, "only" 328,130 sexual assaults were recorded (U.S. Dept. of Justice, 2000; of these, more than 86,000 of them were cases of attempted rape). Of these, approximately 12% were known to be perpetrated by either spouses or relatives. Because of the nature of this survey, however, it may be difficult to know precisely how many sexual assaults take place between strangers versus intimates; the proportion of stranger rape victims who volunteer information may be different from the proportion of intimate rape victims who admit to the assault, even when directly asked.

As with assault and homicide, however, the public fears sexual assault, particularly by strangers. Cases such as Lisa Rene's also serve to fan that flame. Lisa Rene was a 16-year-old girl, staying in her own apartment, when several men claiming to be from the FBI broke into it. She called 911 and was recorded begging for help and screaming in terror as they dragged her away; they spent the next 2 days raping her repeatedly before finally burying her alive (Associated Press, 1995, Oct. 26). Although the data suggest that sexual assault rates are actually decreasing, such gruesome and highly publicized cases, committed largely by strangers, enliven the public's fear that strangers are more apt to commit sexual torture than are family members and acquaintances.

Juvenile Violence

Violence and aggression by children is not a rare phenomenon. Almost half of all persons arrested in 1994 were under the age of 25 (Freeh, 1995). A more recent study of juvenile violence found that 10% of juveniles admitted hitting their parents (Brezina, 1999). Among peers, Duncan (1999) found that 28% of 375 American children surveyed admitted being bullies.

On the topic of street violence, Greenwood (1995) provided an excellent review of crime among juveniles. For example, he pointed out that 3 to 4 out of every 10 boys growing up today in urban America will be arrested before their 18th birthdays. Greenwood also pointed out that the UCR may be the best indicator of youth violence because victim surveys depend on the victims' abilities to determine that their attackers are juvenile. Recent UCR data reviewed by Greenwood reveals that juveniles aged 10 to 17 account for 11% of the U.S. population, but fully 16% of violent felonies. Although the juvenile index arrest rate increased by only 9% between 1985 and 1990—a slower increase than the adult arrest rate (15%)—the decline in juvenile rates is accounted for by property offenses, not by violent offenses. In 1980, juveniles committed 10% of homicides; by 1990 they were committing 13.6%. Between 1984 and 1992, the number of juveniles arrested for homicide who were under age 15 increased by 50%. Although the homicide offending rates of teenagers over 14 increased dramatically after 1985, the rate of homicide offending among this age group has actually declined significantly since 1993 (Fox & Zawitz, 1999). Nevertheless, most experts are not optimistic about rates of juvenile offending continuing to decrease; in fact, the current decreases never declined to pre-1980s levels (Fox & Zawitz, 1999).

Why do juveniles commit violent crimes? Sometimes the motive seems more clear, as in the case of Reiko Imazaki, a high school star athlete who had publicly apologized to his father for "not becoming all that his father wanted him to be" before killing him 2 years later—while telling him he loved him (Associated Press, 1995, Dec. 1). Many cases of youths killing family members are attributed to abuse; Gerard McCra, a 15-year-old, allegedly shot and killed his entire family because of abuse he claimed to have suffered for many years (Associated Press, 1995, Oct. 17). Reporters frequently find that perpetrators often give banal justifications for juvenile violent crimes; John Claypool, who admitted to two murders when he was 14 years old, said he did it "to see what it was like to kill" (Taus, 1995). A 17-year-old high school student punched an elderly teacher as his classmates cheered, claiming later that the 78-year-old man had "bumped him" (Hart, 1995). These apparently frivolous justifications can be particularly upsetting to adults, who often, despite the natural limitations of adolescent cognitive functioning, expect teenagers to have the insight of adults. Nevertheless, it is important to note that despite this lack of insight into the causes of their own behaviors, the causes of juvenile violence run deep, and such offenders usually demonstrate a variety of risk factors for early aggression (as is discussed in the biosocial model of chapter 7).

DOMESTIC VIOLENCE

Child Abuse

Child abuse is usually separated into four subtypes: physical abuse; sexual abuse; neglect; and verbal, psychological, or emotional abuse. Each of these four subtypes has its own definition and incidence rate. The identity of the victims as children is the common thread.

Physical Abuse.　The consequences of physical abuse were originally termed *battered child syndrome* (Kempe, Silverman, & Steele, 1962). Battered child syndrome was identifiable only by x-ray because it was characterized by the presence of several fractured bones in various stages of healing, suggesting ongoing severe physical abuse. However, it became increasingly recognized that the physical abuse of children can take many less severe forms. Today, our knowledge is still evolving, and even definitions can be difficult. Some consider that any physical aggression toward a child constitutes physical abuse; however, most U.S. parents believe that mild physical punishment, such as spanking, is actually good for children. Many who disapprove of more severe violence against children would state that physical punishment could not possibly constitute "abuse." Others would agree that spanking children with the hand is not abusive, whereas spanking them with any object is, because using objects greatly increases the risk of injury to the child. Still others would differentiate belts from other objects in cases in which children are not permanently injured.

As you can see, it is difficult, if not impossible, to arrive at a definition on which everyone would agree. However, for the purposes of this chapter, and with the understanding that there are other definitions, *physical abuse* is defined as physically hitting children severely enough to cause injuries, including relatively mild ones such as bruises or cuts. According to this definition, spanking a child on the buttocks without leaving any marks or injuries would not be abusive. However, shaking a child, which can result in serious internal injuries, would be considered abusive. Similarly, whipping a child or spanking a child and leaving bruises or cuts would be abusive.

How frequently does child physical abuse occur? In 1985, the National Family Survey asked parents in more than 8,000 households how they behaved toward their children. Specifically, the researchers asked parents if they ever engaged in any of the following: kicking, biting, or punching; hitting or trying to hit with an object; beating up; choking, burning, or scalding; threatening with a knife or gun; or using a knife or gun. The rates of "serious" child physical abuse subsequently reported did not include minor violence (such as slapping a child). Furthermore, hitting with an object was kept in a separate category because although it substantially increases the risk of real injury, many parents hit with objects in a strictly disciplinary context.

The NFVS found that 2.3% of U.S. children (23 per 1,000 children) were seriously physically abused in 1985. This percentage suggests that approximately 1.5 million children per year are physically abused in the United States (Straus & Gelles, 1990). Of course, the actual rate of physical child abuse is almost certainly significantly higher than these estimates because many abusive parents may be reluctant to admit that they assault their children. When the rate was recalculated to include children who were hit with objects, the NFVS found that fully 11% of children were physically abused, suggesting that as many as 6.9 million U.S. children may be physically abused each year, depending on the definition used.

Recent correctional records reveal that more than 60,000 inmates nationwide are incarcerated for abuse against a child (Greenfeld, 1996). Almost 1 in 5 inmates were found to be incarcerated for a crime against a child, with more than half of these crimes committed against children under 12 years of age (Greenfeld, 1996).

Child physical abuse can begin in infancy. Michael Bertrand, a 22-year-old father from Warwick, Rhode Island, "beat his 5½-week-old baby son so savagely that the boy suffered brain damage, broken ribs, and spinal cord injuries" (Associated Press, 1995, Aug. 8). Child physical abuse does not end at puberty. As the NFVS showed, many teenagers are also physically abused. Furthermore, even minor violence, such as slapping, carries increased psychological significance during adolescence. Although most parents view slapping small children as normal, the percentage of parents who view slapping, spanking, or shoving teenage children as normal is much smaller. In our culture, it is generally acceptable to hit small children but not adolescent children. Despite these widely shared cultural values, the NFVS found that one third of parents admitted having hit their teenage child at least once during 1985. Further, 7% of U.S. teenagers were victims of severe physical abuse during that year. Adolescents may be better able to defend themselves physically, but because the vast majority remains generally obedient to and dependent on their parents, they remain vulnerable, and thus these rates of physical abuse do indicate a serious problem. Even famous teenagers have been beaten by their parents, as in the case of tennis star Steffi Graf, who was allegedly beaten and kicked by her father while training (Associated Press, 1995, Nov. 6).

The NFVS may be one of the best sources, but there are other sources of statistics on child abuse. The best known is the number of child abuse cases reported by Child Protective Services (CPS); these numbers reflect the cases of child abuse that are detected and treated. In 1984, CPS found that almost 3% of U.S. children were reported to the authorities as victims of abuse; this number includes all types of abuse, such as physical abuse, sexual abuse, and neglect. Only about .68% of the reported cases reflected strictly physical abuse. This small percentage, in contrast to the percentage found by the NFVS, suggests that most victims of child physical abuse are not being detected and treated by CPS. This is undoubtedly due not only to the difficulty in detecting such cases, but also to the limited funding CPS receives and its consequently overworked social workers.

Sexual Abuse.   This type of child abuse involves using a child in a sexual manner to arouse or satisfy an adult. Sexual abuse includes a wide range of behaviors, including (but not limited to) exposure, inappropriate touching, sexual contact, and intercourse. In one court, a father was convicted of child sexual abuse for paying another man to rape his 9-year-old daughter while he watched, although he did not molest the girl himself (Milne, 1995). The child's compliance, coercion, or the degree of force used is not relevant in the determination of child sexual abuse (although it may be important in determining the seriousness of the offense). Children, by nature of their inexperience and lack of maturity, are not capable of consent and thus any sexual contact with a child constitutes sexual abuse on the part of the adult, even if the adult claims that the child "enjoyed" the abuse or "wanted" it. In fact, claims that the child wanted or enjoyed the sexual contact are legally and psychologically irrelevant; sexual abuse is abusive even if there was in fact enjoyment (Hazzard, Celano, Gould, Lawry, & Webb, 1995).

How frequently does child sexual abuse occur in the United States? As in the cases of other crimes against children and other sexual crimes, many victims are too young to report, too ashamed to report, reluctant to report a family member (e.g., a stepfather), or all three. Finkelhor (1988), of the University of New Hampshire, is one of the preeminent researchers in the field of child sexual abuse. His studies indicate that approximately 25% to 33% of women recall being sexually abused as children. Men admit victimization at lesser rates: approximately 10% report that they were molested as children. In 1983, Russell found similar results in a study of San Francisco women; of these women, 28% reported some sexual victimization during childhood (before age 14). Surveys of adult women typically find similar numbers, whereas surveys of pre-teens and teenage girls find lower numbers, usually just under 10% (Saunders, 1999). Finkelhor and other researchers found that most victims never report the offense to authorities (Finkelhor, 1988; Russell, 1983); it may also be that younger victims are even less likely to admit to victimization than are adult victims (Saunders, 1999).

Neglect.   Neglect occurs when a custodial adult fails to see that a child's basic needs are provided for. Basic needs include (but may not be limited to) the need for food, clothing, shelter, schooling, and affection. The precise definition of *neglect* is still evolving. For example, a custodian may feel that a child is not neglected if he or she is fed and clothed; however, a court may rule that custodians who do not force a child to attend school are guilty of neglect.

Adults are not considered to be guilty of neglect when they are unable (rather than unwilling) to meet a child's basic needs; for example, a mother who is starving herself, with no food sources, is not neglectful because she fails to feed her child. Whether or not an adult is neglectful when he or she chooses to meet his or her own needs rather than the child's (assuming that there are only enough resources for one) is a matter of controversy and individual judgment.

The incidence of child neglect rises with poverty (Baumrind, 1994; Jones & McCurdy, 1992). The exact number of neglected children is difficult to estimate because at least some neglected children may never be noticed by authorities (National Research Council, 1993). However, the American Humane Association estimates that neglect is the most common form of child abuse, probably suffered by 8 out of every 1,000 American children (American Humane Association, 1998). Generally, gross neglect of children is categorized with child physical abuse of various sorts and thus is included in physical abuse statistics.

Emotional, Psychological, and Verbal Abuse. Like physical abuse, emotional abuse can be difficult, if not impossible, to define specifically. *Emotional abuse* generally refers to "the persistent degradation or humiliation of children" (Bartol, 1995). A broader definition is "any pattern of behavior which seriously interferes with a child's positive emotional development" (American Humane Association, 1998). A child who is routinely made to feel stupid, ugly, worthless, ashamed, unlovable, or of no value is considered to be emotionally abused. Emotional abuse does not include physical or sexual abuse. However, all child abuse involves the degradation and humiliation of children emotionally (to some degree), and it may be that the key ingredient in the damaging affects of abuse is the emotional abuse that is always present. That is, there may be children who are "only" emotionally abused, but all children who are physically or sexually abused are, in all likelihood, also emotionally abused and damaged.

SPOUSE ABUSE

> Certain women should be struck regularly, like gongs.
> —Noel Coward (*Private Lives*)

For the purposes of studying abuse between spouses, little distinction (if any) is typically drawn between married couples and cohabiting couples. Violence between couples who are not living together is typically termed *dating violence,* although the terms *spouse* or *marital* may be used if the couple has a long-standing relationship (e.g., if the couple does not live together but has been dating for many years, or once lived together in the same household).

Like child abuse, spouse abuse can be roughly divided into different categories: physical abuse and sexual abuse. Neglect is not typically an issue between adults, except possibly in the case of dependent adults (such as those who are ill) or elderly adults (who may be dependent on another person for their basic needs). This section describes physical abuse and sexual abuse between "spouses" (married and cohabiting couples) and between dating couples.

Physical Abuse

Unlike child abuse, the physical abuse of spouses includes even minor violence, such as shoving and slapping. Although it may be legal to use minor violence with a child, any violence (minor or severe) against an adult constitutes assault. The distinction is not crucial, though; however common (or controversial) minor violence against women may be, severe violence is most definitely too typical an event in many women's lives. Domestic violence is the single largest cause of injury to U.S. women, and four women are killed every day by men who batter them to death (Jones, 1990). Of course, spouse abuse also involves male victims (Schafer & Caetano, 1998).

What is the frequency of physical spouse abuse in the United States? The 1985 NFVS found that approximately 16% of U.S. couples had some type of physical, aggressive encounter with each other during the previous year. Of course, the survey also differentiated between all violence, minor and severe, and severe violence (kicking, punching, stabbing, shooting, etc.) only. Across the United States, the rate of severe violence between spouses is, of course, somewhat lower: 6.3% of couples were severely violent with each other during 1985. A study involving face-to-face interviews with 1,635 couples found that as many as 1 in 5 couples experience some violence, with somewhat lower levels for male-to-female and female-to-male violence counted separately (Schafer & Caetano, 1998). Pregnancy is clearly no guarantee of physical safety; a recent study of pregnant women found that 5.7% reported experiencing physical abuse during pregnancy. Of these, 63.3% reported that the perpetrator was her husband, boyfriend, or ex-husband (Muhajarine & D'Arcy, 1999). Interestingly, Schafer's study also found a significant gap between the rates of violence reported by males and females, which made it necessary to estimate frequency ranges, as opposed to arriving at absolute numbers (Schafer & Caetano, 1998). Generally, women were more willing to report violence than were men.

Although child abuse is typically studied as a parent-to-child phenomenon, spouse abuse is a two-way street: That is, it can consist of either husband-to-wife abuse or wife-to-husband abuse. The 1985 NFVS asked about both types of abuse. However, the results are not simple to interpret, because the two types of abuse are potentially different in many ways. First, men are usually physically larger than women are and thus their aggression is more likely to result in the woman being injured. Whereas a man hitting a woman is likely to cause injury, a woman hitting a man is less likely to do so. Both men and women are typically aware of this different potential for injury, and this awareness is a factor in the determination of abuse. That is, violence is more abusive if perpetrators know that they will probably injure their victims; it is less abusive if the perpetrators believe that they are not capable of injuring their victims.

Perhaps the most significant difference between male and female spousal violence is, however, intent. Women and men may behave violently toward their mates for very different reasons. Most notably, men are more likely to hit offensively; women, self-defensively (Adler, 1991; Cazenave & Zahn, 1992; Mann, 1992). It is easier to interpret the 1985 NFVS findings when these facts are understood. Interestingly, although 3.4% of couples were characterized by "wife beating" (husband-to-wife violence), 4.8% of couples were characterized by wife-to-husband violence. This means that at least 1.8 million women were being beaten in 1985, and at least 2.6 million men were being assaulted by their wives. It is probable, however, that these numbers are not strictly comparable. As discussed previously, most severe husband-to-wife violence results in injury, whereas much of the wife-to-husband violence does not. This is one reason why beaten wives are more likely to be noticed: Their injuries are apparent or force them to seek medical or police attention. Second, much of the wife-to-husband violence appears to be an attempt at self-defense. (The use of violence as self-defense by beaten wives is discussed in later chapters.) These arguments are not intended to deny that there are males who are truly victimized and beaten by their female partners, and wife-to-husband violence should not be merely dismissed. Of course, reciprocal blows may escalate a physical fight to the point where real injury may occur. However, evidence does suggest that most of the wife-to-husband cases of violence involve either attempts to strike without expecting to cause any serious injury or attempts at self-defense (Adler, 1991; Cazenave & Zahn, 1992; Mann, 1992). In any case, because couples may understandably be reluctant to admit to violence, these numbers should be considered a probable underestimate of the true incidence.

Sexual Abuse (Marital Rape)

Some scholars in this area have called the marriage license a "license to rape" (Finkelhor & Yllo, 1985). It is true that historically, in the Judeo-Christian culture (among others), the fact that a woman was his wife gave a man full rights to sexual contact with her—her consent, or lack of it, was legally irrelevant. Certainly many moral and ethical people have deplored forced sexual contact, even between spouses. Legally, however, until very recently, a man has had the right to force his wife to have any sexual contact he wanted. In fact, the definition of *sexual assault* has typically been phrased as something similar to: *forced sexual intercourse with a woman who is not his wife*. Forced intercourse with a spouse, therefore, could not be legally termed *rape* or *sexual assault*. Today, many states have rewritten statutes to include spouses in the pool of potential victims of sexual assault.

It is extremely difficult to estimate the incidence of sexual assault between spouses. Until recently, most, if not all, victims believe that it is not possible, technically, to be raped by one's spouse. Therefore, merely asking women if they have ever been raped by their husbands has been likely to elicit an answer of "no," even if forced sexual interaction has occurred. Asking women if their husbands have ever "forced them to have sex" (thereby avoiding the confusion spawned by the word *rape*) is more productive. Of course, a victim of marital rape may decline to admit forced sexual interaction with her spouse because of intense shame; such an admission is tantamount to admitting a disturbed marital relationship. Thus, any statistics on marital rape should be considered underestimates of the true frequency.

The United States has a relatively high rate of sexual assault. Because it is a crime that is frequently unreported, victimization statistics (rather than statistics reflecting the number of arrests or convictions for rape) probably provide the most accurate estimates. In 1983, Russell reported on a sample of 930 women living in California. Her study and others suggested that 25% to 35% of women experience either a completed or attempted rape. Kilpatrick's (1993) data suggested that husbands or other male companions perpetrate 40% of all rapes. We can extrapolate from these numbers to estimate that 36 million women are rape victims each year, 14.4 million of them victims of marital rape. Official statistics based on the number of cases reported to the authorities seem to indicate much lower numbers: that only .07% of U.S. women (only 840,000) are sexually assaulted each year. It is difficult to avoid the conclusion that these official numbers tell us a lot more about the reporting rate of sexual assault than they do about the rate of actual victimization.

Dating Violence

Although dating is usually considered an innocent and exciting form of socializing, it all too often also includes violence between dating partners. In the 1980s and 1990s, media-publicized cases of date rape began to highlight this issue.

Violence is not confined to the marital relationship. Some evidence has suggested that unmarried dating couples may even be more violent than those who are married (Lane & Gwartney-Gibbs, 1985). College students have been asked about the violence in their relationships; about 20% admit to some degree of physical victimization. The studies usually have made no distinction between male versus female victimization; this makes comparisons with married couple data difficult. One study (Stets & Straus, 1990b), in which responses from males and females were analyzed separately, found that the use of violence changes with the progression from dating to cohabitation and marriage. That is, males were least likely to be violent in dating relationships and most likely to be violent in marital relationships. Females, on the other hand, were most likely to be violent in dating relationships, less likely to be violent in marital relationships, and least likely to be violent in cohabiting relationships. The percentage of couples in which both partners were violent was highest among cohabiting couples, compared to dating and married couples.

When severity of violence is considered, a different pattern emerges. When both partners engage in only minor assaults, there appears to be little difference among dating, cohabiting, and married couples. However, in the case of severe assaults, there is a difference. Fully 22% of cohabiting couples are severely violent, in comparison to 10.5% of dating couples and 10.5% of married couples (Stets & Straus, 1990b). When you consider how common cohabiting is today, it is astonishing to think of that figure.

Date Rape. Date rape, as its name implies, involves the sexual assault of a woman by a man, not her husband, with whom she is involved in a social, or dating, relationship—sexual or nonsexual. The incidence of date rape has been investigated in two ways: by surveying young, dating women (typically college women) about sexual assaults they may have experienced, and by interviewing young men about whether or not they have ever forced a date to have sex. (Asking a man if he has ever committed rape is likely to result in a negative answer; many males may not consider forcing a date to have sex as rape.) Surveys of college women generally find that approximately 20% to 28% report having been forced to have some sort of sexual encounter, such as forced intercourse, forced oral sex, and so on (Koss, Gidycz, & Wisniewski, 1987; Yegidis, 1986). The number of males who admit to forcing a date to have sex is, predictably, somewhat smaller: About 5% to 15% of males generally admit to this type of behavior (Koss et al., 1987; Rapaport & Burkhart, 1984). Studies have suggested that about two thirds of date rape occur in "casual" relationships (that is, new relationships with a date who is only an acquaintance), whereas one third occur in the context of an ongoing relationship (Yescavage, 1999). Again, because it is so rare for date rape to be reported, official crime statistics do not, at this time, provide useful information.

Yescavage's (1999) research found that several factors influenced whether or not perpetrators of date rape tended to define the incident as "rape." One of the most important factors was the timing of the woman's refusal to have sex. Yescavage found that the later in the sexual encounter a woman said "no," the greater the probability that the man would not define forced sex as rape. In addition, the later a woman said "no," the more accountable she was held for the rape. Complicating the picture is the fact that men may not attend to earlier protestations, assuming that the woman is only offering token resistance.

ELDER ABUSE

Estimates of the frequency of elder abuse have only recently become a cause for concern. It is difficult to measure elder abuse for two reasons. First, what constitutes abuse of the elderly? Older adults may have varying degrees of physical dependency, but psychologically (unless disease intervenes), they are adults. Therefore, they are probably less vulnerable to verbal and psychological abuse, compared to children. Second, elder abuse is difficult to measure because it is so hidden. Young children are regularly seen in public places: They frequently attend school or day care, for example. These external contacts give society opportunities to discover child abuse. However, apart from medical care, older adults may be entirely housebound.

Until recently, official data on violent crimes against older Americans suggested a rate of approximately 132,000 crimes in 1994 (U.S. Department of Justice, 1994). More recent data estimates that 1% to 5% of elders are physically abused (Swagerty, Takahashi, & Evans, 1999). A similar study in Ireland found that 3% of elders over 65 years of age had been the victims of abuse (Bichard, 1999). A survey of older Americans in the Boston area yielded a similarly high estimate: Pillemer and Finkelhor (1988) estimated that there are approximately 1 million cases of elder abuse in the United States each year, suggesting that many cases may never be reported. The cruelty of elder abuse may be compounded by the victim's complete financial and physical dependence on the abuser. Because older victims (unlike children) are usually dependent for the remainder of their lives, escape is improbable and defense a physical impossibility. Of course, as adults, these victims have advantages that children totally lack, such as a greater psychological ability to withstand stresses and trauma.

PAN-VIOLENCE

Pan-violence is a term that describes violent individuals who are violent both in the home (with family members) and outside the home (violent in the streets). How common is pan-violence? Are most violent street criminals also abusive toward their families? Are most domestic abusers also violent street criminals? Alternatively, are we discussing two distinct, separate types of individuals: those who offend only against family, and those who offend only in the streets?

These may seem to be obvious questions. However, very little research has actually addressed them. The reason for this blind spot is probably overspecialization among researchers. Although criminologists and psychologists tended to focus on street or stranger violence, sociologists (until recently) made up the most important group of researchers studying family violence. Because the two groups of researchers often publish in different journals and attend different conventions, the two kinds of violence are often not examined simultaneously in the same research study (Cervi, 1991; Fagan, Stewart, & Hansen, 1983; Fagan & Wexler, 1987; Hotaling et al., 1989; Kandel-Englander, 1992; Shields, McCall, & Hanneke, 1988). This leaves a fundamental gap in what we know about violent behavior. Are people who are violent, violent everywhere and with anyone? Or do violent people choose their victims and confine their violence to one arena?

A few studies have compared the arrest rates for street violence of wife batterers and nonviolent husbands (Graff, 1979; Straus, 1985). These studies found that those who are violent inside the home (i.e., batterers) are significantly more likely to be violent toward nonfamily persons, compared to nonviolent husbands (Browne, 1984; Fagan et al., 1983; Faulk, 1974; Flynn, 1977; Gayford, 1975; Rounsaville, 1978; Stacey & Shupe, 1983; Walker, 1979). It is difficult to draw any firm conclusions from these studies, however.

First, some of these studies examine only "clinical" samples (samples of people who seek psychological help). Although such samples do give some information, we cannot assume that all violent perpetrators are similar to those who actually seek help for their violence. Second, some studies did not look at violent behavior per se; because it can be difficult to measure violent behavior directly, researchers chose to assess attitudes toward violence or to use other indirect indices. Again, although this approach can yield interesting information, it cannot substitute for a direct approach. Finally, although the rate of street violence in batterers was considered, the researchers failed to ask the opposite question: What is the incidence of family violence among street offenders? Only by examining both sides of this coin can we understand the relationship between family violence and street violence, and estimate the frequency of pan-violence.

One study focused more specifically on the issue of pan-violence (Kandel-Englander, 1992). This study examined, in a representative sample of unincarcerated U.S. males, the proportion of men who offend only outside their families ("street-violent" males); the proportion of men who are violent only toward their wives ("batterers"); and the proportion of men who are violent in both spheres ("pan-violent" individuals).

This study was part of the 1985 NFVS, which included 6,002 U.S. households, chosen randomly (Straus & Gelles, 1990). Half of the time wives were interviewed, and half of the time husbands were interviewed, yielding about 3,000 interviews with men. Of these 3,000 interviews, approximately 2,300 men answered questions about their violent behaviors both inside and outside the home. These 2,300 interviews are the basis for the study.

Each household was contacted by telephone and interviewed for an average of 35 minutes. The researchers set certain criteria that a household had to meet in order to be included in the survey. For example, households had to include adults who were either presently married or cohabiting, or who had been divorced or separated within the last 2 years; single-parent households were also included if they had a child under 18 years of age living in the household. Most of the eligible households agreed to cooperate with the survey; only 16% refused to respond to the interview (Straus & Gelles, 1990).

Violent behavior within the marriage was assessed as part of the Conflict Tactics Scale (CTS), a scale that estimates the level of husband-to-wife violence by asking each husband to reject or endorse any of a list of specific behaviors that he may have committed during "fights" with his wife. This list of behaviors ranges from calm discussion to serious violence. Subjects who were considered batterers were those who admitted doing any or all of the following: throwing something, pushing, grabbing, shoving, slapping, kicking, biting, hitting with a fist, trying to hit with an object, beating up, choking, threatening with or using a knife or gun.

Street violence was assessed by asking the men if they had physically fought with and/or injured anyone who was not in their family. Those men who admitted to this behavior were considered to be men who did have some violent tendencies outside the family.

Sample Characteristics

Before the results of these interviews on pan-violence are examined, we must determine what the sample of U.S. males looked like. Seventy-one percent were White; 11.4% were Black, 9.6% were Hispanic, and the remaining 1.8% were "other" (e.g., Pacific Islanders). Half of the sample were blue-collar workers or farm workers with a high school education or less; the remaining half were white-collar workers, or farm workers, owners, or managers who had more than a high school education. The ages of the men sampled ranged from 18 to 90 years old, with an average age of 42.923 years ($SD = 14.53$). These numbers tell us that the men in this sample were not just high-risk, inner city, poorly educated, or unemployed; rather, they represented a broad range of U.S. men.

Most (95%) of the men interviewed were married or cohabiting with a woman. The remaining 5 % were divorced, separated, or widowed, all within the last 2 years. Thus, this study examined primarily married or cohabiting men.

Results of the Study

Of the men in this sample, 311 (15%) admitted assaulting either a spouse, someone outside their family, or both. Figure 2.1 shows the proportion of violent men who were batterers, street-violent, and pan-violent.

Batterers.   Most of the violent men in this representative sample were men who beat their wives. Although fully three quarters (240) of the 311 violent men admitted assaulting their wives, only 13% (32) of these wife beaters also assaulted individuals outside of their families (i.e., were pan-violent). Most of the batterers (87%) denied that they ever used violence against nonfamily persons.

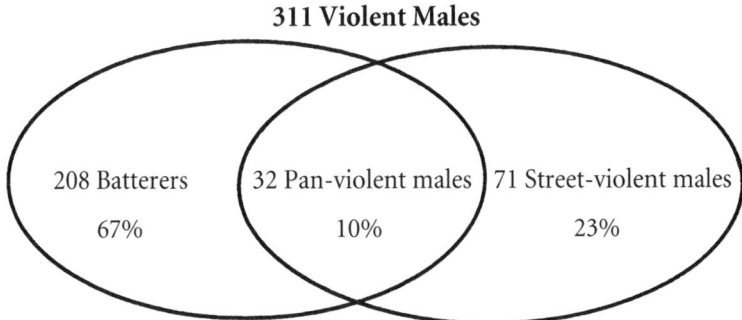

FIG. 2.1.   Proportion of men who are batterers, street-violent, and pan-violent.

This pattern suggests that most criminal violence by U.S. men may be perpetrated in the home and against families, rather than on the street (Gelles, 1985; Saunders, 1992; Shields et al., 1988).

Street Offenders.   Of the 311 violent men, one third admitted to assaulting persons outside their family. Of all these offenders, almost one third were pan-violent (i.e., they also assaulted their wives). Nonetheless, it was still true that more than two thirds of the nonfamily offenders assaulted only extrafamilial victims. Like the batterers, most street offenders "specialized."

One interesting difference between batterers and nonfamily offenders emerged, however. Recall that of the batterers, a mere 13% were pan-violent. In contrast, almost one third of street-violent males were pan-violent. Thus, the chances of being pan-violent are much higher if a man admits to street violence than if he admits to family violence.

Pan-Violent Offenders.   Thirty-two men (10% of the violent men, or 1.5% of the entire sample) admitted assaulting both their wives and people outside their homes. As just noted, the remaining 90% were violent either inside or outside of the family, but not in both spheres. Thus, pan-violence was an unusual phenomenon in this representative sample of U.S. men.

In the debate on the causes of violence, this is an important finding. It suggests that the vast majority (here, 90%) of violent men choose to confine their violence to one arena, either the street or the home. This, in turn, suggests that even if individuals do have marked personality or biological tendencies toward violence, most are still able to control their impulses well enough to choose their victims.

Violent and Nonviolent Men and Their Characteristics.   The four groups of men (batterers, street offenders, pan-violent men, and nonviolent men) were compared across several demographic variables: age, race (White vs. non-White), and social class (defined as white-collar vs. blue-collar employment). The comparisons revealed the following findings:

1. *Age.* Although the violent men were significantly younger than the nonviolent ones, the three groups of violent men (batterers, street offenders, and pan-violent men) did not differ from each other.

2. *Race.* The pan-violent men were different from the other violent men. Although 51.5% of the pan-violent men were non-White, only 35.5% of the batterers and 34% of the street offenders were non-White. The nonviolent group had the lowest proportion of non-White men (28%).

3. *Social Class.* Here, the subjects divided into two major groups: the batterers and nonviolent men versus the pan-violent men and the street offenders. The batterers and the nonviolent men were almost equally as likely to have white-collar as blue-collar jobs. The pan-violent men and street offenders were different; these two groups were disproportionately blue-collar (71% and 76.9%, respectively). This finding suggests that although social class may be an important correlate of both pan-violence and street violence, it is much less strongly associated with domestic violence. It echoes the findings of many previous studies that family violence occurs across all social classes, whereas street violence tends to be more confined to lower income groups (Bartol, 1991).

Why Are Batterers Less Likely to Be Pan-Violent? One explanation for this pattern of violence can be inferred from the social class of the men sampled. In comparison to pan-violent and street offenders, batterers were more likely to be white-collar workers. Perhaps they are motivated to confine their violence to the family because they stand to lose status and income; in contrast, the primarily blue-collar street offenders have less to lose and thus may behave violently wherever they choose.

Why Do Violent Men Tend to Specialize? Remember, fully 90% of violent men specialized. Why is pan-violence apparently the exception?

A spouse or other family member is a relatively "safe" target to assault. Domestic violence is the least likely type of violence to be detected and prosecuted, as can be seen from official statistics reporting that most convicted violent felons are not convicted for family violence (although most violence in the United States is family violence; Straus, 1976). Assault outside the family is a much riskier crime.

Street offenders, already exposed to the risk of societal punishment, do not have the same motive as batterers to confine their violence to the family. However, they may have other motives. For example, some street offenders who have no moral scruples about engaging in bar brawls or fistfights with other men may be repulsed by the prospect of striking a woman or a child. (Recall that all street offenders in this study had families.) In addition, it is possible that men who engage in street violence spend little time at home, thereby lessening their opportunity to assault their families.

This study focused on men who were not incarcerated; because street-violent and pan-violent males are more likely to be incarcerated than are family offenders, it is possible that this sample design resulted in an underestimation of the pan-violent and street-violent groups. Other research that has focused on incarcerated offenders has, in fact, found higher rates of pan-violence; one such study found that most incarcerated men are actually pan-violent. Clearly, more research needs to be done to understand the differences among the four groups —batterers, street offenders, pan-violent men, and nonviolent men—and many questions remain.

Chapter 3

Social Causes of Violence

Probably the most compelling question asked by those who study violence is, "Why?" Why do individuals engage in such horrifying and destructive behavior? Why do parents beat, and sometimes kill, their helpless children? What motivates sexual assault? Why do once-happy marriages deteriorate into violence? Why would an individual randomly kill dozens of people in a fast-food restaurant? What are the causes of violence? This chapter discusses the major theoretical approaches to this question and begin to consider some of the research findings.

Some Basic Questions

1. Are people born violent?
2. Do people learn to be violent?
3. Are violent people "mentally ill"?
4. Are violent people different from other people, apart from their aggressive behavior?

Psychologists and criminologists have studied not only the causes of violence that occur in individuals, but also patterns of the incidence of violent crime. For example, they have looked at the question of whether violent people tend to have certain income levels. Income is one factor that is external to individuals but closely related to their life and choices and thus possibly relevant in the cause of their behaviors. Because external factors can be so important in the causes of all types of behavior, including violence, I begin to examine the causes of violence by looking at factors that are outside the individual. In the next chapters, I examine factors that are internal to the individual and present a model that combines these factors to more accurately explain and predict violent behavior.

External factors can seem deceptively obvious. For example, almost everyone assumes that poverty breeds crime. In fact, this seems like a pretty safe assumption. However, in the history of science, many safe assumptions have had to be tested and qualified or discarded. In the study of violent crime, it is critical to remember that there are many different types of crime with different causes. Perhaps poverty breeds some kinds of crime, but not others. Perhaps poverty is not as important in violent crime as in other types of crime. Perhaps it is *more* important. Furthermore, personal observations can seductively convince us that relationships are much simpler than they really are. Most of us probably feel that we have personally observed that poverty breeds crime—it may appear "obvious" to us that poorer neighborhoods have more crime—yet it is critical to remember that personal observations can be skewed and are therefore not nearly as powerful as empirical evidence.

SOCIAL CLASS, POVERTY, AND VIOLENCE

Many of the causal factors examined in this book are internal, but are nevertheless related to social class and personal income. For example, prenatal health (pregnancy and delivery complications), medical care during childhood (especially regarding head injuries), and similar health outcomes may clearly be influenced by poverty. Although some level of medical care is available to nearly all citizens, there is little doubt that in the United States, those with lower incomes are less likely to have high quality, comprehensive (especially preventative) medical care.

Health is not the only relevant factor related to poverty. For example, children of lower income parents may be exposed to higher levels of violence in their neighborhoods. That exposure, in turn, probably enhances their learning of aggressive behavior patterns.

But let us start with the most basic assumption. How clear is it that lower income persons are more likely to be violent than people in higher socioeconomic classes? Is income inversely related to violence, and to domestic violence?

Tittle, Villemez, and Smith (1978) reviewed 53 studies and concluded that there was no compelling evidence of an inverse relationship between social class and criminal behavior. This conclusion was controversial but important because it motivated the research community to reexamine the relationship between social class and criminal and violent behavior, instead of merely assuming that an inverse relationship existed.

Tittle et al. did not specifically address violent crime, differences between juvenile and adult offending, or different types of criminal behavior (e.g., domestic vs. street violence, or even violent vs. property crime; Braithwaite, 1981). Thornberry and Farnworth (1982) did a comprehensive review and concluded that there was compelling evidence of an inverse relationship between adult crime and social status—the higher the crime rate, the lower the social status. They also suggested that juvenile crime did not show this relationship. More recent studies have confirmed that the typically *less serious* forms of juvenile crime are probably not related to social class (Triplett & Jarjoura, 1997).

Juvenile Delinquency and Social Class

But what about serious juvenile offending? Far from presenting a uniform rejection of *any* relationship between juvenile crime and poverty, the studies in this field suggest that such a relationship might, in fact, exist but be very complex.

For example, one area of research found that any relationship between juvenile offending and poverty could be muddied by the existence of critically important mediating factors, such as academic achievement. School disorder and conduct problems in school were found to be strongly related to the poverty of the surrounding community (Welsh, Stokes, & Greene, 2000). Welsh's study examined predictors of school disorder in more than 40 middle schools in the United States; it attempted to associate community crime, stability, and poverty with problem behaviors in schools among children who were approaching or in adolescence. The important point here is that while the authors found a strong association, they also noted that when the school environment itself was stable and well functioning, the relationship between community poverty and school misbehavior was much weaker (Welsh, 2000).

Other research on juveniles has found similar results. One large study of two waves of the National Longitudinal Survey of Youth examined the relationship between gender, class, and different types of delinquency (Triplett & Jarjoura, 1997). This study looked at more than 4,500 young people in the United States, who were followed over many years to examine their psychological and behavioral development. They measured a variety of factors including social class, education, welfare, and delinquency in the children. One finding was clear: the lower the social class and income of the household, the more likely that the children in that household would commit a violent offense. This was true for both male and female children. Interestingly, the relationship was mediated by educational expectations: when low-income parents expected high academic achievement from their children, the children were much less likely to engage in any violent crime. This was a potent relationship, and its intensity was stronger for males than for females. It is a good example of how a positive psychological environment can mediate the noxious impact of a toxic environmental influence, such as poverty and low socioeconomic status in children. Other research has also found that high parental expectations regarding academic achievement can help children develop positively. Harnish's (1998) study examined 103 children in low- to middle-income neighborhoods and studied the role of parent expectations in protecting against criminal involvement. This study found that parent expectations of academic achievement clearly mediated the relationship between crime, academic achievement, and social class.

Other research examining juveniles and crime and poverty has taken a different tack. As with any correlational relationship, it is possible that any apparent relationship between social class and crime is a spurious one. In other words, there may be a third factor, in itself related to low social class, which is actually causing the resultant rise in crime. For example, perhaps belonging to a lower social class means that you live in a more violent, crime-ridden neighborhood. It may be that neighborhood exposure that causes a youngster to become a criminal, rather than being poor itself.

Along this vein, several researchers have suggested that the statistical correlation between violent offending and lower social class in juveniles is, in fact, actually a spurious relationship. Their studies have found that it is actually factors associated with lower social class, which are, in turn, associated with an increased risk of violent delinquency. For example, one study examining the National Youth Survey data looked at violent delinquency and social class and attempted to understand if, and why, social class was related specifically to violent crime in juveniles. It found that lower social class was indeed related to violent offending, but data suggested that the relationship existed because lower-SES teenagers had learned to regard violence in a more favorable light and had learned this from both parents and peers (Heimer, 1997). The suggestion here was that lower social class presents a risk because of the social beliefs and attitudes it exposes children to, rather than by elements such as material deprivation. Another study hypothesized that low social class increases crime by increasing individuals' social alienation, stress, and by aggravating aggressive tendencies (Entner Wright & Caspi, 1999). A recent dissertation (Ashley, 1999), which examined how adolescent girls become involved in delinquent criminal activities, emphasized how important it is to consider the entire social and developmental situation that a young offender is in, as opposed to considering their socioeconomic status in isolation. Indeed, it is probably impossible to separate a child from the impact of his or her social class; it impacts the child's health, schooling, neighborhood, and family environment.

In summary, it seems probable that social class affects the tendency to be a juvenile delinquent. However, that statement should not stand alone and there are several important caveats. First, the impact of poverty on a teenager's antisocial behavior seems to be strongly nullified by a positive academic environment, or a positive family environment that emphasizes academic achievement. Second, it seems equally important to consider precisely how social class makes its impression on young peoples' development. Future research should probably consider in more detail how growing up in poverty affects a child's psychological well-being by affecting his or her environment and health in a multitude of ways. Keeping these caveats in mind, it is probably reasonable to assert that although poverty, in and of itself, may not cause crime in juveniles, it probably increases the *risk* that an adolescent will become a violent delinquent.

Violent Offending in Adults and Social Class

Is this pattern observed for juveniles the same for adult offenders? If juveniles are more likely to commit a violent crime if poor, then are adults similarly at risk if their income is low? Research on adult crime has found comparable associations between poverty and violent offending. Parker and Pruitt's (2000) study of homicide rates and poverty is a good example. They examined two measures of poverty: traditional income levels and measures of poverty concentration (that is, examining poor people who live in densely populated areas of low social class citizens). They found that poverty was related to homicidal behavior in Black and White offenders. Another study made a more detailed examination of crime, race, and income. It found that different racial groups may be more at risk when poor, but that their risk patterns may differ. This study examined 274 Black, 175 Hispanic, and 114 White inmates in a federal correctional facility (Jackson, 1997). Minority inmates were more likely to come from lower social classes, and were more likely to have family situations that impacted their finances adversely (for example, having dependent children, more siblings, or others dependent on them financially). White subjects were more likely to have been arrested for violent offenses, although this finding may not be representative because it uses a federal prison population and most violent offenses are tried in state courts. In summary, though, the study suggests that stressors associated with lower social classes may affect minorities more seriously than such stressors affect White offenders, although clearly both are impacted by a low socioeconomic status.

Clelland and Carter (1980) noted that social class may be more strongly related to the criminality of certain types of offenders and offenses than to that of others. This is a reasonable concern: we know that different causes of violent crime are clearly of differing importance among different types of violent criminals and individuals. Tittle et al.'s (1978) work clearly implicated the importance of lower social class among the street offenders they studied. More recent and comprehensive research, examining homicide rates among different racial groups and different urban areas, found strong relationships between poverty and an increased risk for committing homicide (Lee, 2000). Further, ameliorating extreme poverty through the use of social programs appears to undermine the impact that poverty has on crime rates (Hannon & Defronzo, 1998).

Some research has suggested that unemployment may be the reason for the association between poverty and violent offending. Increases in unemployment are associated with increases in the number of individuals incarcerated (Grimes & Rogers, 1999). A loss of jobs in sectors that typically employ working-class individuals (such as factory work) has been associated with an increase in violent homicide rates (Shihadeh & Ousey, 1998).

One problem with the literature is that many of the studies conducted focused on crime outside of the family. However, researchers have also examined the relationship between social class and family violence. Studies suggest that men of lower socioeconomic class are more likely to engage in wife abuse than are men of higher socioeconomic class (Kaufman Kantor & Straus, 1987). A meta-analysis of 11 studies examining the husband's educational attainment (one commonly used measure of social class) and the risk of his being abusive toward his wife (Hotaling & Sugarman, 1986), revealed that eight found a significant inverse relationship (i.e., the lower the social status, the greater the violence). Unemployment, found to be a risk factor for street crime, is also a risk factor for a man battering his partner (Kyriacou et al., 1999).

Although this definitely suggests a relationship, like the research on street crime, it suffers from a significant, yet common, limitation: To date, only violence inside or outside the family setting tends to be the focus (Fagan & Wexler, 1987). As pointed out earlier (Hotaling & Sugarman, 1986), researchers tend to look at either family violence, or at crime and violence outside the family—not both. It is not unreasonable to speculate that that family-only and street offenders could be quite different (Kandel-Englander, 1992; Englander, 1997) and in fact evidence has been found to support that idea (Young, 1993).

Kandel-Englander's (1992) study of a group of violent males, culled from a large, representative sample of Americans studied in 1985 as part of the National Family Violence Survey, separated offenders into four groups: family offenders, street offenders, pan-violent offenders, and nonviolent men. One of the difficulties in more conventional studies that compare, for example, spouse abusers versus nonviolent spouses, is that the group designated as "spouse abusers" will likely include (a) spouse abusers who *also* offend outside the home and (b) spouse abusers who *only* offend against their families—two arguably different groups. In Kandel-Englander's (1992) study, these different types of offenders were separated: "family-only" offenders had not offended outside the home, and "street" offenders had not offended inside the home; in contrast, "pan-violent" offenders had offended in *both* spheres.

Next the social class backgrounds of the four were examined. Notably, there were differences between different types of violent offenders. Street-violent men and pan-violent men were from a lower social class than nonviolent men, but family-violent men were *not different* from nonviolent men in social class. This finding makes it apparent why it is important not to just assume that poverty breeds crime. It may breed some kinds of crime, but not others. This does not mean that family violence is unrelated to social class, but is merely *less strongly* related to social class when compared to street and pan-violence.

The summary here is a good one for all offenders in the study, but how valid is it for different racial, ethnic, and gender groups?

Racial groups were similar. White subjects mimicked the group as a whole. Social class scores suggest two major groups of White subjects: pan-violent and street-violent men, who come from lower social classes; and family-violent and nonviolent men, who come from higher social classes. For non-White subjects, the findings on income were similar: the street-violent and pan-violent are from a lower social class, the nonviolent and the family-violent from a higher (and are similar to each other). Other studies have suggested that poverty may have a similar effect on different racial groups (Shihadeh, 1998; Lee, 2000; Parker, 2000).

In keeping with most research related to a complex social behavior like violence, one would expect to find mediating variables. And in fact that is exactly what several studies have found—that other social factors may affect how, or how much, poverty and social class affects crime and violence. One such mediating variable may be gender. Males and females may also show differences in their relationship to social class and crime. Triplett and Jarjoura's (1997) study found that although both males and females are more likely to commit violent offenses when they come from lower family income levels, property offending was more strongly related to lower SES in males. Family factors may also affect how strongly SES affects violent crime risk. One recent dissertation found that parental expectations and discipline played a strong mediating role (Harnish, 1998). Lykken (1998) argued that factors like poverty are strongest when associated with inadequate parenting.

EDUCATION AND VIOLENCE

Does the level of education an individual achieves have an impact on his tendency to be violent, either across the board, with his family, or on the street? One approach to this question is to compare the number of years of school completed by violent and nonviolent men. In my 1992 study, I began by lumping together all three groups of violent men (street, family, and pan) into one "violent" group, and comparing them to nonviolent men. It is interesting to note that although violent and nonviolent men did not differ in the average number of years of school completed, nonviolent men showed a wider distribution than their violent counterparts. In other words, they were more likely to have either very little education or a great deal of education, whereas violent men tended to complete a "middle" number of years of school; they did not tend to drop out of school very early and they did not tend to complete many years.

What might account for this pattern? Perhaps one difference between violent and nonviolent men is how their cultures view education. In some cultures, such as those in more remote rural regions, education is viewed as less necessary, yet there remain strong social controls on violence. Perhaps one group of nonviolent men comes from cultures such as these. On the other hand, nonviolent men were also more likely to have attained a great deal of education (e.g., they were more likely to have gone to college). In most cultures, more education means more investment in society and more to lose by prosecution as a criminal; thus, it is not surprising that more education should be associated with less violence. Finally, perhaps violent men tended to cluster in the "middle" area of educational attainment because they did not succeed in school, on the one hand, but also did not come from cultures that would deemphasize education while strongly controlling their violent behaviors. Further research will have to investigate these possibilities more closely.

Interesting as this picture is, as we know by now, these patterns may be very different for White and non-White violent men. When the two groups were considered separately, it became apparent that the violent versus nonviolent education differences hold only for non-White subjects—and are sufficiently marked in them to cause the differences found in the group as a whole. Violent and nonviolent White subjects, it turned out, did not differ much in years of schooling completed. Violent and nonviolent non-White men did. Education, therefore, may be a more important contributor to violence among non-White, than among White, men.

As we have seen, there are real differences between those men who are street- and pan-violent, and those who are violent only with their families. These differences were correlated with differences in education. Overall, family-violent men stayed in school as long, or longer, than nonviolent men. The pan- and street-violent attained, on the average, much less education. When only White men are considered, however, education appeared not to differ between the family-, pan-, and street-violent males. (Note that this analysis only considers the years in school, not the quality of school experiences.) A very different pattern characterized non-White violent men. The family-violent and nonviolent had completed a similar number of years in school; the street- and pan-violent had completed significantly fewer years. A more recent study, which examined the differences between domestically violent men and nonviolent men, found a gap in years of education (Gerstein, 2000). Unfortunately, it is difficult to incorporate such research into other findings because (as has often been the case in studies of social class) men who are *only* domestically violent are lumped together with men who are violent *both* on the street and in the home. Clearly, at least in some offenders, there is an association between domestic and street crime (Englander, 1997; Kandel-Englander, 1992; Marks, 1999).

More recent research has suggested that it may be academic achievement per se, rather than education, that really impacts a person's risk of developing violent or criminal behavior. By "academic achievement," I mean an individual's commitment to and achievement levels within school. In contrast, studies of "education" often only measure the number of years a person attends school, rather than studying the quality of their work in the school setting.

McEvoy and his colleagues' (McEvoy & Welker, 2000) review of the field found that academic failure or success, specifically, seemed strongly related to whether or not students became delinquent and if they did, to the seriousness of their involvement in criminal or violent behavior. The associations seemed clear, as did the protective role that high academic achievement seemed to play in students who were at risk but resilient. Further, many of the cognitive and attentional problems found in children who are at high risk of criminal involvement (see chapter 4) are also found in students with persistent academic problems. Other research has also found that at-risk but resilient students may be protected from delinquency or violent behavior by parents who have high expectations for academic achievement (Nettles, Mucherah, & Jones, 2000). McEvoy concluded that any program that increases the odds that a child will achieve academic success will also reduce criminal involvement by that child.

However, he acknowledged that the relationship between academic success and delinquency is likely to be a two-way street. That is, although academic failure may help "make" a criminal, coming into school with disruptive behavior is probably just as likely to, conversely, cause academic problems (McEvoy & Welker, 2000). Other studies have found that being exposed to violence has an important, negative impact on a student's mathematics and reading achievement in school (Nettles et al., 2000). A study of college students (Gibby-Smith, 1995) found that children born to adolescent mothers presented a significantly higher risk of both educational underachievement and juvenile delinquency. The U.S. Department of Justice released a 1999 report finding that "programs monitoring . . . academic progress increased . . . academic achievement" (Catalano, Loeber, & McKinney, 1999). A recent study of 144 children found that parental verbal abuse, even in the absence of any physical abuse, contributed to academic failure (Solomon & Serres, 1999).

To summarize, then, educational achievement is one indicator of the social status attained by a person. The number of years a child goes to school may be important in determining whether or not that child will become violent, but if this is the case, it is less true for White men than for non-White men. While researchers continue to find links between education and violence, they need to continue to draw distinctions between different types of violent behaviors. Finally, whether or not a child succeeds at school, and is invested in school, may be a more important predictor of criminal involvement than simply measuring years of schooling. And it appears highly probable that the link between academic failure and criminal behavior is a two-way street, with failure associated with subsequent criminal behaviors, and problems behaviors in school, in turn, associated with problems in academic achievement.

RACE AND VIOLENCE

Although we have discussed the importance of considering race when analyzing crime and violence patterns, there are basic questions left. Are members of some races or ethnic groups more likely to be violent than members of other groups? Are some types of violence related to race, whereas other types are not?

White-dominated media may have fostered the perception that race is a key factor in violent crime. In 1988, when George Bush was running against Michael Dukakis for president, he accused Dukakis, then governor of Massachusetts, of being "soft" on crime and of releasing hardened criminals before they had served their full prison terms. To illustrate the accusation, he ran an advertisement telling the story of the early release of a dangerous-looking, violent inmate named Willie Horton.

Horton evoked an emotional response from many viewers of the advertisement for a variety of different reasons. Some people felt that Horton perfectly matched their stereotype of an African-American violent felon—his frightening face evoked profound fears of crime and violent victimization. Others felt that the Horton campaign was an attempt to manipulate voters into being so afraid of racially motivated crime that they would vote for Bush. In any case, the campaign left open some basic questions about race and crime.

The evidence that Blacks in the United States are involved in criminal activity to a much greater extent than their proportion in the population is consistent (Block, 1977; Hewitt, 1988; Humphrey & Palmer, 1987; Wolfgang, 1958). However, the extent of involvement may vary depending on the crime. For example, in the 1970s the National Youth Survey (completed on 1,700 male and female adolescents) found no difference between the races when only low frequency, minor offenders were examined. In sharp contrast to this is the picture of homicide, the most serious violent crime in our society. Although Blacks comprise only 12% of the U.S. population, it is estimated that more than half of all homicides are committed by Black individuals (Conklin, 1986; Freeh, 1995; Greenfeld, 1992). Similarly, Blacks perpetrate about 4 in 10 assaults. Most victims of Black violence are Black as well, a fact that has led many African-American community leaders to seek an end to Black-on-Black violence.

That said, a number of experts have noted that Blacks and Hispanics are more likely than Whites to be suspected, arrested, and, if charged, convicted of violent crimes (Elliot & Ageton, 1980; Freeh, 1995). Whites are more likely to be given probation than are Black or Hispanic offenders (Jackson, 1997). There is little doubt that racism plays at least some role in the U.S. criminal justice system, and at least part of the impression that African-Americans are more violent than other ethnic and racial groups is probably due to the prejudicial handling of minorities within it.

On the other hand, it seems unlikely that prejudicial handling accounts for the entire ethnic discrepancy in crime rates. What other factors cause violence to be more prevalent in minority communities and among minority individuals? Socioeconomic factors seem to affect both Black and White homicide rates equally; in a study of the impact of the disappearance of low-skill jobs in industrial areas, researchers found similar affects across racial groups (Shihadeh,

1998). Furthermore, biological variables that have been linked to crime appear to apply equally to different races. For example, several studies have found that the relationship between abuse and violence and health during pregnancy and delivery remains valid even when race is controlled for (Kandel & Mednick, 1991; Shanok & Lewis, 1981). It seems most likely that minority individuals and communities are under social pressures and stresses that increase their vulnerability to violence in general. They are more likely to live in violent neighborhoods, to have larger families without social support, to have fewer financial resources, fewer job opportunities, and so on. In fact, one study examining the background stressors among a group of federal prison inmates found that Black and Hispanic prisoners were more likely to have lower incomes and more people who were potentially financially dependent on them (such as children). Although education levels were similar between racial groups, some evidence of preferential treatment did emerge: White convicts were less likely to face imprisonment, in comparison to their non-White counterparts (Jackson, 1997).

OTHER FAMILY CHARACTERISTICS AND VIOLENCE

Social class, education, and race are not the only areas of interest in the development of street and family violence. For example, does marital status (being single, married, or divorced) affect the likelihood that someone will become violent with his or her family? And what about family size (coming from a family with many vs. fewer children)?

There is little doubt that pressures like financial distress can increase the probability of family abuse, whereas support can decrease at least child abuse (Cicchetti, 1990). Support is usually found in the presence of a helpful spouse, family, and/or friends. Even studies of mothers who were abused as children found that if they have good support as adults, they are unlikely to abuse their own children (Egeland, Jacobvitz, & Sroufe, 1988). Other research pointed out that parents who have unstable relationships (i.e., they shift from relationship to relationship) may be at greater risk of being abusive (Belsky, 1988; Cicchetti, 1990). Therefore, it is important to study not just the existence of a marital relationship, but also its quality.

Similarly, a large family size may increase the risk of violence in the offspring. Parents with many children generally are under more stress and have more responsibilities, and almost any factor that increases stress levels in a family also increases the probability of violence. One researcher examined family size and family violence to see if there was a link between the two, and found that larger families did indeed display more family violence (Gil, 1971). In addition, another researcher studying biological factors in violence noted an interesting pattern: he found that low monoamine oxidase (MAO) levels in humans are associated both with violent criminality and with larger family size (Ellis, 1991). More recent research has also found that as the number of children increases, so does the rate of childbirth complications (also linked to violence later in life); this effect was found to be particularly important among the offspring of women who have 10 or more children (Babinszki et al., 1999). This line of research suggests that having many children may actually have an impact on the physical status of those children, and that it may be these physical changes in addition to the psychological pressures of a large family that are responsible for an increase in violent behavior. Other research has noted that the children from larger families appear to have an increased risk for a number of developmental problems (Wagner, Schubert, & Schubert, 1985), including scholastic and achievement problems (specifically, lower SAT scores; Zajonc & Bargh, 1980). Clearly, different parents cope differently with large families, and having many children does not inevitably lead to problems in their behavior. It is not simply the presence of many children that is important, but how family size affects stress that determines the relationship to abuse and violence. Furthermore, the mechanism by which larger families develop this increased risk status may be biological, social, intellectual, or academic.

How do these family characteristics affect the probability that someone will become violent on the street or at home? It is clear that single people are more likely than married people to be involved in street crime; however, this difference probably has to do with age rather than marital status per se. The relationship between youth and violent crime is indisputable; people younger than 29 commit most violent street crimes (U.S. Department of Justice, 1988), and are also less likely than are older age groups to be married.

Little research has focused directly on the relationship between the number of children a person has and his or her propensity for violent street crime; however, the research on crowding in the home may be related to this issue. Although densely populated neighborhoods are not necessarily more high crime, densely populated households do produce more violent criminals (Mueller, 1983). This finding suggests that a large family living under stressful conditions, in a limited space, may contribute to the development of a violent street criminal.

SOCIOLOGICAL PERSPECTIVES

Sociological models emphasize the social characteristics or the social environment of a person, rather than that individual's biology, personality, or developmental history. Sociologists note that an increase in violence within a society is often accompanied by extreme social change, such as cultural conflict, when a dominant society imposes its values, structure, educational methods, and so on, on a politically or economically subordinate culture (Lee, 1995). Generally, sociology emphasizes causal factors that are close in time to the target violence and are external to the individual (Nagin & Paternoster, 1994).

Hirschi's Social Control Theory

One major sociological theory pertaining to antisocial behavior is *social control theory* (Heimer & Matsueda, 1994; Hirschi, 1969, 1990; Nagin & Paternoster, 1994). The premise of social control theory is that individuals who are adequately invested in a society are deterred from behaving antisocially by their investment. In other words, people who are invested in and committed to a society will not misbehave because if they do, they stand to lose their investment (Nagin & Paternoster, 1994). The most obvious example of this is property crime: People with more money are less likely than poor people to become involved in property crime. Presumably, becoming a criminal is simply not worth the risk of being apprehended if you already have substantial material gains. Researchers have suggested that if people need to be more invested in society in order for crime to decrease, then the current emphasis on incarceration is not the answer to today's violent crime problem in the United States (Gottfredson & Hirschi, 1995). Despite the popularity of social control theory, some researchers have argued that antisocial behavior is not particularly related to attachment and/or commitment to mainstream society (Heimer & Matsueda, 1994).

Sutherland's Differential Association Theory

In the first half of the 20th century, Sutherland theorized that antisocial behaviors are due to association with persons who have beliefs that encourage law-breaking behaviors. The premise is that a criminal would have learned to become a criminal by acquiring these belief systems (Sutherland, 1947). A recent review of studies that test Differential Association Theory (Williams & McShane, 1999) confirmed that associating with individuals who encourage law breaking is one of the strongest predictors of criminal behavior.

Mental Illness and Violence

In the area of family violence, sociology has taken a different view from psychology and psychiatry. In contrast to models that view family violence as the result of an aberrant individual, this model notes that family violence is neither a rare event nor do extremely "different" individuals perpetrate it. Rather than focus on personality disorders or mental illness, sociological theorists often point out that violence is usually perpetrated on a family by an individual who is not "mentally ill" or even noticeably deviant in any other way (Pagelow, 1993). Similarly, contrary to some early psychological expectations, sociological research evidence suggests that female victims are neither pathologically "masochistic" nor mentally ill.

Female Victims and Mental Illness

Some theorists have suggested that battered wives "permit" their husbands to abuse them (Frieze & Browne, 1989). Megargee (1982) noted that other theorists believed battered women to be secret masochists, allowing the abuse to occur because they enjoy it. Such ideas were probably based on early psychoanalytic theories that held that masochism was normal for women, and that women could be expected to display masochistic tendencies much more frequently than men (J. H. Williams, 1987). However, Pizzy (1974) asserted that such theories were without scientific foundation and that women do not like or desire the abuse that they suffer. Indeed, empirical support for the idea that female victims of abuse are masochistic or in other ways mentally disturbed has lacked consistency (Megargee, 1982), although some studies found positive correlations between mental illness and being a victim of spouse abuse. Interestingly, Gayford (1983) discovered one possible source of the confusion. Although almost 50% of the battered women in his study had received psychiatric services and almost 75% had been given psychoactive medication, in most cases this intervention occurred after the marital violence had started. This fact makes it unlikely that the women's psychological difficulties could have been a causal factor in the violence. Although it is possible that the battered women had preexisting, causally relevant disorders but simply failed to seek treatment until after the abuse began, this is an improbable scenario to be coincidentally present in so many cases. Neither Gayford (1983) nor other researchers (P. Scott, 1974) found that masochism was a significant factor in wives' "tolerating" abuse.

Sociological theorists have studied the social factors that keep women in abusive relationships, rather than emphasizing the personality factors that may or may not do so. Several social factors have in fact been identified as key in maintaining the presence of the victim in an abusive relationship: financial and social dependence on the spouse; lack of marketable skills; having children in need of support; being burdened by continual childbearing (thus limiting mobility and independence); feeling uncertain about the seriousness of the problem; being fearful of being single, alone, and poor; and lack of knowledge about other options (such as government assistance). (Why women stay in abusive relationships is discussed in more detail in chapter 12.)

The Mental State of Violent Offenders

It is not uncommon for studies of violent offenders in general to find high levels of mental illness. One typical study found that 220 out of 500 homicidal offenders had evidence of significant mental illness, most commonly some type of personality disorder (Shaw et al., 1999). Other studies also found high levels of psychiatric problems among individuals who commit the most serious violent offenses (Lewis et al., 1986, 1988).

Such findings may not be true for all types of violent offenders. Sociologists in particular have studied family offenders for evidence of mental illness. Being an abusive husband and parent has been linked to many personality factors, such as alcohol abuse, inadequacy and poor self-esteem, extreme jealousy, and general immaturity (Bartol, 1991; Gayford, 1983). Abusers frequently do show such characteristics, but attempts to form psychological typologies of abusive males have not been successful; although psychologists may be able to form psychological profiles of individual offenders, it is much more difficult to form a psychological profile that fits all family abusers (Megargee, 1982). Sociological theorists point out that social factors may be more important in predicting *when* a male will become violent (Wilson, 1995); such researchers study factors such as crowding (Bower, 1994; Calhoun, 1961; Evans & Lepore, 1993; Frankel, 1992; Freedman, Levy, Buchanan, & Price, 1972; Gaes, 1994; Gove, Hughes, & Galle, 1979; Ruback & Riad, 1994; Sechrest, 1991), the mass media (Centerwall, 1992; Friedrich & Stein, 1973; Huesmann & Eron, 1986; Huston, Watkins, & Kunkel, 1989; "Reel Violence," 1994; Singer, Singer, & Rapaczynski, 1984), high temperatures (C. Anderson, 1987; C. Anderson & D. Anderson, 1984; C. Anderson, Deuser, & DeNeve, 1995; Rotton, 1993), and their relationships to the onset of violence.

Crowding, Temperature, and Violence

The relationship between crowding and violence has been investigated in both rats and humans. Among rats, crowding seems to lead to a breakdown of normal mating and nesting behaviors and to an increase in aggression and violence. Among humans, "private" space seems more relevant to violent tendencies than "public" space; that is, population density in a neighborhood appears to be relatively less important than density within private living spaces.

High temperatures and individual violence seem to be strongly related; for example, violence increases during the summer and is more prevalent in hotter climates. However, this relationship may be complicated by factors such as increased alcohol consumption during hotter summer months. In addition, political or mass violence seems to be mediated by cultural ideals of masculinity that emphasize aggression, as well as by temperature (Van De Vliert, Schwartz, Huismans, Hofstede, & Daan, 1999). Finally, social factors such as the mass media (particularly television) are clearly related to aggression (although this is a far from simple relationship, and is discussed in much more detail in later chapters).

Family Violence Across Cultures and Societies

The United States has led the virtual explosion in research in the incidence and causes of family violence, and as a result, many assume that family violence is predominately a U.S. problem (Gelles & Pedrick Cornell, 1983).

However, less interest abroad does not mean less violence in the households of other cultures and countries. Leading U.S. researchers have pointed out that there is no evidence to suggest that Americans are particularly violent with their families (Gelles & Pedrick Cornell, 1983).

Furthermore, much important research has been accomplished abroad. However, different countries tend to have different approaches to the problem of family violence. For example, although western Europe and the United States have acknowledged for decades that child abuse is a problem, some other countries (such as China and Russia) appeared to deny—as late as the end of the 1970s—that such abuse even occurs (Tauber, Meda, & Vitro, 1977). Another example may be seen in the area of public policy and childrearing. In contrast to the United States, where the right to use corporal punishment on children often seems to be jealously guarded, more than a decade ago Sweden passed a widely accepted law making corporal punishment of children illegal (Feshbach, 1980). In the United States today, nearly all parents hit their children as a disciplinary measure (Straus, 1983).

Thus, it is clear that despite some pockets of consensus, different cultures take different approaches to the very idea of family violence. Sociologists make the point that what is criminal violence to an American, or to a Westerner, may be perfectly acceptable in other cultures. To date, however, most research on family violence has been conducted by Western nations, who share both the financial resources to investigate these problems and the cultural belief that family violence is a problem.

POPULATION DENSITY

Does violence occur more often in rural, relatively unpopulated places, or in highly populated urban cities? There is no doubt that more street violence occurs in major cities; this high-visibility violence has led most people to assume that population density, or crowding, must be related causally to violence in some way. That assumption aside, what is the evidence that crowding is linked to violence?

In an imaginary world, we could subject human beings to crowded and uncrowded conditions and study the effects on their behavior. Obviously, however, this would be unethical and unthinkable. Therefore, much of the research on crowding and violence has been conducted on rats, rather than on human beings. The most interesting studies were conducted in the 1960s by Calhoun (1961), a researcher who found that crowded conditions significantly affect and change the normal lifestyles of rats. For example, male rats in crowded conditions, in comparison to males in uncrowded nests, showed no interest in their offspring and in their mates. They also behaved very aggressively, attacking and destroying other nests. These rats attacked both other males and females, and in general behaved violently and antisocially. On the other hand, studies of crowding in rhesus monkeys found absolutely no increase in aggression—in fact, rhesus monkeys appeared to cope with crowding by increasing their prosocial grooming behaviors, not by attacking each other (Bower, 1994). Thus, although the rat results are interesting, it seems likely that crowding affects different organisms in different ways. At the very least, the relationship is unlikely to be so simple in human beings. The most straightforward analysis of the crowding–violence question in human beings was conducted as a study of the relationship between U.S. violent crime rates and population density (Freedman, 1975). Despite the common assumption that violent crime occurs more frequently in urban areas, this study found that when social class (poverty) is controlled for, there are actually fewer crimes of street violence in high-density cities (per capita). Overall, of course, there are more violent street crimes in cities, but it appears that this may be only because there are more people, rather than because the crowding of cities makes people more violent. Of course, this analysis only took into account street violence; it did not really address domestic violence undetected by authorities. In support of this finding, a more recent study (Frankel, 1992) found that suicide rates (albeit a very different form of violence) were highest in states with low population densities, such as Nevada and New Mexico. The lowest suicide rates were in densely populated states, such as Washington, DC, Massachusetts, New Jersey, and New York.

Other recent studies point in a different direction. One study (Rand, 1991) found that between 1985 and 1989, the percentage of urban households victimized by crime rose from 28% to 31%, whereas the percentage of rural households victimized by crime dropped from 20% to 17%. This study is limited because it focused on crime in general, rather than on violent crime; however, its recent date implies a more accurate accounting of both family and street crime. It is not unusual for different studies to come to different conclusions; before deciding which results are more plausible, let us examine the experimental evidence on human crowding and aggression.

Some researchers have either studied "natural" pseudoexperiments, or conducted laboratory experiments wherein they expose groups of individuals to crowded rooms and observe their reactions. Of course, laboratory experiments have limitations: Aggression there cannot be equated with aggression in the home or on the streets, and crowding in a room for a short period of time undoubtedly has less of an effect on human behavior than chronically overcrowded conditions. Nevertheless, there have been interesting results. One typical study (Freedman et al., 1972) found that crowding did make males more aggressive and hostile, although it did not have this effect on females. When males were in uncrowded rooms, they did not show this increase in aggression and hostility. On the other hand, pseudoexperiments in prisons (in which rates of violence have been studied in conjunction with increases in crowding) have found no increase in violent behavior among inmates as crowding increases (Gaes, 1994;

Sechrest, 1991). Sechrest pointed out that jail populations in the United States grew 10% each year between 1978 and 1987. He studied both inmate-on-inmate assaults and inmate-on-staff assaults in a facility for 1,406 men, and found that the location of the assaults was more important in predicting them than was density or crowding. Of course, studies of prison crowding and violence also may not be representative of street violence, although they do involve "real" violence.

Studies of the effects of crowding in "natural" conditions are also apparently mixed. Research on younger school-aged children living in crowded conditions in India found that residential crowding was associated with increased blood pressure, behavior problems, and academic problems (Evans, Lepore, Shejwal, & Palsane, 1998). In contrast, research on college-aged students found no physiological effect from crowding (Rousseau & Standing, 1995). Such differences in research may suggest that people of different ages experience crowding differently. Another study attempted to explain such differences in findings by pointing out that crowding may not have a direct effect on physiology, aggression, or general psychological outcomes, but rather may alter typical patterns of social support and social withdrawal, which in themselves may be the more important influence (Evans & Lepore, 1993).

Overall, the evidence that crowding contributes to violence appears to be mixed. Earlier studies of violent crime suggested no relationship between urban or rural crowding and violence, although domestic violence was probably not taken into account. More recent population studies of crime in general suggest that urban (crowded) areas do experience more victimization, although not necessarily violent victimization. Studies examining general psychological outcomes from crowding are mixed. Experimental studies of the crowding of animals and the short-term crowding of humans do suggest an increase in aggression, although the aggressive responses observed cannot be equated with human violence as we see it occurring in the home and on the street. Crowding in prisons, a more natural environment, does not appear to increase the rate of violence in those institutions. Reviewers have noted the marked inconsistency of the data on this relationship (Gaes, 1994). One possible mechanism, and confound, may be differential reactions to crowding. For example, one study compared males and females on their reactions to high density (Ruback & Riad, 1994), and found that although males reacted to high density with more psychological distress, females did not. This study is tangential but suggests that different types of samples may provide different results in the study of crowding and aggression. Undoubtedly, firm conclusions must await more research.

Chapter 4

Biological and Psychological Bases of Violent Behavior

Violent crimes can be as baffling as they are repelling. In England, two 10-year-old boys lured a 2-year-old away from his mother at a shopping mall; they took him down to the local railroad tracks, where they beat him to death and left his body to be run over by a train. In the United States, a group of teenagers shot and killed a man whose car they were stealing—even though the man had willingly handed over his car keys and was not resisting the theft in any way. In Massachusetts, a group of young teenage schoolgirls planned to murder their English teacher because she was too strict:

> After the final bets were in, Okiki, a 13-year-old honor student, sat stone-faced at her desk in English class, silently preparing to collect a couple of hundred dollars on a dare. She had settled on a simple plan. Just wait for the bell to ring, reach into her book bag, grab the 12-inch fillet knife she had brought from home and stab the teacher in the chest. . . . But there is something that troubles [Sergeant] Cambarere even more [than this plan]: his first glimpse of the girls when they were brought into the police department. "They were giggling." (Hull, 1993, p. 37)

In some social circumstances, it is not so difficult to understand why violence happens. For example, soldiers shoot other soldiers in a battle because failing to do so may mean their own death. Even John Hinckley's assassination attempt on President Ronald Reagan had some purpose behind it: He was attempting to impress Jodie Foster, an actress whom he admired. Other violence, however, seems completely devoid of motive or sense. How could 13-year-old girls possibly plot to kill their teacher "because she 'got in my face'"? How can it be that they were unafraid of repercussions and unconcerned by the idea of committing such a terrible crime? Why would 10-year-old children kill a completely innocent 2-year-old? Why would car thieves risk being charged with murder, when killing their victim was completely unnecessary?

To understand the causes of violence, it is not always enough to understand the external circumstances that often drive other types of criminal behavior. It is true that violence sometimes results from factors such as an individual's desire for financial gain or from an individual's repeated exposure to violent behavior in his or her social environments. Sometimes, however, it also happens in an apparently motiveless fashion. *Violence is never truly without motive,* but its motives may be so complex and elusive that it *appears* motiveless. In all cases, but particularly in cases of violence that appear to have no motive, internal or individual factors may be critical in understanding the cause of such behavior. A variety of different biological and psychological influences and mechanisms have been considered over the years. I summarize them here and attempt to construct a more comprehensive model of the causes of violent behavior.

BIOLOGICAL PERSPECTIVES

One of the first people to think seriously about why violent people behave the way that they do was a man named Cesare Lombroso. Writing in 1876, Lombroso discussed his belief that criminal behavior resulted from a primitive instinct that increased some people's likelihood of behaving in a criminal manner. Lombroso also assumed that people who behave like criminals have biologically different brains. That is, he was interested in the idea that criminals are born biologically destined to behave violently or antisocially, regardless of their social environment. At the time of his work, our understanding of human biology was primitive and thus Lombroso could not discuss specific biological mechanisms. In addition, he was not particularly interested in the interaction between a person's biology and their psychosocial influences. However, Lombroso was one of the first major figures to publicly advance the theory that violence is primarily, if not completely, due to biological causes.

Types of Biological Influences

There exists a mistaken tendency to use interchangeably the terms *biological* and *genetic.* In fact, genetic influences are only one type of biological influences on behavior. There are (at least) two different types of biological influences: genetic influences and biological environmental influences. *Genetic influences* refer to the blueprints for behavior that are contained in a person's chromosomes. Chromosomes contain deoxyribonucleic acid (DNA), the genetic material a person inherits from his or her biological parents, which is referred to as *genotype* (Johnson, 1991). An individual's *phenotype* is the outward expression of his or her genotype. For example, one may carry genes for both blue and brown eyes; that would be one's genotype. One's phenotype would be brown eyes only, however, because brown-eye genes dominate over blue-eye genes. Similarly, it is theoretically possible for a person to carry genes that influence behavior; the behavior they actually express would be the phenotype of those genes. We know that DNA predetermines some aspects of an individual's phenotype, such as eye color or hair type. Whether, and how strongly, it affects the behavior of an individual is the question many researchers study.

Biological environmental influences, unlike genetic influences, are events that affect a person biologically but are not encoded into the person's DNA. For example, consider a head injury from a car accident, which subsequently changes the victim's personality. The head injury is unmistakably a biological environmental influence. But no genotype determines that someone will have a car accident; however, such an accident, and its accompanying head injury, can still have an important biological effect on the person's behavior.

Lombroso, the 19th-century biologist discussed earlier, was interested in *genetic* influences, and considered them the single most important influence in determining criminal behavior. He did not consider the differential biological influences of genetics versus environment. He concluded that people who behaved in violent and antisocial ways were "born criminals"—destined to be criminals by their genes. He believed that a life of crime was the inevitable destiny of people who had certain biological features. Finally, he made the classic error of assuming that genetics exert an *immutable* influence on behavior—that is, that a person's psychological environment cannot mold or influence a behavior if it is genetically encoded—an assumption we now know to be often untrue. Genetic influences on behavior are often influenced heavily by a person's psychological environment ("Mind and murder," 1994).

The Nature–Nurture Debate

Lombroso's announcement that biology was the only important factor in causing crime eventually set off a firestorm of controversy. However, Lombroso was not the only person who believed that biology was the most important factor influencing behavior. Around the turn of the century, as today, the major discipline examining human behavior was psychology. At that time, most psychologists, like Lombroso, were convinced of the primary importance of genetic influences and did not question the idea that criminal behavior was "inborn" (West, 1988).

> Adler had ... selected a feature, aggressiveness, common to all instinctual life, and then regarded it as the one and only key to the understanding of all psychological problems. (Jones, 1955, p. 262)

The error made here was clearly one of oversimplification. Early psychologists often put forward theories that attempted to ascribe all behavior, or huge classes of behavior, to one simple cause or theory (such as genetics). Today we know that behavior is an immensely complex issue that is typically influenced by many different factors. But in 1914, old theories held sway and new theories were regarded with suspicion. At that time, however, a young, bold psychologist by the name of John Watson (1878–1958) began a revolution. Watson concluded that the genesis of troubled behavior lay in the individual's *psychological environment,* and that it was that environment that exerted the most profound influence on behavior, rather than any biological influences. Rather than examine a patient's physiology or inner mind, Watson proposed to focus simply on overt behavior. He called his new approach *behaviorism* (Reed, 1989). For more established psychologists, these ideas represented a rejection of all their beliefs and work. But these ideas have penetrated criminology, and most criminologists today believe that Lombroso was at least partially wrong about the origins of criminal behavior, and that the *psychological environment* (also called *social learning*) is responsible for crime and violence. This controversy, between those experts who believe that biology is the key to criminality and those who believe that people *learn* to be criminals, is called the *nature–nurture debate.*

Modern Biological Theories

As the 20th century wore on, psychologists continued to make interesting discoveries about learning and violent behavior. However, one finding consistently emerged: Although learning was clearly related to violent behavior, learning theories alone could not fully explain violence in human beings.

As an example, consider the principle of *imitation:* It states that children may learn to be violent by imitating an adult's aggression. According to this principle, one would expect that children who grow up watching violent parents would be

---

Does Violence Run in Families?

Most people believe that if a child either witnesses or is the target of violence from a parent, then he or she is destined to become a violent person. In fact, this isn't really the case. Having a violent parent does increase the risk. However, most children of violent parents do not grow up to become violent themselves. If you compare children of nonviolent parents to children of violent parents, you would indeed see that proportionately, more children of violent parents were violent themselves. Therefore, it is clear that having violent parents is detrimental, in that it increases the risk of violence in a child. However, having violent parents by no means "dooms" any given child to becoming violent. As stated before, most children of violent parents still won't grow up to become violent.

violent themselves. As the theory predicts, a higher proportion of children who witness violent parents are violent, in comparison to other children; however, despite their higher risk, many children of violent parents do not, in fact, behave aggressively as adults (Spatz Widom, 1989a).

Some children who are exposed to violent psychosocial environments do become violent; many other children who are similarly exposed do not (Kandel et al., 1988; Spatz Widom, 1989a, 1989b; Werner & Smith, 1982). This fact led researchers to hypothesize that some children are *vulnerable* to noxious circumstances, whereas others are *resilient* or *invincible*—that is, resilient children survive and cope well despite terrible circumstances (Werner & Smith, 1982). For example, consider two siblings—a brother and a sister—who grow up watching their parents fight violently with each other. The brother is ultimately violent with his own family, but the sister never uses violence as an adult. Why did the brother adopt and imitate his parents' violence, whereas the sister remained relatively less vulnerable? Westley Dodd, a notorious serial killer who kidnapped, sexually abused, and brutally murdered several children in the northwest United States, had siblings who evidenced no signs of seriously violent behavior.

What makes one child resilient and another child vulnerable? One possible difference between resilient and vulnerable children is their biology. Perhaps unfortunate genetic influences or biological environmental influences serve to weaken some children, thus making them vulnerable. On the other hand, perhaps positive biological influences strengthen some children, thus making them resilient. The fact that children are differentially vulnerable suggests that biology may be an important difference among violent versus nonviolent people.

Another piece of evidence has emerged that supports the importance of biology as one cause of violence. In the past few decades, researchers have conducted longitudinal studies that track the same group of people over long periods of time, usually years. Several important studies (Eley, Lichtenstein, & Stenvenson, 1999; Farrington, 1978; Olweus, 1979) have found that aggressive behavior is (in some children) a stable characteristic from very early childhood until adulthood. Both boys and girls may show that stability of aggression, which seems to become more stable as the child grows (Loeber & Hay, 1997). When a behavior begins very early in life, before a child has been exposed to any psychological environment for a lengthy period of time, it likely that this behavior is strongly influenced by biological factors. Thus, the evidence from longitudinal studies suggests that early biological factors (such as genetic influences, or early biological environment) may operate during an individual's entire lifetime to affect their tendency to be violent.

In summary, there are two major pieces of evidence that suggest the importance of biology as well as learning: (a) the early emergence of aggressive behavior as a stable characteristic in some individuals, and (b) individual differences in vulnerability to noxious environmental influences (such as having violent parents). The question that remains is: What biological influences are important in making a child more or less vulnerable to poor psychosocial environments?

Physiology and Anatomy

One type of biological factor that might influence the development of violence is anatomical differences between the brains of violent individuals and nonviolent individuals—in shape or matter.

One type of anatomical difference that has been studied in relation to violence is the presence of a brain tumor. A brain tumor is an uncontrolled growth mass in the brain. There are two types of brain tumors: those that actively destroy healthy brain tissue, and those that cause problems by compressing brain tissue until it is unable to function normally. Brain tumors, which offer gross (large) insults to brain integrity, undoubtedly cause changes in behavior, including personality changes. A few violent criminals have been found to have brain tumors upon autopsy (Mark & Ervin, 1970). Some testing has also found brain dysfunction in forensic populations (Friedt & Gouvier, 1989). One study found a high incidence of focal (that is, small and localized) abnormalities in the left hemisphere of violent individuals who also tended to be mentally retarded, epileptic, or who had suffered from earlier brain damage (Pillmann et al., 1999). In general, however, there was no relationship between EEG abnormalities and violent behavior (Pillmann et al., 1999). The pattern of this research suggests that while focal abnormalities such as tumors might exacerbate violence in some individuals (probably those who have multiple impairments), in general they are not a typical cause of violent behavior. The earlier findings of tumors had caused some excitement in the scientific community; these individuals raised the possibility that extreme, senseless violence may be due, at least in part, to brain tumors that radically affect normal brain function, or that worsen more subtle brain deficits. In reality, however, this scenario would only fit a small number of violent offenders. Most violent offenders do not have brain tumors, and research in this area suggests strongly that brain tumors (and other types of massive brain damage) are not an important factor in the etiology of the majority of violence. To date, the hypothesis that violence is due to massive brain dysfunction appears to have little support, and autopsies of chronically violent offenders usually find no noticeable (i.e., major) brain damage (Goldman, 1977).

However, not all damage to the brain is massive. Damage to the brain ranges from extremely minimal to extremely major. Most cases of brain damage are at the minimal end of the spectrum, although it is the major cases that are the most noticeable.

Minimal Brain Damage. Also called *minimal brain dysfunction,* minimal brain damage does not "look" like major brain damage. A person with minimal brain dysfunction will not have "obvious" brain damage; however, minimal dysfunction may affect behavior, emotions, learning, or memory—that is, the more subtle (or "higher") functions of the brain. For example, although major brain damage might result in severe mental retardation, minor brain dysfunction might result in a learning disability that would not necessarily affect intelligence in any way (e.g., dyslexia). Because we know that minimal brain dysfunction appears to be related to problems such as learning disorders and hyperactivity (Halperin & Newcorn, 1997; Lynam, 1996; Waldrop & Goering, 1971; Weiss, 1990), it is logical for scientists to be interested in the possibility that minimal brain dysfunction is related to behavioral problems like violence.

Minor Physical Anomalies.   The problem is, how does one measure minimal brain dysfunction? Most neurological tests, including brain scans, only show major damage. Because there are no brain scans for minor damage, we can only measure it indirectly. One indirect way to measure minor brain dysfunction is through external physical markers called *minor physical anomalies.* Minor physical anomalies are minor external malformations of the skin or external features. Examples of minor physical anomalies are having the second toe of your foot be longer than your big toe, or having only one crease on your palm, instead of three. Such minor malformations are common; almost everyone has one or two minor physical anomalies. However, people who have four or more have an unusually high number. Why would having four or more minor physical anomalies suggest that minor brain dysfunction was present?

During fetal development, the brain develops from a more primitive structure called the *neural tube.* Part of the neural tube is called the *neural crest.* The neural crest is the basis for both the formation of the brain and the formation of other tissues, including skin and bones. This means that pregnancy disturbances that affect the development of the neural crest could result in both minor external malformations and minor brain dysfunction (Geschwind & Galaburda, 1987). Indeed, we know that pregnancy difficulties in rats can result in both minor brain malformations and minor external malformations (Geschwind & Galaburda, 1987).

If minor physical anomalies are an indication of minor brain dysfunction, then individuals with a very high number of anomalies might display violent behavior and other behavioral problems. But has there been any link found between minor physical anomalies and violent behavior?

Interestingly, a series of studies has found a relationship between minor physical anomalies and childhood behaviors related to adult aggression (such as hyperactivity) and criminal violence as an adult. Studies of children with behavior disorders related to delinquency often find that the children have high numbers of minor physical anomalies (Arseneault, Tremblay, Boulerice, Seguin, & Saucier, 2000; Fogel, Mednick, & Michelsen, 1985; Nichols, 1987; Waldrop & Goering, 1971). One longitudinal study followed 170 Montreal (Canada) boys from kindergarten through adolescence; they were examined at age 14, when their minor physical anomalies were assessed. This study found that MPAs were related to an increased risk of violent delinquency by age 17, as measured by both self-report and official records, although MPAs were not related to property offending (Arseneault et al., 2000). Another study, which followed children from birth until adulthood, found that subjects with high numbers of minor physical anomalies as children were at significantly higher risk of recidivistic, violent criminal activity as adults (Kandel, 1988; Kandel, Brennan, & Mednick, 1989).

Neuropsychological Testing.   Minor physical anomalies are only one indirect way of assessing minor brain dysfunction. A second way is *neuropsychological testing.* Neuropsychological. tests are verbal or visual tests that measure subtle brain functions such as learning and memory abilities. These tests may reveal subtle brain deficits that go undetected by more conventional neurological testing. Researchers have administered neuropsychological tests to violent criminals, and have found evidence that such individuals often have subtle brain impairments (Elliott, 1978; Friedt & Gouvier, 1989; Guillette, Meza, Aquilar, Soto, & Garcia, 1998; Krynicki, 1978; Landrigan et al., 1999; Robinson & Kelley, 1998; Spellacy, 1977, 1978; Yeudall & Fromm-Auch, 1979; Yeudall, Fromm-Auch, & Davies, 1982). One recent study found that a low score on a neuropsychological frontal lobe task predicted aggressiveness among 72 White males (Giancola & Zeichner, 1994). Studies on children found links between behavior problems, aggression and acting out, and neuropsychological abnormalities (Guillette et al., 1998; Landrigan et al., 1999). An in-depth study comparing chronic violent offenders to nonviolent offenders found that the violent offenders were significantly more likely to demonstrate a number of indicators of abnormal neuropsychological function, including head injuries, seizures, headaches, hypoglycemia, dizziness, poor coordination, and speech and vision problems (Robinson & Kelley, 1998). Furthermore, subjects with poor neuropsychological functioning, particularly in the frontal lobe region, are more aggressive when provoked (Lau, Pihl, & Peterson, 1995). Other studies also linked frontal lobe dysfunction and antisocial behavior (Kandel & Freed, 1989).

Head Injury.   A third way of measuring minor brain dysfunction is through studying the medical history of a person to reveal head injuries that did not result in gross brain damage. Head injuries can cause anything from extremely minor to extremely major brain damage. If a head injury seems severe enough to be noticed (e.g., if the patient was knocked unconscious), but the injury did not result in major brain damage, then it is at least possible that it resulted in minor brain damage. One study compared 27 control children to 27 children who had suffered brain injuries. The children who had suffered the injuries were significantly more likely to show problems with aggression and antisocial behavior; this was true even for the eight children who showed mild brain injuries (Andrews, Rose, & Johnson, 1998). Ommaya and his colleagues studied military discharges and found that individuals with mild brain injuries were much more likely than others to be discharged for "behavioral" reasons, including criminal convictions (Ommaya, Salazr, Dannenberg, Chervinsky, & Schwab, 1996). One bizarre case was recently presented at a meeting of the American Academy of Physical Medicine and Rehabilitation. The case involved a 47-year-old graphic designer with no history of psychological problems or antisocial behavior, who suffered a mild head injury and developed impulsive behavior including property crimes (Moon, 2000).

Researchers, like Dorothy Otnow Lewis of New York University, have combed the medical histories of some of the most violent people in our society. Lewis and other researchers found that the medical histories of violent delinquents reveal unusually high levels of head injuries (Busch, Zagar, Hughes, Arbit, & Bussell, 1990; Lewis, Shanok, & Balla, 1979; Rosenbaum & Hoge, 1989).

In summary, although both major and minor brain damage may cause violence, the weight of the evidence suggests that the most important type of brain dysfunction in people who are chronically violent and criminal is minimal brain dysfunction. Although it is almost certain that most people with minimal brain dysfunction will never be violent, a noticeably high number of repeat violent offenders show some level of brain dysfunction (usually minimal).

Neurotransmitters

Neurotransmitters, commonly referred to as *brain chemicals,* are chemical messengers that transmit information between neurons in the central nervous system. Because neurons do not physically touch each other, they must send out neurotransmitters to communicate. There are many different types of neurotransmitters, and they tend to specialize in function. How much, or how little, of any particular neurotransmitter chemical is in your brain is an important determinant of many types of behavior. Both biology and psychosocial environment affect the levels of different neurotransmitters, and thus affect behavior. Several psychological disorders, such as schizophrenia (a common form of psychosis or insanity), are at least partially caused by too much or too little of one type of neurotransmitter or another. A logical question, therefore, is whether violent behavior is related (at least in part) to the level of certain neurotransmitters in the brains of violent people.

As stated previously, there are many different types of neurotransmitters in the brain. However, monoamine neurotransmitters have been most significantly linked to aggression (Berman & Coccaro, 1998). Past research has linked low levels of serotonin with violence, particularly with impulsive aggression (Brown, 1990; Virkkunen & Linnoila, 1993). Of the monoamines, low levels of *serotonin* have been implicated most strongly in recent research. One study of rhesus macaque monkeys found that low levels of a serotonin metabolite were found in dominant monkeys and that levels in general were negatively correlated with aggression (Westergaard, Suomi, Higley, & Melham, 1999). This study pointed out that low levels of serotonin were, in fact, adaptive for some monkeys in that it enabled them to attain a dominant status. Studies in humans, however, have generally failed to note positive results of low levels of serotonin. One study of adolescent boys with conduct disorders found a negative correlation between their levels of serotonin and the severity of their violent offending (Unis et al., 1997). The study found that this relationship was particularly strong in boys with childhood onset of conduct disorders (as opposed to boys whose conduct disorders did not emerge until adolescence). Another recent study injected both male and female subjects with a serotonin-releasing agent, but interestingly found that although a link between hostility, aggression, and low serotonin was found, it was only noted in male subjects (Cleare & Bond, 1997). Stanley and her colleagues (2000) studied serotonin levels in 64 psychiatric patients with a variety of diagnoses. They found that serotonin levels were lower in aggressive subjects —and that this was true for all types of psychiatric diagnoses. The researchers also noted that impulsivity was also linked to serotonin function. This suggested the possibility that aggression and impulsivity may share common biological roots. Yet another study linked serotonin levels to aggression *other* than inter-personal aggression: New and her colleagues found an association between low levels of serotonin and self-injurious, suicidal behavior among a sample of personality-disordered, suicidal subjects (New et al., 1997).

One criticism of this body of research is that the subjects involved are pre-dominantly drawn from clinical populations: that is, they are all individuals with behavioral and mental disorders. However, one large-scale study examined sub-jects who were participating in a cardiac study—not a psychiatric population (Manuck et al., 1998). This study is also interesting because it examined men and women between the ages of 30 and 60, which are significantly older than the highest risk ages for violent and aggressive behavior (16–24 years). The study found that among the male subjects, reduced serotonin activity was in fact linked to aggression and hostility, even in this mentally healthy population of middle-aged males. Among the females, low serotonin had no effect with one exception: Post-menopausal women tended to exhibit higher hostility levels (although their aggression levels remained unaffected).

A second criticism of the literature focuses on its conceptual use of "aggres-sion" as a measure, as opposed to measuring actual violent criminal offending. Berman and Coccaro (1998) acknowledged the connection between serotonin function and aggression, but pointed out the paucity of studies that use violent *criminal offending* as a measure. However, an excellent large-scale study of 781 21-year-olds in a birth cohort found results that are very consistent with the lit-erature in general: Whole blood serotonin levels were, in fact, found to be asso-ciated with violent criminal offending, although again that finding was true for males but not true for females (T. E. Moffitt et al., 1998).

Other studies found data that indirectly implicates serotonin function. David-son and his colleagues studied 500 violent individuals through a study of their brain scans and found a high rate of defects in the prefrontal cortex—an area that regulates serotonin function (Davidson & Putman, 2000).

Both Davidson (Davidson & Putman, 2000) and Stanley et al. (2000) suggested that psychoactive medications may be useful in controlling serotonin function and thus potentially controlling violent behavior. However, at the current time data do not suggest that simply controlling the levels of these neurotransmitters would eliminate violent behavior in humans. Furthermore, it is not likely to be such a simple fix. Other neurobiological researchers have brought up the possibility that any one biological factor may be partially responsible for certain types of violence but not necessarily all types (Raine, Meloy, et al., 1998). Furthermore, the effects of neurotransmitters are particularly complex and are both caused by, and cause, changes in behavior. None of these caveats are meant to dismiss the potential importance of neurotransmitters in violence, but at present, there probably needs to be a better understanding of the role and mechanism of neurotransmitters, the complex relationships they have with human behavior, and the potential role of mediating environmental variables (Kruesi & Jacobsen, 1997).

Hormones

Hormones are also chemical messengers within the body; they are similar to neurotransmitters, but are also different in several important ways. First, neurotransmitters are very fast messengers, whereas hormones carry messages much more slowly. Second, although neurotransmitters only work within the brain and the spinal cord, hormones are chemical messengers that are distributed throughout the entire body.

Two hormones have been the focus of most research on aggression and criminality: *testosterone* and *cortisol*. Testosterone is one of the male sex hormones, called *androgens*. Both males and females secrete androgens, but males secrete a much greater quantity than do females. Androgens are frequently cited as an important cause of aggressive behavior, particularly intermale aggression. What is the evidence that this is true?

A 1995 study of 692 male prisoners compared those who had committed sex and violent crimes with those who had committed only property crimes on salivary testosterone levels (Dabbs, 1995). Interestingly, the higher testosterone levels were associated both with sexual and violent offending as well as with generally more intractable and confrontational behavior—what might, in another interpretation, be seen as dominance behaviors. Dabbs and his colleagues found a wide variety of behaviors marking the high testosterone males, of which more sexual and violent offending was only one.

A study of 13 elderly men suffering from dementia, however, found that although testosterone was related to aggressive behavior, it was not found to be related to agitated and confrontational behavior (Orengo, Kunik, Ghusn, & Yudofsky, 1997).

In 1996, Banks and Dabbs published a study in which they compared the testosterone levels found in young adult delinquents to levels found in a group of college student controls. The researchers compared 36 students to 29 delinquents, and matched them for age, sex, and race. Some of the delinquents had drug offenses and some had violent offenses. Generally, the violent offenses tended to be milder, although two subjects had committed homicide. Banks and Dabbs found that the delinquent subjects had higher testosterone levels than the student controls. Furthermore, this was true for both male and female offenders (Banks & Dabbs, 1996).

Again, some inconsistencies emerge. For example, a Spanish study of preschoolers uncovered slightly different findings. Sanchez-Martin et al. (2000) studied 28 male and 20 female preschoolers. They examined the children's play behavior via videotaped sessions. The play was "free play"—that is, not scripted activities. Finally, the researchers measured salivary testosterone in the children. Interestingly, although they did find a significant relationship between hostile aggression and testosterone in male children, they found no such association in female children (unlike Dabbs' earlier research; Sanchez-Martin et al., 2000). They also found no association between testosterone and the tendency of a child to engage in playful (not hostile) aggression.

Another study of domestic violence also found an association between testosterone and aggression. Soler and colleagues studied 54 men from low socioeconomic backgrounds. They asked these men to self-report on their aggression levels with their domestic partners, and a high percentage reported some form of verbal or physical aggression. Furthermore, testosterone levels were significantly correlated with these types of self-reported aggression (Soler, Vinayak, & Quadagno, 2000). Of course, inasmuch as this study utilized self-report measures of aggression, it is possible that aggressive men were mistakenly included in the "low aggression" group if they failed to report their own violent behavior.

Finally, if high testosterone helps cause aggression, will low testosterone help reduce it? A newer way to study the impact of androgens on aggression is through the forensic use of chemical castration. This process involves the administration of the female hormone medroxyprogesterone acetate (Depo-provera) that decreases the functioning of testosterone (one of the androgens). The theory is that such an administration will decrease a male's sexual drive and permit the release of repeat sex offenders into society (Spodak, Falck, & Rappeport, 1978). Despite some anecdotal reports of success in stopping sexual offense recidivism, clinicians have noted that chemical castration does not work in all male offenders and that as many as half are still able, despite treatment, to function sexually (Sheremata, 1997). Another study used a different approach: Some researchers examined the impact of artificially reducing testosterone levels without castration. This experiment involved eight normal men, so its findings may or may not be generalizable to violent criminal offenders (Loosen, Purdon, & Pavlou, 1997). Loosen and his colleagues found, interestingly, that some effects were the same for all men whereas other effects happened only in some of the men. For example, all eight men showed marked reductions in "outward-directed" anger, but only half exhibited reductions in anxiety and sexual desire (Loosen et al., 1994). Neither study really suggests that lowering testosterone, either through castration or through chemical means, is decidedly effective on violent males.

The literature that implicates testosterone as an important cause of violence may seem strong, but research is rarely as clear as it appears at first glance. There are inconsistencies. Some research points to aggression and dominance/hostility as being related to testosterone, and other research fails to find that dominance/hostility measures are related to sex hormones. Some research notes a testosterone–aggression relationship in both males and females; other research finds it only for males. Reducing testosterone demonstrated that in different men, it plays different psychological roles, and there is no clear evidence that it might effectively reduce violence in all violent males. Despite this, some consistencies emerge: Clearly testosterone may play *some* role in causing aggressive behavior in at least some offenders. What factors might account for the inconsistencies found in the aforementioned literature?

Bernhardt has suggested that perhaps more than one biological factor must go wrong for testosterone to truly have a deleterious effect. He pointed out that although studies have linked high levels of testosterone to aggression, this relationship cannot be a simple one because successful athletes and businessmen also tend to have high testosterone levels, although they are usually not violent individuals (Bernhardt, 1997). Bernhardt pointed out that testosterone may be acting in accord with low serotonin in violent individuals, and that it may be this "double whammy" that results in criminally violent behavior. He pointed out that serotonin, in addition to being linked to aggression, is also linked to hyperresponsiveness to bad events. Possibly, what is happening is that when a high testosterone male is thwarted in his dominance attempts—when he fails—then if he "hyperresponds" to this bad event, he will evidence aggression. Thus, Bernhardt's intriguing theory suggested, as many other researchers have, that there probably needs to be more than one system malfunctioning to achieve a truly violent individual.

Another theory suggests that high testosterone levels might have social and psychological implications as well as biological ones, and that a person might need to be exposed to social problems *in addition* to the biological factors to develop a markedly violent tendency. Raine and his colleagues studied 1130 male and female children from the Indian Ocean island of Mauritius as part of a prospective cohort study. They found that children who were taller and heavier at age 3—correlates of higher testosterone—were also more aggressive, more fearless, and sought more stimulation then their peers (Raine, Reynolds, Venables, Mednick, & Farrington, 1998). Raine speculated that these children might be expected to have suffered socially as well. For example, taller and heavier children might bully more both because they are more likely to have been exposed to more testosterone, and because, being bigger, they find it easier to be a bully. Thus, this study exposed the complex nature of human social interaction and biology. Our biology impacts us all, and in turn, it impacts our ability to socialize with other human beings, which in its own turn, helps to determine our own behavior.

One final theory, and one of the most compelling, has to do with the timing of exposure to testosterone. We assume that because higher testosterone is measured in grown men that it is *then* that it must be making its greatest impact. However, a significant body of research has implicated prenatal exposure to testosterone as a likely source of influence on brain development and thus on behavior (Fishbein, 1992; Kim & Rubin, 1997). Fetal exposure to high levels of androgens (male-typical range or clinically-high range) may affect the tendency to be violent in two ways. First, prenatal exposure to androgens appears to actually lower the tendency of a person to behave in a prosocial manner (L. Ellis, 1990). Second, levels of prenatal testosterone are theoretically related to levels of MAO, which affects general aggressiveness and feelings of anger and frustration (L. Ellis, 1991). Like androgens administered to transsexuals, androgens administered prenatally may also affect emotions related to aggression. A series of studies that examined individuals who were exposed to unusually high levels of androgens prenatally found that such persons have an increased risk of being aggressive and violent, supporting the notion that it may be androgen exposure during fetal brain development that is most critical (Berenbaum & Hines, 1992; Berenbaum & Resnick, 1997). Finally, a fascinating study of twins (E. Miller et al., 1998) studied the behavioral differences in females who had a female twin versus a male twin. Theoretically, his team expected the female twins who had a male twin to hold more "masculine attitudes" then females who had female twins. The reason for this, theoretically, was because female twins are exposed to more testosterone in utero if they have a male twin than in they have a female twin. Although there are other possible interpretations of these findings—most notably, the social influence of having a male twin—it remains possible that being exposed in utero to unusually high levels of testosterone can have an effect on brain development.

A second hormone that has been implicated more recently is *cortisol*. Cortisol is the hormone that regulates our bodies' reactions to stress. It is involved with the immune system and with sex hormones as well. A few studies have linked low levels of cortisol with a tendency to be aggressive. For example, one study looked at 38 boys, aged 7 to 12, who had been referred to a clinic for behavior problems. The boys were enrolled in a long-term study, and their behaviors were recorded for 4 years, based on reports from their teachers and parents. There were also some reports from the boys themselves and some from their peers. Finally, the researchers also studied levels of cortisol in the boys' saliva. Not only was low cortisol associated with aggression in general, but also it was associated with boys who were the *most* aggressive and who showed aggressive symptoms the *earliest* during the study years (McBurnett, Lahey, Rathouz, & Loeber, 2000). Boys who had higher cortisol levels were spread across categories—some exhibited symptoms earlier, some later. But of the boys in the low-cortisol group, almost every single one exhibited aggressive symptoms by age 10. Thus, although low cortisol levels indicated that a child would develop an earlier onset of aggression, having a higher cortisol level did not protect from also developing an earlier onset—at least, it only protected some children.

Another study found similar results. Pajer and her colleagues studied 47 adolescent girls with conduct disorder and 37 controls. They measured cortisol in all subjects, and found that those with conduct disorder had significantly lower cortisol levels, relative to the control subjects. This was found even when they controlled for probable confounds such as age and socioeconomic status (Pajer, Gardner, Rubin, Perel, & Neal, 2001).

In summary, evidence suggests that hormones play a significant, but not a simple, role in determining violent behavior. This is not surprising, inasmuch as hormones are known to impact many human behaviors, and in every case they have a profound, complex impact that is mediated by a variety of variables— both biological and social.

Genetics

For decades, researchers have searched for the "aggression gene." In one Dutch family with at least 14 men with strong violent tendencies, researchers did find a genetic mutation on the X chromosome (Morell, 1993). Despite such cases, the majority of researchers agree that violence does not appear to be a behavioral tendency that is transmitted via a simple, directly acting gene (Mednick & Kandel, 1988; Mestel, 1994; Smedley, 2000). In any case, it is clear that if genetic bases for aggression and violence exist, they are clearly mutable and changeable by a person's psychological environment; the old idea that genetics determines one's behavior *absolutely* is clearly mistaken.

The case for genetics as a cause of aggression and adult criminal violence has to be pieced together from a number of different areas of study. First, we know that children with violent parents do have a higher tendency to be violent themselves (Spatz Widom, 1989a, 1989b). In fact, one study that found that adolescent murderers tend to have violent fathers suggested that genetics might be an important cause of the teenagers' aggression (Lewis et al., 1985). Despite this earlier research, however, the field needs to make the critical distinction between biological *heredity* versus family psychology. Parents provide a psychological, as well as a biological, environment for their children. What do parents teach their children, and what do they pass to them through their genes?

Twin Studies.   Twin studies are studies that typically compare identical (monozygotic) to fraternal (dizygotic) twins. Identical twins are the only human beings alive who are genetically identical. Fraternal twins are genetically siblings only; they carry similar genes, as siblings do, but not identical genes as identical

> **Genetics or Environment?**
>
> Don was a mean and violent young man, unhappily married, with three children. Although he was frequently absent due to his repeated incarcerations on petty property and violent crimes, when he was home he often beat both his wife and his children. His oldest son, Joe, started to get into trouble as soon as he turned 12; at age 19, he was arrested and convicted of sexual assault with a deadly weapon and attempted murder. He had tried, but failed, to kill his victim. Did Don pass on "violent" genes to his son, or did he "teach" him to be violent by being a violent role model?

twins do. Therefore, if a behavior is found more commonly in both identical twins and less commonly in both fraternal twins, then one conclusion is that that behavior may be genetically heritable. This is called *concordance*. For example, suppose you take a group of identical twins, and you pick out every single Twin A who is a nail-biter. Then, you look to see what percentage of Twin Bs are also nail-biters. If 25% of Twin Bs are nail-biters just as Twin As are, then you have a concordance rate of 25% for nail-biting. Some psychological disorders have much higher concordance rates. For example, schizophrenia has a concordance rate of 50%; if one identical twin has schizophrenia, then there is a 50% chance that the other twin will also have schizophrenia. Researchers examining aggression and violence ask this question: Is there a higher concordance rate for aggression among identical twins than among fraternal twins? For example, if 50% of identical twins were (theoretically) concordant for aggressive behavior, but only 20% of fraternal twins were concordant for aggressive behavior, than one might conclude that aggression has a genetic component that both identical twins share, but that fraternal twins might or might not share.

Hudziak and his colleagues, who studied 492 twin pairs (comparing identical to fraternal twins), recently completed one classic twin study on aggression. The researchers surveyed the twins' parents about a broad range of behaviors, including aggression, and then cross-checked to see if aggressive behavior was more commonly found in both identical twins than in both fraternal twins. Indeed, that was precisely what they found, and the researchers estimated that, in their sample, genetics accounted for 70% to 77% of the variance in aggression (Hudziak, Rudiger, Neale, Heath, & Todd, 2000). Such a finding suggests a strong genetic influence on aggression.

Another twin study, which mostly focused on female twins, compared 183 monozygotic (identical) with 64 dizygotic (fraternal) twins. All the twins were same-sex and adults; most were female. This study examined aggression in more detail: The researchers counted fully 18 measures. They studied both physical and verbal aggression and aggressive attitudes (e.g., hostility). They found that not only were individual measures of aggression heritable—that is, more commonly found in both identical twins—but that there was a great deal of overlap between different types of aggression. In other words, not only might aggressive behaviors be heritable, but also this study suggested that the same genotype might produce a variety of aggressive behaviors. The researchers did point out that their sample was predominantly female—not male, as is most research on violence and violent crime.

Twin studies are compelling, but they suffer from a common flaw: Not only do identical twins share genes, but also they often share an environment that treats them similarly. Because they look alike and appear alike, society in general may, to varying degrees, treat them as one person or as two "versions" of one person. Because of this, identical twins are not the perfect genetics–environment experiment. Another method, which seeks more fully to separate genetics from psychological environment, is the method known as *adoption studies.*

Adoption Studies.   Adoption studies are studies that examine children who have been adopted away into a different family. Adopted children are children who have one set of biological parents, and a different set of psychological parents. By comparing the children's behavior with both their adopted parents and their genetic parents, it is possible to ascertain which behaviors are genetically inherited and which behaviors result from family environments.

Imagine that an adopted boy is having problems with violent or aggressive behavior. If both his biological and his psychological parents are violent people, then there is little we can learn from this case. If neither of his sets of parents are violent, then there is similarly little information. But what if his biological parents are violent, but his adopted parents are not? If the adopted child is aggressive in the same way as his biological parents, this suggests that violence is primarily inherited genetically, rather than learned. But what if the opposite were true—what if his adopted parents are violent, but his biological parents are not? If the adopted child is aggressive in the same way as his adopted parents, then genetics are probably relatively unimportant in causing violence.

Earlier studies, which studied children prospectively in long-term studies, found that the latter scenario appeared to be truer. Several studies found that adopted-away children are as aggressive as their adopted parents are, rather than as their biological parents are (Mednick, Gabrielli, & Hutchings, 1984). In a more recent study, researchers used a different design and obtained somewhat different results. Instead of studying child–parent behavioral traits, they studied how similarly siblings behaved (van den Oord, Boomsma, & Verhulst, 1994). They compared 221 pairs of biologically unrelated siblings to 111 pairs of biologically related siblings. All the children were adopted, but the biologically related siblings should show a higher concordance of aggression and crime if such behavior is genetically heritable.

The researchers found mixed results. Although both aggression and delinquency were heritable, aggression was much more heritable than delinquency.

Genetics accounted for 70% of the variance in aggression (similar findings to the twin studies), but only 39% of the variance in delinquency. This suggests that earlier research, which studied official records of delinquency, might not have been off-target. It is certainly plausible to find different degrees of heritability for aggression per se, versus official criminal records of offending—two measures of behavior that are clearly not the same thing. Some researchers have argued that earlier adoption studies do not rule out genetic influences, but rather point out that they are strongly mediated by environmental influences (Cadoret, Leve, & Devor, 1997).

Both twin studies and adoption studies suggest a definite degree of heritability for aggression, although neither body of research by itself draws one to the conclusion that violence is the result of a simple genetic transmission. However, there is a third body of research that is relevant here: studies that examine the heritability of *childhood precursors* of violence in adulthood. Certainly we know that violence does not simply appear in adulthood, but rather, follows disorders that appear, to greater or lesser degrees, in children who are at high risk of growing up to become aggressive or violent. What evidence is there that these childhood disorders that are linked to adult violence are at least partially caused by genetics?

Heritability of Disorders Related to Violence.   Attention Deficit/Hyperactivity Disorder (a disorder with strong ties to adult violence) may be heritable (Halperin & Newcorn, 1997). D. Sherman (1997) examined 576 twin boys between the ages of 11 and 12 and found that the data demonstrated that hyperactivity, impulsivity, and inattention were behaviors significantly influenced by genetics. Another study used a classic adoption design by examining the relatives of a group of children with ADHD (Sprich, Biederman, Crawford, Mundy, & Faraone, 2000). This study compared the biological and the adopted relatives of these children for indicates that they, too, had ADHD. They found that whereas only 6% of the adopted parents were ADHD, fully 18% of the biological parents of ADHD children exhibited ADHD symptoms.

Conduct disorders (CD) are another set of childhood disorders that are strongly linked to adult crime and violence. Studies examining this disorder also found evidence for its heritability. One recent twin study examining 2,682 adult twin pairs revealed substantial concordance for CD among identical twin pairs (Slutske et al., 1997). The behavior, which they found to be more concordant in identical twins, included weapons use, physical cruelty to animals or people, and aggression. The researchers also found, interestingly, that identical twins were more concordant for choice of playmates—a finding that might be interpreted as suggesting that their psychological environments were also more similar. However, their data yielded an estimate of heritability of approximately 71%, very much in line with other research on the heritability of these types of behaviors—"a substantial genetic influence on risk for conduct disorder," according to researchers in the United States and Australia. Symptoms of CD, usually identified in childhood, include chronic stealing, lying, bullying, arson, property destruction, weapons use, physical cruelty to animals or people, fighting, aggression, truancy, and/or running away from home.

Another twin study on the heritability of Conduct Disorders found similar results. Again, researchers studied 43 monozygotic ("identical") and 38 dizygotic ("fraternal") same-sex twins (McGuffin & Thapar, 1997). They surveyed the twins about their antisocial behaviors and found that behaviors indicative of Conduct Disorders were more concordant in identical twins. The researchers concluded that these behaviors have a significant heritable component.

Finally, Coolidge, Thede, and Jang (1999) compared 70 identical and 42 fraternal twins between the ages of 4 and 15. They were seeking to uncover the causes of a range of behavior disorders, and found that several of these disorders were significantly more concordant in identical twins. Conduct disorder was in fact one of the disorders most strongly influenced by genetics—Coolidge estimated that it demonstrated a heritability of 68% (very consistent with past research).

In summary, much of the data on the genetic basis of violence is suggestive of a significant, but not total or direct, heritability. Twin studies are interesting but cannot be definitive, because they do not separate the effects of psychological environment and genetics. Adoption studies are mixed; and studies that are indirect in nature—that is, which do not study violence directly but study other disorders related to it—suggest a heritability index of approximately 70%. In general, the data suggest that there must be a heritable component of violence; perhaps impulsivity, hyperactivity, or aggressive tendencies are genetically transmitted, but clearly this is not a simple or direct relationship. Even if one were to broadly apply the heritability estimates of 70%, such a number would imply that 30% of the reasons that people become violent is unrelated to genetics. As with most behaviors in human beings, no one simple answer suffices.

XYY Syndrome.   There is another possible way that genetics could influence violence, apart from heredity. Genetic factors may affect behavior through chromosomal anomalies—that is, mistakes in how the person's DNA copies itself. Because DNA must copy itself millions of times to create a new person, it is almost inevitable that some errors will occur, and these errors may affect behavior. One such error that has been studied in relation to violence is called the *XYY syndrome.*

The XYY syndrome is an error involving the genes that determine gender. The gender of a developing fetus is determined by the 23rd pair of chromosomes, one of which is inherited from the mother and one of which is inherited from the father. The mother always contributes a gene known as X. The father contributes either an X gene or a Y gene. If you are a female, your father contributed an X gene, and your gender genotype is XX. If you are a male, your father contributed a Y gene, and your gender genotype is XY. Most people have, thus, two genes that determine their gender: one from their mother, and one from their father.

Some males, however, have two Ys contributed to their genotype, rather than the normal one Y. Thus, their genotype is XYY instead of XY. The fact that some notorious criminals have been XYY has raised the question of the role of XYY in determining behavior. If one Y causes you to be a male, do two Ys cause you to be a "super-male"? Would two Ys cause an exaggeration of male qualities, including the higher rate of violence among males? Some scholars have suggested that XYY males are predisposed to aggressive behavior (Horan, 1992). The problem with this theory is that most violent male criminals are not XYY. Although research has indicated that there are some features associated with being XYY (such as unusual height and severe acne), violence does not appear to be one of them (Freyne & O'Connor, 1992).

PSYCHODYNAMIC PERSPECTIVES

Sigmund Freud, a brilliant, stubborn, and opinionated physician who was born in 1856 and who spent most of his life in Vienna, developed original hypotheses about the causes of human behavior. He wrote a great deal about childhood development, although ironically all of his patients were adults. The basis of Freud's hypotheses was his therapy sessions with them.

Interactions with patients led Freud to postulate that a person's behavior, including a tendency to be violent, was the product of unconscious forces in his or her mind. Freud did believe that childhood events were key in determining adult behavior, but he also felt that many of the most important childhood events were innately predetermined (Rizzuto, 1991). Freud called his school of psychology *psychoanalysis*. Modern versions are sometimes called *psychodynamic psychology*.

Unfortunately, he was also a stubborn, headstrong man who had trouble tolerating any serious challenges to his beliefs. Although he attracted a great many talented students and followers, he also broke professional relations with many of them due to his inability to entertain opinions that differed from his own. Since Freud's death in 1939, his school of psychology (and its followers) has developed and changed. Nevertheless, psychoanalysis today still emphasizes the role of the unconscious in shaping behavior.

Psychoanalysis and Violence

Freud believed that aggression was a normal but unconscious impulse that is repressed in well-adjusted people. However, if the aggressive impulsive is particularly strong or repressed to an unusual degree, then some aggression can "leak" out of the unconscious and the person may be aggressive against a random, innocent victim. Freud called this displaced aggression, and this theory might explain an attack of "senseless" violence, labeling it as aggression that was too repressed and has broken through to the surface.

Displaced Aggression?

A young boy sits in the front passenger seat of an old Ford as it cruises through his neighborhood. It is a hot summer day and he is uncomfortable and irritated. He is cradling a gun on his lap. As he passes a group of 12- and 13-year-olds playing in the street, he suddenly, and for no apparent reason, points the gun out the car window, aims at one boy, and opens fire. He pulls the trigger three times, each time hitting the child, before the startled driver of the car accelerates sharply.

The most significant criticism of Freud's hypotheses is that they were based on his personal interactions with patients, rather than on any data obtained through experimentation. Despite this, some psychoanalytic theory is widely accepted as valid. For example, the idea that unconscious motives and childhood events are important in understanding adult behavior is a cornerstone of much modern psychological theory. However, other ideas of Freud's are much less widely accepted. For example, the notion that every person has a natural, built-in aggressive impulse that must be repressed does not have scientific support (Adams et al., 1990).

OTHER PSYCHOLOGICAL AND PSYCHIATRIC PERSPECTIVES

This area of study asks: Is violence a mental illness? Do other mental illnesses cause violence, or do they increase the risk that someone will become violent? There have been intriguing case studies suggesting that violence and/or criminal behavior may at least sometimes be the result of mental illnesses. One such case involved a "baby snatcher"—a woman who repeatedly stole other people's infants (McNulty, Cahil, & Tom, 1999). The 36-year-old woman had multiple psychiatric symptoms, including seizures, borderline retardation, and aggressive behavior, and it was later determined that, following seizures, she would develop delusional beliefs about babies she saw—namely, that the babies were hers and that they had been stolen from her. Antiseizure medication controlled the seizures and the delusions, and thus the criminal baby-stealing behaviors.

This case illustrates the dream of psychiatry: that violence or criminality will be revealed to be either (a) a psychiatric problem, treatable with psychiatric medication; or (b) the result of a treatable psychiatric problem. But how often do cases like this emerge? How frequently is violence, or criminality, the result of a mental illness?

The Association Between Mental Illness, Violence, and Criminality

Are mentally ill individuals at higher risk of being violent or criminal? One study of 893 mental patients in Sweden looked at the criminal records across a variety of different diagnoses (Belfrage, 1998). Of those discharged, 28% had committed a crime within 10 years, and these crimes were both property and violent in nature, although most of the violent offending was petty (e.g., making threats). Interestingly, only schizophrenics had committed severely violent offenses—no other patients. This study showed a clear increased risk for criminality among the mentally ill, but a less clear picture emerged about an increased risk for *violent* criminality. Although violent offending did occur in the study sample, most (but not all) of it was petty.

In a review of several studies (Tardiff & Marzuk, 1996), it was noted that more recent, well-designed studies leave little doubt that there is a link between criminality and mental illness. For example, one study compared the criminal records and psychiatric records of more than 300,000 people and found a clear association between criminality and mental illness; however, there was no specific association that implied that those who are mentally ill tend to commit violent offenses as opposed to offenses in general. That is, subjects tended to commit more offenses but not any one type. Other studies of female convicts in prison populations have revealed high rates of psychiatric illnesses.

The review article also pointed out that although mental illness in general does not point specifically to increased violence, some diagnoses are clearly more closely associated with violent offending than others. One study of 693 Finnish murderers found the likelihood of violence linked to two diagnoses: schizophrenia and antisocial personality disorder (also called psychopathy).

In general, recent research seems to suggest that mental illness does increase a person's capacity or tendency toward crime, but not necessarily toward violent crime. The consensus of current research is that the mentally ill are only slightly more likely to be violent than are other members of the general population (Juss, 1997; Monahan, 1992). The fact that the media tends to focus on violent crimes committed by mentally ill individuals at least partially explains the public's concern. However, the mentally ill may become more violent than other people when other risk factors, such as substance abuse, are introduced into the equation (Juss, 1997), or when they have specific diagnoses.

Psychiatric Disorders Studied in Connection With Violent Crime

Affective Disorders. Does being depressed make a person more likely to commit a crime, or a violent crime? According to Modestin and Ammann (1997), some types of depression may place people at risk for criminal behavior. This study looked at 261 male patients diagnosed with bipolar affective disorder or with major, minor, or intermittent depressive disorder. They compared criminal records to control subjects and found that the patients with bipolar disorder (sometimes called manic–depressive illness) were in fact more often convicted of crimes than controls. However, they did not find any relationship between *serious* or *major* unipolar depression (those individuals who only become depressed, never manic) and crime. Interestingly, the patients who were only slightly depressed did have increased crime rates. Thus, although mild unipolar depression or bipolar depression increased risk, major unipolar depression did not. It may be that major depression is too crippling a disorder to permit someone to form the intent, and the action, to commit a crime.

Another study of juveniles found again that mania and bipolar depression were significantly associated with an increase in criminal behavior (Pliszka, Sherman, Barrow, & Irick, 2000). This study examined 50 adolescent boys and found that their affective disorders were associated with antisocial behavior and with drug abuse. A similar study of 74 depressed adolescents found high reports of aggression in the home and aggression at school, with 14% actually being arrested for aggressive behavior problems (Knox, King, Hanna, Logan, & Ghaziuddin, 2000). This research is noteworthy because other studies found links between depression and criminal behavior, but not violence specifically. However, it is worth pointing out that this study examined primarily aggression that did not reach "serious" levels necessitating involvement with the criminal justice system, and that parents tended to be less aware of this aggressive behavior (again suggesting that it was somewhat less serious). Thus, it may be mild to moderate unipolar depression, and bipolar depression or mania, that are linked to antisocial and criminal behavior and *possibly* to aggression and violence that is not of the most severe degree.

Panic Disorders. Is it possible that some people who are impulsively violent suffer from a disorder related to panic disorders? One intriguing study suggests that this might be so. George and his colleagues performed an experiment on 34 individuals (mostly men) who had histories of domestic violence. They gave these subjects (and a control group of nonviolent subjects) either a placebo or a dose of sodium lactate. Sodium lactate is a substance that induces panic attacks in almost all people who get panic attacks anyway. Generally, lactate does not induce panic attacks in people who typically do not get them. This was a double-blind study: Neither the researchers nor the subjects knew if they were getting or giving lactate or the placebo. Results were very interesting. The violent individuals reacted to the lactate very differently from the controls; the lactate induced in them panic, fear of losing control, and rage. One abusive man reported that the lactate induced in him the same feelings he experienced when violent. These findings suggest that some violent individuals may in fact experience the same physical problems that precede panic attacks in other people. In other words, perhaps at least some violent people are in essence having panic attacks that manifest as violence, rather than merely as overwhelming emotions.

Clearly, more research is needed to confirm this finding, but it remains an intriguing possibility.

Personality Disorders and Psychopathy. The psychiatric disorder that has been most commonly linked to crime and violence is called *antisocial personality disorder* (ASP), or *psychopathy*. This is a *personality disorder,* which is a psychological disorder that exists in a person who is not insane or psychotic, but whose psychological disturbances nevertheless affect their behavior significantly in a more or less permanent manner. The behavior of a person with ASP is characterized by constant conflict with society. These individuals are incapable of loyalty to any groups or persons and are grossly selfish, callous, irresponsible, and impulsive. They are marked by a lack of shame or guilt over their behavior; they tend to deny any responsibility for their problems and seem unable to learn from punishment or experience. ASP is diagnosed most frequently in males and in lower class individuals.

According to Hare (1996), probably the most eminent researcher who studies psychopaths, they are "intraspecies predators who use charm, manipulation, intimidation, and violence to control others and to satisfy their own selfish needs" (p. 25). Although most criminals are not psychopaths, those who are, are exceptionally dangerous. Hare estimated that 15% to 20% of the criminal population meets the diagnostic criteria for psychopathy. Fisher and Blair (1998) studied 39 boys between the ages of 9 and 16 on a series of tasks and found that psychopaths differ from others in two basic ways: (a) their ability to change and adapt responses in reaction to changing circumstances, and (b) their ability to learn the basic moral premise that it is wrong to do something if it injures another person. Larsen (2001) wrote in his book *Bad Boys, Bad Men:*

> Adults who defy social norms often establish a pattern of misbehavior in childhood, sometimes seeming to live without a conscience, to shirk the rules and expectations that keep most of us in check. They show a disturbing lack of empathy and fail to learn from their experiences, always blaming someone else for their problems and misdeeds. Such people can explain why the shopkeeper deserves to be robbed, why the spouse asks to be beaten, why their every betrayal is justified. ... While antisocials can understand the concepts of right and wrong on an intellectual level, they have no emotional connections to commonly held standards of behavior. (p. 5)

What causes psychopathy? What are the defects, if anything, that are found in people with this diagnosis? Traditionally, psychopathy was blamed on poor parenting skills or emotional deprivation, but increasingly research is pointing to very real brain differences between those who are psychopaths and those who are not. One study used magnetic resonance imaging (a detailed brain scan) to study the brains of 21 men with antisocial personality disorder and compared them to control subjects. These scans revealed that the 21 psychopathic men showed an 11% reduction in the volume of their frontal lobes (Raine, Lencz, Bihrle, LaCasse, & Colletti, 2000). Specifically, the reduction was in the cortex over the frontal lobe—the grayish "cover" over the brain that modulates our responses to stress and fearful situations. The frontal lobe has been linked to both learning and adaptability problems and reckless, impulsive, behavior. In his discussion, Raine noted that other studies have found similar problems in frontal lobe functioning. One such study compared 30 psychopaths to 30 non-psychopathic criminals, measuring how well their prefrontal cortexes were functioning (LaPierre, Claude, Braun, & Hodgins, 1995). Some areas of the prefrontal cortex showed significant impairment in the psychopaths but not in the controls. Other areas showed no differences. Interestingly, the psychopaths were unable to complete a task that required them to label an odor. This is a task that patients with frontal lobe damage also often have trouble completing.

A recent study (Charman & Blair, 2001) pointed to the temporal lobes as also being potentially involved in psychopathy. This study examined nine children with psychopathic tendencies and nine control children. The children were asked to label pictures of facial expressions, and the psychopaths had no problem with happy or angry expressions but had difficulty labeling sad and fearful facial expressions. This specific type of impairment, the researchers hypothesized, might be due to problems in the temporal lobe.

Other physiological oddities have been noted in psychopaths. One study compared 54 prisoners who were psychopaths to those who were not. They then recorded their skin, cardiac, and facial responses to fear-inducing sentences. One aspect of fear in human beings is that when a person is afraid, he or she experiences involuntary changes in skin and in heart rates. People cannot control these involuntary changes; they are instinctive and hard-wired. In this study (Patrick, 1994; Cuthbert & Lang, 1994), the psychopaths showed much lower rates of these involuntary changes. They *reported* feeling afraid but their physical data indicated that they were actually feeling much less fear than "normal" people. This indicates a physiological difference between controls and psychopaths.

In general, the data on brain dysfunction and physiology in psychopaths is compelling evidence that this disorder leads to an increased risk of crime and violence and is probably caused by dysfunctions in the frontal and possibly in the temporal lobes of the brain. Clearly, not all criminals and violent people are psychopaths, so this area of mental illness only explains a minority of offenders. Further, researchers are generally hesitant to assert that the brain deficits they see in psychopaths are a simple cause of the behaviors these people exhibit. It has been pointed out that behavior typically involves multiple brain regions (LaPierre et al., 1995).

Some researchers, noting that psychopathy appears to be a biological disorder leading to crime, have suggested therapies that might help reduce the crime and violence rate. However, one interesting paper pointed out that psychotherapy does not seem to work with psychopaths—in fact, psychotherapy may actually *increase* the ability of a psychopath to commit crime, by teaching him how other people think and feel and how to effectively "play the game," thereby increasing his ability to connive or fool people (C. Sherman, 2000).

Overcontrolled and Undercontrolled Violence

In the press and in the consciousness of the U.S. public, it is possible that nothing is more fascinating than the prospect of a mild-mannered, introverted, law-abiding citizen who suddenly goes "berserk" and brutally slaughters his or her family or other individuals. Certainly, many people are able to grasp the distinction between habitually violent, uncaring individuals and those rigid, well-behaved individuals who once in a lifetime "break out" and become violent.

That distinction was of particular interest to Megargee (1966), who described these two types of violent offenders as *undercontrolled* and *overcontrolled* individuals. Persons with few or no inhibitions against violence, and thus used violence frequently as a response, were described as *undercontrolled*. Such individuals are frequently extroverts. In contrast, *overcontrolled* individuals have very strict moral codes against misbehavior of all types, including violence. These people are introverted, rigidly self-controlled and oversocialized; they conform to society's standards obsessively. According to Megargee, it is precisely these overcontrolled individuals who will be the most violent, although undercontrolled individuals will be violent much more frequently. In more recent

---

An "Overcontrolled" Offender?

Paul Bernardo was a 30-year-old bookkeeper who "might be Joe Ordinary, from Anytown, Canada" (Nickerson, 1995). A handsome man who had been characterized as domestic and quiet, Bernardo had no criminal record. Apparently, however, he had long harbored fantasies of sexually assaulting young girls and then killing them, fantasies that he allegedly was able to fulfill with the help of his wife. Although Bernardo had no criminal record, he was charged with sexual assaults on women as far back as the early 1980s, leading some to question whether "overcontrolled" offenders truly have no history of violence, or whether they are merely better at hiding their crimes than other offenders. Certainly, Bernardo went to significant lengths to hide the bodies of the girls he had killed: After cutting one body into 10 pieces with a power saw, he allegedly encased the parts in cement and then sank them in a fishing pond (Nickerson, 1995).

years, Megargee extended his theory to explain that although different types of offenders are overcontrolled or undercontrolled, other factors might still help explain why violence appears when it does. For example, the theory now asserts that issues such as a person's psychological environment while growing up, the strength of his or her moral beliefs, and biological factors such as genetics help influence why an undercontrolled or overcontrolled offender might offend violently (Stephenson, 1996).

Extroversion has, in fact, been linked to habitual violence and aggressiveness (L. Ellis, 1991). In addition, some research has suggested that violent offenders with no previous record of violence are much more likely to show features of the overcontrolled personality than are violent offenders with a history of violence. However, it appears that the overcontrolled versus undercontrolled dichotomy may be more descriptive than useful as etiological information; that is, it may help us understand different types of offenders more than it may help us understand why some people offend and others do not. More recent evidence has pointed out, for example, that many overcontrolled and undercontrolled individuals are also found in the nonviolent population (Henderson, 1983). Why do some overcontrolled individuals break out in extreme violence, whereas others do not? Although the distinction drawn here is very interesting, it may be less significant in understanding what drives violent behavior in general.

Hostile Interpretation of Ambiguous Events, or Cognitive Distortions

In 1996, a 17-year-old boy attacked a total stranger, unprovoked, with an ax. He knocked on the man's door and when it was opened, he attempted to attack before he was driven off by his intended victim. His defense in court? That he was mentally deranged and unusually paranoid by late-stage Lyme disease. Before he became ill, this boy apparently had no behavioral problems, but his Lyme disease caused him to develop the unusual, but not unheard of, symptom of paranoid delusional misperceptions (Dee, 1999).

Cases this like are certainly rare. But are paranoid misperceptions rare among violent individuals? One theory suggests that such biased misperceptions may in fact help explain why some people are violent. Indeed, as the theory goes, under certain circumstances, aggression may be a normal and adaptive response. This may particularly be the case when an individual is faced with hostile or threatening forces, and violence is perceived as a necessary response. Given that a hostile environment might provoke an aggressive response in almost anyone, some researchers have investigated the possibility that violent individuals are not people who inappropriately choose violence; rather, they are people who inappropriately perceive hostility where most people would not (Dodge, Bates, & Pettit, 1990; Dodge, Price, Bachorowski, & Newman, 1990). That is, perhaps it is not the response that is skewed, but the perception of the environment.

Dodge studied aggressive and nonaggressive children, and found that aggressive children have two perceptual tendencies that nonaggressive children lack. Aggressive children were more likely to believe that other people had hostile intentions, and they were more likely to evaluate the results of aggression positively. One study furthered this by comparing reactive to proactive aggression (Crick & Dodge, 1996). This study examined how children's cognitions develop and maintain aggression of two different types, and found that hostile biases were particularly characteristic of reactive–aggressive children.

Dodge and colleagues also studied adolescent offenders in a maximum-security prison and found that although these biases were also found in this population, they were only found in undersocialized delinquents. This line of study sheds some light on why it may be so difficult to treat violent offenders. Trying to teach such offenders to be nonviolent may, in fact, be trying to teach them to react nonviolently to what they perceive to be intensely threatening situations. For example, imagine that you are standing in a field holding a gun, and an elephant is charging toward you at full speed with his tusks aimed right at you. Trying to teach violent offenders to be nonviolent might be like trying to teach them not to shoot that elephant, even though there is every indication that that elephant is deadly.

Other research has noted similar findings. Some of Dodge's later research (e.g., Dodge, 1993) also found that both moderately and severely aggressive children have a number of problems with "social cognition," among them, attributional biases. Another study (Coleman & Kardash, 1999) compared 27 aggressive to 27 nonaggressive boys and examined the way these boys recalled and recognized information. The boys were given a series of ambiguous and unambiguous sentences, and tested for how well they remembered the sentences. Some of the sentences had aggressive content and some did not. The main difference she found between these two groups of boys was that the aggressive boys were significantly better at recognizing the aggressively slanted items. Salzer Burks, Laird, Dodge, Pettit, and Bates (1999) conducted a longitudinal study, following a group of children from kindergarten through the eighth grade. In this study she and her colleagues studied what immediate factors preceded aggression in children. They found that children with biased "knowledge structures" (that is, memories that emphasize hostility) process information in a more negatively biased way and are more likely to develop stable negative cognitive biases and stably aggressive behavior.

Other similar studies have found that aggressive children attribute fewer positive intentions to people in problem-solving scenarios (Vitaro, Pelletier, & Coutu, 1989) and that sexually aggressive men use a "suspicious schema" in interpreting women's statements (Malamuth & Brown, 1994). Finally, Downey and Walker (1989) looked more closely at this phenomenon and noted that attributional biases did not appear to mediate the link between high risk and aggression, but rather, appeared to serve as a protective factor against aggression.

That is, children who are at high risk for violence—for example, children who have been abused—are not at even higher risk if they also make biased attributions. Rather, those children who do not make biased attributions are at lower risk of becoming aggressive, even if they have been abused. In other words, making accurate rather than biased attributions may be a protective factor that makes children resilient.

Other research examined different types of violent offenders and found cognitive misinterpretations and biases that appear to be specific to the type of offense. For example, rather than making general, nonspecific hostile misinterpretations, adults who commit child abuse tend to misinterpret children's behavior. Specifically, they tend to regard children's misbehaviors as more intentional than they really are—possibly paving the way to righteous anger and abuse (Zebrowitz, Kendall-Tackett, & Fafel, 1991). Sexually aggressive men, rather than suffering from blanket distortions, may differ from other men primarily in their distortion of women's communications (Malamuth & Brown, 1994). As research continues into the factor of cognitive distortions, it becomes increasingly likely that violent offenders may be individuals who distort perceptions in such a way that it predisposes them to behave in certain, specific criminal ways. "All violent feelings produce in us a falseness in our impressions of external things" (John Ruskin, cited in Cohen & Cohen, 1993).

RECIDIVISM AND VIOLENCE

The term *recidivism* refers to a criminal offender who commits crime a second time. A *chronic recidivist* is the term usually used for an offender who commits the same crime several, or many, times. What are the psychological risk factors for a person becoming a recidivist?

The first risk factor is the type of violent crime the person engaged in the first time. Are some groups of violent offenders more likely to repeat their offenses, once released, then others? Answers to these questions have important implications for public safety; the U.S. public is growing increasingly outraged by the discovery that a violent crime has been perpetrated on an innocent victim after the offender was released from prison following an earlier violent offense. In Connecticut, a young schoolteacher was shot and killed by her boyfriend just outside the elementary school where she taught. Even though just 4 months earlier he had put a gun to her head and attempted to kill her, he was free on bail. How likely is it that a murderous young man—or any given offender—will repeat his crime? The answer, not surprisingly, is that it depends on the type of crime perpetrated.

When we examine street-violent crime, a clear pattern emerges. Most street-violent criminals will not, in fact, ever commit more than one violent crime during their careers. This statement may seem erroneous in the face of a great deal of publicity to the contrary, but in fact, it is a few chronically violent offenders who are responsible for the majority of violent crime (Mednick, Harway, Mednick, & Moffitt, 1981; Piper, 1985). Nationwide data suggest that a mere 5% of offenders in 1989 were charged with 45 or more offenses each (Beck & Shipley, 1989). Furthermore, some research has suggested that recidivistic violent offenders are much more apt than nonrecidivistic offenders to inflict severe injuries on their victims (Convit, Isay, Otis, & Volavka, 1990). Official records show that only about one third of violent offenders are rearrested within 3 years for a violent crime, with the remaining 67% staying out of trouble (Greenfeld, 1992). In street-violent criminals, furthermore, biological variables are most strongly related to recidivistic violence; in one study, 100% of recidivistic street-violent criminals had strong biological markers for violence such as highly disturbed prenatal development, high numbers of minor physical anomalies, or high numbers of head injuries (Kandel, 1988; Kandel et al., 1989). All these data suggest the existence of a small but highly recidivistic group of street-violent criminals, with the majority of street-violent criminals likely to be only one-time offenders. Is this pattern the same for family violence?

Unfortunately, it appears not. A larger proportion of family violent offenders appears to offend again—particularly those who victimize children. For example, abused children who are left in formerly abusive households without intervention have a 40% to 70% chance of being reinjured and a 5% chance of being killed (Jellinek et al., 1992). The first NFVS (Straus & Hotaling, 1980) found that 94% of abused children were abused repeatedly during the year they were studied, suggesting very high recidivism among physical abusers of children. More than half of sexual abusers report that they have committed sexual abuse multiple times (Bernard, 1975). Many sexual abusers of children refuse treatment or fail to cooperate with it, contending that they do not want to be "cured" of their sexual preference for children—an attitude that certainly suggests recidivism (Bernard, 1975; Marshall & Barbaree, 1988).

Similar patterns of recidivism are found in spouse abusers and people who abuse the elderly. Thus, in contrast to street violence, recidivism in family violence appears to be the rule rather than the exception. Why are family violent offenders so much more likely to repeat their offenses, in comparison to street-violent ones? One major reason is undoubtedly opportunity. A physical abuser's victim is present, in his or her domain, a good deal of the time—there is no need to seek out targets for aggression. One conveniently and repeatedly appears. Similarly, most child sexual abuse is perpetrated by someone who knows the child, and therefore has repeated access to the victim. And a spouse is a "handy" victim; always there, and perhaps too frightened to retaliate. A second reason is impunity, or an offender's lack of fear that he or she will be caught and punished. Physical and sexual abuse occurs in the privacy of the home, with few or no witnesses; any witnesses there are typically have strong motivations to keep silent. Furthermore, police and other authorities are noticeably more reluctant to "interfere" in family violence than in street violence, and tend not to view family-violent individuals as "criminals." In fact, family-violent offenders may not view themselves as criminals.

Apart from victimizing family versus strangers, what other characteristics are common in recidivists? They are more likely to be men and more likely to be young—in fact, the older the prisoner, the less likely that he or she will reoffend (Beck & Shipley, 1989). This study also found that the more education a prisoner had, the more likely he or she was to remain out of the criminal justice system after a first offense (Beck & Shipley, 1989). Interestingly, the length of the initial prison term was *not* associated with risk for recidivism. Another study found that attempting to predict whether a person would become a recidivist based on his or her tendency to become angry quickly was ineffective. This study of 252 Canadian inmates found that anger proneness, despite its possible association with violence in some individuals, was unassociated with recidivism (Loza & Loza-Fanous, 1999).

Perhaps the most important information about the relevance of individual factors in violence comes from recidivism data. Only a small minority of offenders become chronic recidivists, and these individuals both commit the majority of criminal acts and show the strongest relationship to internal markers for violence (Convit et al., 1990; Kandel et al., 1989; Kandel & Mednick, 1991; Piper, 1985).

Chapter 5

Developmental Factors
and Social Learning

DEVELOPMENTAL PERSPECTIVES

Developmental psychologists have noted that violence does not simply "appear" in previously healthy adults; it is an adult behavioral disorder that is preceded by disturbed behaviors during childhood (Denno, 1990; Dilillo, 2001; Herrenkohl et al., 2001; Herrera & McCloskey, 2001; Hunt & Joe-Laidler, 2001; Lewis et al., 1985; Marks, Glaser, Glass, & Home, 2001; Ornduff, 2001; Weiss, 1990; Weisz, Martin, Walter, & Fernandez, 1991; Zagar, Arbit, Hughes, Busell, & Busch, 1989). Thus, understanding what behaviors precede adult violence may enable society to prevent such violence before it ever happens.

Longitudinal research is the tool researchers use to uncover the childhood antecedents of violent behavior. By studying a group of children—both those who behave normally and those who have behavioral disorders—and then subsequently measuring the violence of all these individuals as adults, researchers are able to discover that having behavioral problems as a child increases the risk of adolescent and adult violence.

Developmental psychopathology is a special field that studies behavioral disorders and diseases that arise during development, or disorders that are caused by problems in development. Developmental psychopathologists are most interested in identifying the type of behavior problems during childhood that best predict adult violence and aggression. Their research has revealed a number of behavioral styles and disorders of childhood that noticeably increase the risk of violence during adulthood.

Temperament and Aggression

A child's *temperament* is that child's habitual emotional responses to a variety of circumstances. Temperament is usually considered to be congenital (that is, a child is presumed to be born with his or her temperament) and hereditary ("Emotion and Temperament," 2001; Gallagher, 1994; Kagan, 1988). In that sense, temperament may be a genetic factor that *contributes* to violence later in life, in contrast to a model that postulates a direct genetic cause of violent behavior (Garbarino, 1999; see chapter 4). Of course, nothing in this theory rules out the possibility that temperament could also, as with other behavioral factors, be influenced partially or even primarily by biological environment. Researchers have noted that temperament may, in turn, affect the psychological environment a child is exposed to, and that children who are difficult to parent because of their temperament may be exposed to parenting that (possibly inadvertently) causes or reinforces aggressive tendencies (Garbarino, 1999; Nichols, Gergely, & Fonagy, 2001). Personality characteristics included under the rubric called *temperament* include distractibility and adaptability (Garrison & Earls, 1987), extroversion and introversion (Kagan, 1988; Woodward et al., 2001), impulsivity (L. Ellis, 1991; Garbarino, 1999) and generally being characterized as "difficult" (especially in infancy; Garbarino, 1999; Sanson, Oberklaid, Pedlow, & Prior, 1991).

Much research links temperamental styles in childhood to aggression during either childhood, adolescence, or adulthood. Research has associated temperamental difficulties with childhood disorders associated with aggression and violence, such as ADHD (Pisecco, Baker, Silva, & Brooke, 2001). Studies of preschool-aged children typically find a positive relationship between "difficult" temperament and aggressive behavior (Tschann, Kaiser, Chesney, & Alkon, 1996). A prospective study in New Zealand sought to find a relationship between temperament at age 3 and behavior at age 18. These researchers found that an "undercontrolled" temperament early in life was linked with aggression later in life (Caspi & Silva, 1995). Garbarino (1999) pointed out that children with certain temperamental and parenting characteristics might tend to make aggressive, antisocial peer choices that further reinforce aggressive tendencies. Several other researchers have noted similar findings, namely, a positive link between temperamental characteristics and aggressive behavior (Denno, 1990; Garrison & Earls, 1987; Kingston & Prior, 1995; Loeber & Hay, 1997). More specific research has taken the study of temperament a step further. For example, Fitzpatrick found that the temperamental characteristic that was most important in predicting violent victimization among children was a confrontational temperament—an inability to walk away from a fight. Another study found that a difficult temperament was primarily related to *stably* aggressive subjects, as opposed to subjects who were characterized by only *transient* aggression (Kingston & Prior, 1995). Finally, a study of several hundred kindergarten children asked if temperament and aggression were directly linked or possibly mediated by parenting variables. This study found that temperament influenced the level of maternal stress, which in turn influenced the level of aggression in the child (Adessky, 1997). This finding suggested that although temperament may be important, it may also affect other parenting variables which in turn exert a significant influence on a child's tendency to develop aggressive behavior.

Temperamental differences during adulthood have also been linked to some forms of aggression. One study of workplace anger and aggression found a correlation between scores on a scale of temperament and workplace anger and verbal aggression (Calabrese, 2000). That study, conducted on hospital personnel, found that those whose temperament was predominately characterized by a tendency to be "sensitive to morals, believing that manners are decaying and that 'no one shows respect anymore'" were those who were both most likely to express verbal aggression and those who were most likely to be angry at the expression by others of verbal aggression or sarcasm. Grof (2001) explored longitudinal research on overall psychological functioning in adults in a comprehensive longitudinal study and noted that temperament appears to be related to negative emotions in general—particularly to anxiety and depression. Thus, longitudinal research on adults does suggest that temperament continues to have an influence on behavior. The developmental data on children argues, in turn, that one of its influences is in the realm of aggression and violence.

Conduct Disorders

A conduct disorder (CD) is a persistent pattern of behavior in which the child repeatedly violates the basic rights of others or age-appropriate norms of social behavior (Sroufe, Cooper, & DeHart, 1996). The phrase *violating the basic rights of others* refers to behaviors such as stealing from other people, hurting them, or forcing them to do something that they would prefer not doing. Violating "age-appropriate" norms, on the other hand, refers to the child's violation of the behavioral standards that society reasonably expects from a child of that age. For example, no one expects 2-year-olds to sit quietly at desks in a classroom. However, we do expect 10-year-olds to do so. Therefore, sitting quietly at a desk is an age-appropriate norm for a 10-year-old, but not for a 2-year-old. It is not pathological for a 2-year-old to fail to sit quietly; but persistently failing to "act their age" may be a symptom of a CD. A very important word in this definition is *persistent*. All 10-year-olds, at some time or another, misbehave and fail to sit quietly in class. As any teacher or parent knows, all children do not have CDs. However, a behavioral problem becomes indicative of a CD when it occurs on a persistent, continuing basis.

What causes children to have CDs? Several biological factors have been linked to CDs. For example, one study found that males with CDs have distinctive secretion levels of androgens (Dabbs & Morris, 1990; van Goozen & van den

Ban, 2000), hormones that have also been associated with violence, especially prenatally (see previous chapter). In addition, males with CDs, when given a serotonin-releasing medication, experienced some reduction in some types of aggressive behavior (Cherek, 1999). These findings seem to suggest that serotonin might be involved both in aggression and in some of the aggression symptoms seen in children with CDs. Hormones and neurotransmitters, and other biological factors, do not appear to singlehandedly "cause" the disorder; rather, they probably increase a child's vulnerability (Mednick & Hutchings, 1978). Correlational studies suggest that the family environment is important in causing this disorder; negative parenting skills and poor family interactions appear to be relevant factors (Kunitz & Levy, 1998; Maxwell, 2001). Studies of children of battered women find high rates of this disorder, suggesting that being exposed to parental violence may be at least partially responsible for CDs in some children (Ware et al., 2001). One representative study found that children with CDs came from families characterized by poor cohesion and higher conflict than children with other psychological difficulties (e.g., anxiety disorders; Haddad, Barocas, & Hollenbeck, 1991). However, it is difficult to tell if the child's disorder has caused the family problems, or if the family problems helped cause the child's disorder; depending on the family, one or both of these scenarios may be true. In any case, family environment is doubtless important in the development of CDs, as evidenced by the success of therapies based on social learning principles in treating the disorder (Miller & Prinz, 1990; Mpofu & Crystal, 2001).

Several studies found relationships between CDs, aggression, and violence later in life (Cornwall & Bawden, 1992; Hay & Castle, 2000; Webster-Stratton, 2000; Weisz et al., 1991). Other research has looked at more specific characteristics of aggression and conduct disorders. One study (Dodge, Price, et al., 1990) examined CDs and their relationship to violence in 128 adolescent boys, ages 14 to 19. These boys were in a maximum-security prison for juvenile offenders. The researchers found that factors that were positively related to the number of violent crimes, such as hostile biases in the interpretation of ambiguous events, were also positively related to aggressive CDs. These findings were true even when race, intelligence, and socioeconomic status were accounted for. Another study found that CDs were related to proactive, but not reactive, aggressive behaviors in a sample of 742 teenage boys (Vitaro, Gendreau, Tremblay, & Oligny, 1998). A smaller study, comparing boys with conduct disorders to a comparison peer group, found that the boys with CDs were less able to empathize with persons in experimental vignettes (Cohen & Strayer, 1996)—and of course, a lack of empathy has been related to violence in other circumstances as well (Duncan, 1999; Jones, 1995; Milner, Halsey, & Fultz, 1995; Rice et al., 1994). Finally, a prospective study found that cognitive deficiencies at age 7 were related to conduct disorders and aggression at age 17, suggesting that the cognitive problems noted in many violent offenders (see chapter 4) may be causally related to later childhood disorders such as CDs, which in turn may be causally related to violence in adulthood (Schonfeld, Shaffer, O'Connor, & Portnoy, 1988).

Attention Deficit Hyperactivity Disorder

Hyperactivity is a word that has crept into our colloquial speech. As a result of its common usage, most people believe that hyperactivity simply refers to children who are particularly energetic. However, hyperactivity is actually a clinical disorder that, in order to be diagnosed, must meet certain basic criteria. The condition referred to here as *hyperactivity* is also known as *attention deficit hyperactivity disorder* (ADHD).

There are three features of ADHD. The first feature of the disorder is the feature that most people are familiar with: a persistent pattern of impulsive and overactive behavior. In everyday life, children might be unable to control their behaviors appropriately; for example, a 7-year-old may occasionally have trouble sitting still in a circle of children during storytime. Hyperactive children may try very hard to sit still, but they are simply unable to control their own motor behavior.

The second feature of hyperactivity is a tendency to be very easily distracted and to have significant difficulty concentrating appropriately on a task. This feature is usually labeled *distractibility* or *concentration difficulties.* Children with this symptom are distracted by events that would not typically distract other children. For example, when a teacher is explaining a lesson, a hyperactive child might be distracted by someone walking past the classroom or by the sound of a car driving by. Most individuals are able to screen out distracting noise when necessary; for example, you are able to concentrate on this sentence, even if you are reading it in a noisy room. The target stimulus is this paragraph, and the extraneous stimuli are noise, lights, voices, and other stimulation that you are screening out, rather than concentrating on. Hyperactive children are very sensitive to extraneous stimuli, and may lack the ability to effectively filter them out, thus interfering with their ability to focus on the target stimuli. Their high level of distractibility makes it very difficult for them to concentrate.

The third feature of ADHD is aggression, and this feature is the one that may be most relevant to the discussion here. Hyperactive children have an increased tendency to be aggressive with their playmates. They may be much more likely than other children to become involved in fights with schoolmates and to have playground problems. This is especially true of hyperactive boys (Boyajian, DuPaul, Handler, Eckert, & McGoey, 2001; Hubbard & Newcomb, 1991; Pope, Bierman, & Mumma, 1991; Treuting & Hinshaw, 2001). Some research has even suggested that it might be this childhood aggression specifically, rather than the general syndrome of hyperactivity, that really predicts later violence (August, Stewart, & Holmes, 1983).

The diagnosis of hyperactivity may be made on any combination of these three features; all three need not be present. Alternatively, all three features may be present in any given hyperactive child. Hyperactivity is different from many other childhood syndromes. Some behavior disorders of childhood are transient, lasting only a few years and having no long-lasting impact. However, hyperactivity is significantly related to adult outcomes, including violent crime (L. Ellis, 1990; Hughes et al., 1991; M. Walker, 2000; Weiss, 1990; Young, 2000). It appears that hyperactivity affects so many facets of a child's life that permanent repercussions (in an untreated hyperactive child) may result. For example, hyperactive children (again, if left untreated) may have trouble making friends (Blum, 1999; Nolan & Gadow, 1997; Pope et al., 1991); they are difficult playmates because of their impulsive, overactive, aggressive behavior and their inability to concentrate on the task at hand. It is not unusual for other children to avoid hyperactive playmates (Hubbard & Newcomb, 1991), or at least to fail to form close friendships with them. Thus, hyperactive children may lack the opportunities other children have to learn how to form close relationships (Pope et al., 1991). Similarly, hyperactive children may not absorb basic skills in their early years of school because of their inability to concentrate and focus on classroom lessons (Garrison & Earls, 1987). Because all advanced learning is built on basic skills, a lack of these skills can affect school performance for many school years to come. Whether or not ADHD results in lasting impairment in the form of adult violence or aggression may depend on what type of ADHD a child has, and what comorbidity exists (i.e., what other disorders the child may show); some subtypes of ADHD appear to be significantly more related to aggression than others (Bonafina, Newcorn, McKay, Koda, & Halperin, 2000).

The causes of hyperactivity are of particular interest to criminologists because hyperactivity has been linked to adolescent and adult crime and violence (E. Taylor, Chadwick, Heptinstall, & Danckaerts, 1996). One important cause appears to be biological factors (Andrews et al., 1998; Comings, 1997; Deckel, Hesselbrock, & Bauer, 1996; L. Ellis, 1990; Hughes et al., 1991; Kandel, Brennan, & Mednick, 1989; Sanson et al., 1991; Sherman, 1997, 2000; Swedo et al., 1998; Thomas, Garrision, Slawecki, Elhers, & Riley, 2000). For example, childhood hyperactivity occurs more frequently in children with poor perinatal health (health problems during pregnancy and delivery; Kandel, 1989; Sanson, Oberklaid, Pedlow, & Prior, 1991; Thomas et al., 2000). It has also been found in children who sustain head injuries (Andrews et al., 1998) or with troubled brain function (Sherman, 2000), and evidence suggests a genetic influence as well (Comings, 1997; Sherman, 1997). One study has even linked hyperactivity to bacterial infections (Swedo et al., 1998). The biological factors that contribute to hyperactivity are linked to violence in adulthood as well (see chapter 4). Although hyperactivity is found disproportionately in the histories of violent criminals, it is important to note that most hyperactive children still do not become violent as adults (Hughes et al., 1991; Kandel et al., 1989; G. Weiss, 1990; Zagar et al., 1989). Clearly, however, hyperactivity constitutes an increased risk for adult violence (Taylor et al., 1996), and most researchers believe that this body of research implies common biological antecedents for hyperactivity and violence. As usual, though, there is an alternative hypothesis: The interpersonal and social consequences of hyperactivity (rather than the biological bases) may help cause violence (Kandel et al., 1989). Both of these explanations have merit, and both are likely to be partly true.

The family and the other psychosocial factors in a hyperactive child's environment may also be relevant in understanding the causes of this problem, and by association, the causes of violent behavior. Hyperactive children can be found in many different types of families; however, a few studies have found links between parenting styles and hyperactivity in children (Jacobvitz & Sroufe, 1987; Scahill & Schwab-Stone, 1999). In contrast to CDs, however, hyperactivity appears to be significantly related to biology (Halperin & Newcorn, 1997) and less strongly related to family and social factors.

Treatment of hyperactivity is important because of its potentially far-reaching consequences into the lives of the children it affects. Although it may be tempting to simply wait for children to "outgrow" hyperactivity, its relationship to peer problems, learning problems, and adult outcomes makes this a risky approach. In addition, failing to treat hyperactive children can lead to poor basic academic skills and school failure that persists even after the worst behavioral symptoms are gone; and failing to form significant peer relationships early in life can affect interpersonal skills later on. Treatment for hyperactivity is controversial because it frequently involves medication—most often the drug methylpheniclate (trade name Ritalin), which is a stimulant. Stimulants usually have paradoxical effects on children; although Ritalin would arouse an adult, it calms hyperactive children. It is particularly helpful for concentration problems and helps hyperactive children succeed in school. Although stimulant use with children is controversial and has been criticized (Divoky, 1989; Kohn, 1989), most evidence suggests that approximately 80% of hyperactive children do respond favorably to stimulants (Fischer & Newby, 1991; Gainetdinov & Wetsel, 1999; Pliszka, 1991; "Ritalin Study," 2001; Whalen, 2001). Techniques such as behavior modification are less effective than medication for most children, although they can be the treatment of choice for the remaining 20% (Pliszka, 1991). No one likes administering behavior-altering drugs to children, but the side effects of such medication appear to be less detrimental than the consequences of leaving hyperactivity untreated.

Ideally, psychotherapy should always accompany medication, to help children learn to control their behavior, adjust to having this disorder, and ensure that they maintain positive self-esteem. Parent training and psychotherapy are usually beneficial for any hyperactive child and the child's family (Barkley, 2000; Hinshaw & Owens, 2000; Whalen, 2001). Like stimulants, therapy can help control the disorder and help alleviate the consequences but is not a perfect cure.

Learning Disorders

About 100 years ago, physicians started to describe peculiar disorders termed *learning disorders*. Learning disorders are sometimes called *learning disabilities*. This is a label that is attached to children who have problems in one or more of the basic processes that humans use to process understanding of language or numbers (Shalev, 2001; Tanner, 2001). Many learning disabled children can process much information normally, but have difficulties in performing particular tasks. These children have normal intelligence, but have reading, writing, drawing, or spelling abilities that are at least 2 years behind those of normal children of the same age (Shalev, 2001; Tanner, 2001).

An example of a learning disorder is dyslexia, the inability to read with understanding (Herschel, 1978). Approximately 5% of the population has dyslexia, meaning that they are of normal intelligence but have difficulties reading. A dyslexic child may reverse letters (e.g., the child sees a "b" when a "d" is written). How does one learn to read when the words "read," "doggie," and "hard" appear as "reab," "boggie," and "harb"? In dyslexia, the order of letters may also be affected: Rather than seeing "read," a child may see "erad."

Learning disorders do not affect intelligence per se, but do affect a child's self-esteem and psychological functioning (Stringer, Morton, & Bonikowski, 1999; Valas, 2001). Obviously, a child who must struggle to read even the most basic words is apt to consider him or herself "dumb" or even "bad" (i.e., uncooperative). Children with undiagnosed learning disorders may be regarded as naughty or stubborn, or as refusing to learn and cooperate with their classes. Because of the possible psychosocial side effects of learning disorders, it is not surprising that violent criminals often have such disorders in their histories. Several researchers have investigated the possibility of a link between learning disorders and crime.

Most studies find that learning disabilities, and their causes, have indeed been linked to an increased risk of delinquency and criminal behavior (Cherkes-Julkowski, 1998; L. Ellis, 1991; Guillette et al., 1998; Robinson & Kelley, 1998; Wasserman, Pine, Workman, & Bruder, 1999). In one recent study, Robinson and Kelley (1998) compared 19 repeat violent offenders, 19 repeat nonviolent offenders, and 18 first-time offenders. They found that the repeat violent offenders demonstrated the highest levels of neuropsychological dysfunction, such as learning disorders and speech and vision problems. Another researcher studied premature infants in a longitudinal study and found high levels of language disabilities and delays and high risk for involvement in criminal behavior (Cherkes-Julkowski, 1998). Poor verbal skills may predispose some children to antisocial behavior and drug abuse (Wasserman et al., 1999). One intriguing study found links between pesticide exposure in young children and the level of both learning disabilities and aggressive behavior (Guillette et al., 1998). Researchers agree that the link is clear: although most children with learning disabilities will never be violent criminals, having such disabilities does increase a child's risk of developing aggressive or violent criminal behavior.

Development of Aggression in Normal Children

Remember, violence is aggressive behavior with the intent to cause physical or psychological harm. Intent is central to this definition; accidents are not aggression.

Infants do commit physically rough acts, babies like to tug at things, and they may be painfully adept. However, an infant is not a violent being; although an infant may hurt his or her mother by roughly tugging at her hair, the infant has no intention of causing harm.

Like infants, toddlers may engage in rough play, but they are usually surprised when their aggression causes harm. Typical toddlers still lack deliberate intent to harm. However, aggression later in childhood may be related to behavior during the toddler stage of development. The critical process called *socialization* begins during toddlerhood, whereby toddlers begin to acquire the rules and values of their society (Sears, 1961; Sears, Maccoby, & Levin, 1957). Although at first toddlers only obey these rules, after a while they internalize them; that is, they begin to believe that they are correct. This belief, this *internalization* (Grusec & Goodnow, 1994), is the heart of socialization, and socialization is the heart of law-abiding and peaceful behavior.

Preschoolers (in a stage also called *early childhood;* Sroufe et al., 1996) do begin to understand that aggression hurts others, and this understanding results in the ability to form intent, which is the basic underpinning of interpersonal violence (Arsenio & Cooperman, 2000; Vissing, Straus, Gelles, & Harrop, 1991). Other developments during early childhood are also related to aggression. For example, *social competence* emerges. This is an ability seen in a child who plays regularly with peers and is liked by peers, and is related to behavior problems in preschool years (Campbell, 1994). Children with adequate social competence are able to play in a friendly manner with other children, which is important because such play enables them to learn about many different issues—including the acceptability (or unacceptability) of aggression and violence. Children with high social competence are better able than children with poor social competence to absorb peer lessons about prosocial and aggressive behavior (Arsenio & Lemerise, 2001; S. B. Campbell, 1994; Frey, 2000; Marks et al., 2001; Vaughn, Hogan, Lancelotta, Shapiro, & Walker, 1992). It is during early childhood that both the capacity for prosocial behavior and the capacity for aggression increase dramatically.

What affects a young child's tendency to be aggressive or prosocial? One of the most important events in a child's life (possibly the most important), attachment to a parent or parents, is probably strongly related to the child's tendency to be either prosocial or aggressive. *Attachment* refers to the emotional bond between a child and his or her caregiver. This relationship between the quality of attachment and aggression appears to work in two ways. First, it seems likely that violence in a family—the presence of either spouse or child abuse—interferes in the formation of a strong, positive attachment (Cicchetti & Olson, 1990; Draijer, 1999). Some researchers have reported that being exposed to domestic violence "blunts" a child's emotions, thereby possibly reducing the likelihood of the child becoming attached to caregivers (Schneider-Rosen & Cicchetti, 1984). Second, just as violence may interfere with attachment, insecure attachment may help cause aggression in children. Secure attachment to parents predicts a high level of prosocial behavior (Denham, 1994; Eberly & Montemayor, 1999; Troy & Sroufe, 1987), and infant attachment problems seem to lead to hostile aggressive behavior during the preschool years (Denham, 1994; Lyons-Ruth, Alpern, & Repacholi, 1993). Attachment is also related to social competence (Page, 2001). The findings that violence interferes with attachment, and that a poor attachment may help predict antisocial behavior, might help explain the relationship between parental violence and an increased risk of aggression in the family children (Halford, Sanders, & Behrens, 2000; Spatz Widom, 1989b). It is possible to speculate that the resilient children of violent households may form positive attachments to parents despite the domestic aggression they are exposed to, and that it may be this positive attachment that protects them from the noxious influence of domestic violence.

During middle childhood (the school years), developmental changes in peer interaction occur. Generally, most children become more altruistic and kind toward their playmates, and come to understand better that friendship involves caring and understanding, not just mutual play interests. In most children, there is a decrease in *instrumental aggression;* they generally cease to use aggressive behavior merely to get something they want. However, there may be an increase in *hostile aggression* (aggression aimed at hurting the victim; Atkins, Stoff, Osborne, & Brown, 1993; Dumas & Neese, 1996). This may be seen especially in the form of verbal aggression between children; and it is during middle childhood that an increase in hostile aggression emerges among children who have witnessed adults deliberately trying to hurt each other.

Interestingly, an examination of peer groups in middle childhood reveals many of the potential bases of adolescent gang activity. First, peer networks during middle childhood are relatively stable clusters of friends. Second, there are interesting gender differences (Matthys, Cohen-Kettenis, & Berkhout, 1994). Peer groups of boys during this age are generally larger clusters, where the group emphasizes loyalty and activities that members participate in together. As with older boys, peer groups of this age are very interested in competition between members and achievements of peers, and their groups tend to have formal and rigid rules, with some clearly dominating members. Emotional intimacy is not usually present or, if present, is not emphasized.

Girls' peer groups, on the other hand, usually consist of smaller groups and do emphasize emotional intimacy and support of each other. The group activities usually revolve around noncompetitive activities such as playing and talking together, rather than competitive activities such as sports. Girls tend to be significantly more emotionally attached to their peers than are boys (Nada Raja, McGee, & Stanton, 1992). Whereas boys' peer groups tend to emphasize feelings of inclusion, girls' tend to emphasize feelings of intimacy (Vernberg, 1990).

Parenting style during middle childhood and adolescence also has a significant impact on aggressive behavior. Parents who are warm and loving, regardless of their disciplinary practices, usually produce cooperative, prosocial children; however, parents who are highly controlling and feel a strong need to assert power over their children, and who are less warm and loving, tend to produce children who are more aggressive (Denham, 1994; Eberly, 1999; Weiss, Dodge, Bates, & Pettit, 1992). One typical study found that parents who maintained a secure attachment and had a positive influence on their young teens had children with more prosocial behavior (Eberly, 1999). Alternatively, a different study found that parents who exercised a high degree of physical control had adolescents with significantly more behavior problems (Barber, Olsen, & Shagle, 1994). Of course, this relationship is a two-way street; different types of children provoke different types of parenting. Parents who feel a need to control one child may not feel that need with other children. Doubtless, every child's unique personality provokes a somewhat unique parenting style.

SOCIAL LEARNING PERSPECTIVES

Social learning theory grew out of the behaviorist movement; social learning theorists are thus interested in *overt behavior* (behavior you can actually see and measure), as opposed to inner or unconscious processes (such as biological influences of cognitive biases) that cannot be directly seen or measured. This theory stresses that people learn how to behave as a result of the psychosocial environment they live in, both as children and as adults. Early on, social learning theory was used to understand the causes of violent behavior (Sutherland, 1947).

There are two major learning mechanisms that are important to criminologists. The first mechanism is called *observational learning* or *modeling* (Akers, 1985; Lance & Ross, 2000). Modeling refers simply to the imitation of other people. Do people learn to become aggressive or violent through watching and imitating others who are aggressive? Many criminologists and psychologists believe that they do, and research on the influences of the family and mass media certainly supports this contention (Curtis, 1963).

A classic experiment on modeling and aggression demonstrated just how strong an influence observational learning can be. Bandura, a famous psychologist, decided to conduct an experiment to see if children would behave aggressively after watching aggressive adults (Bandura & Huston, 1961; Bandura, Ross, & Ross, 1963). While a child played in a room, Bandura had an adult enter the

Learning To Be Violent

In 1992, the newspaper *Education Week* published a story entitled "Children in Boston Exposed Early to Violence." This study reported that 1 in 10 children whose mothers responded to a survey at a Boston health clinic had witnessed a knifing or a shooting by age 6.

Shocking as that number was, data in years to follow confirmed that American children routinely witness violence. A review of the literature (Berman, Silverman, & Kurtines, 2000) found that since 1992, several researchers have been investigating how often children are actually exposed to violence that might be teaching them that the best way to cope is by using aggression. Is seeing violent behavior a rare occurrence among American children, or is it a common event? If it is common, that would suggest that many children witness violence without becoming violent themselves—what psychologists call *resilience*. Is it possible that some children learn to be violent by seeing it, whereas others do not?

Berman et al. (2000) reviewed several studies to see if children frequently see violence in their homes while growing up. Their meta-analysis suggests that this type of event is not unusual or rare for American children at the turn of the 21st century who live in urban, lower income, higher crime areas. Although the 10% number found by the *Education Week* study was high, these other studies found that generally between 50% and 85% of children living in these areas (cities in the studies included Washington, DC, New Haven, CT, and Miami, FL) have witnessed violence by the time they are teenagers. The same literature generally finds that in high-risk areas of the United States, approximately 40% to 45% of children have witnessed a murder by their adolescent years. Although it is likely that this number is very different in lower risk areas, it is still clear that witnessing violence is a potentially important part of the reason some children learn to be violent themselves.

room and begin aggressively playing with a large Bobo doll. For approximately 10 minutes, the adult kicked and socked the Bobo doll, saying aloud "Kick him!" while the beating went on. Next, after watching the adult, the child was told that he or she would not be allowed to play with a group of very enticing toys. (The goal here was to frustrate the child.) Finally, the child was led into another room where several toys—including a Bobo doll—waited.

The children who had seen the adult assault the Bobo doll were more likely to imitate the adult's aggressive behavior and attack the Bobo doll themselves. Other children, who had also been frustrated but who had not seen the aggressive adult, were much less likely to hit the Bobo doll. Thus, observing an aggressive adult appeared to dramatically increase the likelihood of aggression in the child.

A second principle of behaviorism emphasizes *reward and punishment* as shapers of behavior (Lance & Ross, 2000; Winder & Rau, 1962). Sometimes this principle is called *operant conditioning*. Operant conditioning means simply that behaviors that are rewarded are more likely to occur again, and behaviors that are not rewarded (or are punished) are less likely to recur. A reward is any pleasant event or feeling, such as a cookie, pride, parental admiration, or acceptance as a member of a group. *Punishment* is anything that makes it less likely that the behavior will repeat.

More recent research has also demonstrated support for social learning theory's role in influencing the development of violent behavior. One study, which examined college students' perceptions of violence in sports and the factors that contribute to violence in sports, found that college students did perceive social learning variables to be important (Lance & Ross, 2000). A second study found that violence in the family of origin did in fact lead to an imitation in the form of dating violence—exactly as social learning theory would predict (Foshee, Bauman, & Linder, 1999). Another study used social learning principles to construct an intervention that attempted to change attitudes toward date rape— successfully (Lanier & Elliot, 1998). Finally, Garrett studied covictimization in African-Americans and found that being the victim of violence was the strongest

---

An Example: The Rewards of Sexual Assault

Until recently, a general misunderstanding about the rewards of sexual assault led to very poor reporting and conviction rates of this violent crime. Traditionally, sexual assault was assumed to be motivated by sexual desire, and the reward of the assault was obtaining sexual intercourse with the most attractive victim possible.

Believing this, investigators were baffled by offenders who reported assaulting elderly women or children; offenders who reported that they did not experience an orgasm or an erection during the assault (a common occurrence) equally baffled them. Without these events occurring, they tended to believe that the assault did not even happen.

Today we know that sexual assault is most often motivated and (more importantly) rewarded by a feeling of intense power over the victim; thus, it is a crime that can happen between any two people (even a husband and wife) and need not involve sexual intercourse for the offender to be satisfied. If the victim is rendered powerless, the offender has his reward.

In the case of sexual assault, better understanding of the rewards of the crime has led to dramatically increased detection and conviction rates.

predictor of being violent oneself, exactly as social learning theory principles would predict. In general, a wide range of studies finds that behavior and learning of violence frequently tends to support, rather than refute, social learning theory.

One final point about this theory: social learning would predict that violence occurs because the person has been *rewarded* for being violent, or has seen others rewarded for being violent. Operant conditioning is a very powerful shaper of behavior, and an important step in understanding anyone's violent or criminal behavior lies in understanding what the rewards of violence or criminality are for them. In real life, however, discerning exactly what these rewards or punishments are is frequently a very difficult task.

Chapter 6

Media Exposure and Violence

One frequently hypothesized cause of contemporary violence is the enormous impact that mass media sources have on individuals, particularly on children. Although the most pervasive and best-studied of these sources is, of course, television, the recent surge of popularity of video games has also been targeted by researchers interested in how people learn from mass media sources to be violent.

VIOLENT VIDEO GAMES

Violent video games have become increasingly popular toys with children, both in the home and in video arcades. One result of this surge of popularity has been a heightened level of concern about the possible impact of playing such games. Several different sources have suggested that violent video games might cause aggressive or violent behavior in people who play them (Irwin & Gross, 1995; Larkin, 2000; Scott, 1995). The methodology of studies coming to this conclusion varies somewhat. One study asked college students how often they played violent video games, and linked more video-game-playing to a higher level of aggressive behavior and lower academic performance (Larkin, 2000). A second study had college students play either a violent or a nonviolent video game and subsequently "punish" their opponent by exposing them to a loud unpleasant noise; the students who played the violent video games used the noise against their opponents longer than did the other students (Larkin, 2000). Another study on school-aged boys found that children who played video games in a laboratory setting played more aggressively, both when frustrated and when not frustrated, than controls

(Irwin & Gross, 1995). Although these studies are typical of many similar pieces of research, not all such studies have found a positive relationship. Scott's (1995) research found the opposite: he attempted to associate aggressive feelings with violent video games, and found no significant relationship. Other studies found this lack of an association as well (see Scott's 1995 review).

Studies that attempted to more precisely define the relationship between video game playing and aggressive behavior have pointed out that other variables may mediate the relationship. For example, several studies have suggested that males may be more vulnerable than females to the impact of playing violent video games (Anderson & Dill, 2000; Dill, 1999; Irwin & Gross, 1995). Irwin's (1995) sample (cited earlier), as part of a positive study finding an association between playing video games and aggression, was comprised solely of young boys aged 7–8 years old. Anderson conducted two studies: one attempted to associated "real-life" video game playing with "real-life" aggression (i.e., aggressive behavior and delinquency outside the laboratory), and a second study examined exposure to violent video games in a laboratory and its short-term effect on aggressive thoughts and behaviors. Both Anderson's (2000) and Dill's (1999) studies found the relationship between video games and aggression, both in the short term and in "real life," was stronger for males than for females. Another factor that may mediate the relationship is the age of the child: Griffiths (1999) reviewed the literature in this field and found that one of the few consistencies across studies is the finding that younger children are more vulnerable to the impact of video games, relative to older (adolescent) children. In addition, a preexisting tendency to be aggressive seems to increase the influence of violent video games (Anderson & Dill, 2000; Dill, 1999). This last factor would indeed be consistent with a great deal of other research suggesting that individuals are differentially vulnerable to violent influences, and that an important part of these differences is any preexisting tendency to aggression (see chapter 4).

Finally, although academic performance problems have been linked to violent video games, it does not appear that children who are already academically suffering (such as learning-disabled children; see chapter 5) are drawn to violent video games that, in turn, increase their aggressive tendencies. Rather, studies have found that the drop in grades associated with violent video game playing is probably due to the time spent in playing and thereby lost to academic pursuits such as studying (Anderson & Dill, 2000; Larkin, 2000).

TELEVISION VIOLENCE AND AGGRESSION IN CHILDREN

Some groups of experts have long maintained that television is an excessively violent influence on children (Burne, 1993; Centerwall, 1992). Some researchers have even linked television violence to violent crime (Centerwall, 1992), although others have found only weak correlations between television violence and aggressive behavior or other undesirable outcomes (Gortmaker, Salter, Walker, & Dietz, 1990; Harris, 1992; Janokowski, 1985). The same was once said many years ago of radio, which featured shows in which heroes aggressively conquered villains. Recently, however, there has been a major shift in public opinion and mounting concern about a possible link between the epidemic of youth violence and the effects of television violence on children.

The question of whether or not television has a destructive impact on children may be controversial, but there are some facts no one disputes. First, it is clear that U.S. children watch a great deal of television. The average 4-year-old watches 2 hours each day (Huston, Watkins, & Kunkel, 1989), and older children may watch 40 hours or more every week. In Huston's study (Huston, Wright, Rice, Kerkman, & St. Peters, 1990), young children spent more time watching television than doing any other activity. In addition, there is no doubt that much of the content of television programs is violent. Some estimates hold that a U.S. child views 3,000 acts of violence every year on television; these acts include murder and robbery, assault, beatings, and torture (Pierce, 1984; Strasburger, 1985). Whereas 85% of prime-time shows were nonviolent during the 1950s, only 20% to 30% were nonviolent in the mid-1990s ("Reel Violence," 1994). The reality is that television is a business, not a public service (for the most part), and is run by individuals who are trying to sell commercial airtime. In order to succeed, sponsors must entice people to watch as much television as possible, and violence has dramatic appeal. Interestingly, however, it is not the shows aimed at adults that are most violent, but the shows aimed at children. Prime-time (or "family-oriented") shows include, on the average, 6 violent acts per hour; children's Saturday and Sunday shows (e.g., cartoons), in contrast, about 26 violent acts per hour (Gerbner, 1990). Before the average U.S. child even reaches high school, he or she has seen about 100,000 acts of violence on television, 8,000 of which are murders (Radecki, 1989; "Reel Violence," 1994). When asked, many children protest that they know the difference between television "fake" violence and "real" violence; in fact, this may be true for most, if not for all (Atkin, 1983). Nevertheless, it remains possible that even "fake" violence has an impact. The only way to test this hypothesis is to review the research on exposure to television violence and the development of violent behavior. If it appears that amounts of exposure are related to levels of violence, then there must be an effect. If no such relationship exists, then perhaps children *are* able to distinguish between fantasy and reality, and the issue is as simple as that.

Two types of studies have been conducted: correlational studies and experimental studies. A correlational study addresses the question of whether behavior becomes more violent as a child watches more violent television; that is, whether the two factors vary together. If they do, then a child who watches 1 hour of violent television might (theoretically) be mildly aggressive in his or her play, whereas a child who watches 3 hours might be more aggressive, and a child who watches 5 hours might be extremely aggressive. Such a pattern, in which one measure increases as a second measure increases, is called a positive correlation. In fact, a positive correlation between violent television watching and aggressive behavior has been reported in several studies (Eron, 1987; Huesmann & Eron, 1986; Turner, Hesse, & Peterson-Lewis, 1986). Other studies have found that violent television watching only increases aggressive behavior in children who already tend toward aggressive behavior (Friedrich & Stein, 1973). Do these studies prove that violent television watching causes an increase in behavior (at least in some children)? Unfortunately, they do not. Correlations are highly suggestive but do not prove the direction of influence. In this case, the positive correlation could equally suggest one of three interpretations:

1. Violent television watching causes violent behavior to increase.
2. Children who are violent choose to, and prefer to, watch violent television more than their nonviolent counterparts.
3. Some third factor—for instance, lack of parental involvement—is responsible for both the increase in violent television watching and the increase in violent behavior.

Because correlational studies cannot tell us which of these three interpretations is the correct one, experimental studies have been conducted in an attempt to sift them apart. An *experimental* study is one in which the researcher controls one factor (such as television watching) while measuring changes in a second factor (such as aggressive behavior). The dilemma is how a researcher, in a society in which almost everyone has a television at home, might completely control a child's exposure to television violence. The truth is that total control is impossible. A child may agree to watch only certain programs, or at certain times, but may be exposed to television violence in other settings—for example, at a playmate's house, or home alone without parents to control television viewing. Therefore, investigators have been limited to attempting to see whether aggressive responses rise immediately after exposure to violent television. A typical experimental study might proceed according to this scenario:

1. The investigator randomly separates the subjects into two groups: Group A and Group B.
2. Group A is exposed to 1 hour of violent television.
3. Group B is exposed to 1 hour of nonviolent television.
4. Then both Groups A and B are given some task that frustrates them.
5. The investigator watches both groups closely: Are the members of Group A more likely to react aggressively than the members of Group B?

Suppose Group A does react more violently; there are several possibilities. Perhaps Group A members tended to watch more violent television before the experiment ever began. Alternatively, perhaps Group A just happens to contain individuals who tended to be more aggressive before the experiment ever began. In a well-designed study, where the subjects are picked for the study randomly, the two groups should be equal and these two possibilities can be ruled out.

In fact, in well-designed research adults do appear to react more violently after they have been exposed to violent television compared to adults who have been exposed to nonviolent television. This suggests that television violence may have the immediate effect of causing an increase in violence (Huston et al., 1989). But what about long-term effects? Do years of television violence "build up" in children and cause them to be violent as adolescents and adults? That is the question that remains unanswered. What we can conclude is that correlational studies suggest that television violence may be related to violent behavior as an adult, and that television violence appears to provoke more aggressive behavior in the short term.

"I Watched Violent Television as a Kid, and I'm Okay"

This is perhaps the most common argument presented in favor of dismissing the impact of violent television on behavior. On the surface, it makes sense. How can violent television be destructive if everyone watches it, and most people are never violent? The answer lies in an understanding of risk factors and behavior. Violence never has one single cause; there are a multitude of important influences, including biological predisposition, temperament, and family experience. Sometimes a universal influence, something experienced by everyone, can contribute to violent behavior, but only in people who have other risk factors (such as a violent family life) as well. In these at-risk individuals, television violence may in fact be a very important influence. This observation is consistent with the findings of some of the research previously reviewed, which have also suggested that violent television has its most destructive impact on children already at risk for violence.

By what mechanisms might exposure to television violence lead to more aggressive behavior? There are three major theories:

Learning and Imitation. According to this theory, television may model violent behavior that some children (and adults) will imitate (Lance & Ross, 2000; Lanier & Elliot, 1998; Sutherland, 1947). The assumption is that television teaches people how to be violent.

Trigger Mechanism. According to this theory, television violence may "trigger" violent behavior in those few people who already tend to behave violently ("Viewing violent sports," 1997; Wickelgren, 1993; Wood, Wong, & Chachere, 1991). In this view, television violence may be the "final straw," not the only or even the most important influence, but the influence that finally leads the already at-risk individual toward violent behavior. Evidence supporting or refuting this theory is unclear. Some studies have suggested that TV can "trigger" violence in individuals already at risk (Wickelgren, 1993), but others have found no association ("Viewing violent sports," 1997). One theory has held that, for example, watching violent sports on television has "triggered" domestic violence; despite such theories, at least one study found no link between child abuse and the watching of violent spectator sports ("Viewing violent sports," 1997). Viewing violence on television or in the mass media may be a trigger, but if so, it does not seem to apply to all individuals or to all situations.

Desensitization.   According to this theory, television violence may so accustom people to violence that they do not notice it anymore (Davis & Mares, 1998; Linz, Donnerstein, & Adams, 1989; Payne, 1997; Potter & Smith, 2000). It occurs when people encounter something shocking so often that after a while it fails to provoke any emotional response at all. One example of desensitization is the response of most people in major U.S. cities to homeless individuals. Many years ago, the sight of someone living on the street was shocking and upsetting to most Americans. Today, however, most New Yorkers can walk past a homeless person and feel virtually nothing because they see homeless individuals so frequently. Several studies have suggested that the same principle may operate in the case of television violence (Davis & Mares, 1998; Linz et al., 1989; Payne, 1997). These researchers have found evidence for desensitization after the watching of shows such as violent talk shows (Davis & Mares, 1998) and more typical depictions of TV violence (Payne, 1997). Perhaps watching hundreds of thousands of violent acts on television desensitizes us to violence so much that we consider "real" violence to be ordinary and unavoidable. On the other hand, the literature is not in complete agreement here: At least one recent study has found no evidence for desensitization. That study examined reactions to graphic depictions of extreme violence and found that, in fact, people tended to evidence normal fear reactions rather than become desensitized (Davis & Mares, 1998). In general, this suggests that while desensitization may take effect for more typical depictions of violence, more extreme forms of violence generally still evoke a reaction in individuals who are watching.

All of these theories contribute to a possible explanation of the relationship between television violence and aggression in television watchers. However, because all three theories postulate a causal relationship, they must at this point be viewed as speculative.

Chapter 7

The Biosocial Model

INADEQUACY OF SINGLE-FACTOR EXPLANATIONS

Most investigators examine the causes of violence as they relate to only one factor. For example, one study might examine the association between television and violence, whereas a separate study might focus on the relationship between a biological factor and aggression. Although this is an effective method for expanding our knowledge, it distorts our perspective. Separate research studies can demonstrate that individual factors are related to violence, but no single-factor model has been effective in fully explaining why some individuals are violent and others are not. For example, as chapter 6 showed, exposure to television may be linked with violent behavior in children; but almost all U.S. children watch television, so the question of why it affects some children strongly and not others remains.

A more accurate approach to the explanation of violent behavior is an epidemiological perspective. Epidemiology seeks to understand what factors increase the risk of disorders, rather an attempting to pin down the cause of a problem disease or behavior. *Risk factors* are any factors that increase the risk of getting a disorder or a disease. For example, driving without a seat belt increases the risk of injury in an accident. Driving without a seat belt is not a cause of an injury, but wearing no seat belt is associated with higher levels of injury. *Protective factors,* on the other hand, are factors that promote health. Wearing a seat belt is a protective factor against auto injury. Although wearing a seat belt does not guarantee against injury, it is associated with lower levels of injury.

Similarly, having four or more minor physical anomalies (MPAs) is associated with higher rates of recidivistic violence. Watching violent television is associated with higher rates of childhood aggression. This is not to say that MPAs and television single-handedly cause violence; rather, these are risk factors that increase the probability of violence. No one risk factor alone is enough to cause the behavioral disorder we call *violence;* rather, multiple risk factors must be present.

Just as there are risk factors, there are protective factors against violence. Living in a family that clearly rewards prosocial behavior and punishes aggression and violence is one protective factor; although such a family cannot guarantee that no child in it will grow up to be violent, the risk of such a disorder is clearly lower.

Conceptualizing the causes of violence as a risk and protective factor equation can clarify the role that all of the factors discussed in chapters 3, 4, 5, and 6 must play. Furthermore, it helps explain why some factors seem relevant in some violent offenders, although they seem clearly irrelevant in other violent offenders. Rather than emphasizing any given theoretical approach (e.g., theorizing that individuals learn to be violent, or theorizing that media sources are the primary influences on violence today), epidemiology seeks only to identify factors that clearly affect the risk that an individual will demonstrate a disorder. Accordingly, the biosocial model can account for the potential contribution of both biological and psychosocial factors. It seems clear that neither set of factors alone can explain the existence of human violence.

In addition, several important risk factors associated with violent behavior are clearly influenced both by an individual's internal makeup and by his or her external conditions. These risk factors, being among the most important in predicting violent behavior, clearly demonstrate the importance of both types of influences.

GENDER AND VIOLENCE

One of the most intriguing aspects of violence is how gender-based it is. In other words, males and females differ in their rates of violent behavior to a greater extent than they differ in their patterns of most human behaviors. We have seen the increased vulnerability of males to childhood disorders related to violence, and the potential importance of some types of androgens (most possibly prenatal exposure) in the etiology of violence (L. Ellis, 1990, 1991). But how large is the male–female difference? Is it really true, as we frequently assume, that males are responsible for most violence? Although some researchers have argued that gender differences in aggression are exaggerated, particularly if different types of aggression are accounted for (Bjorkqvist, 1994), most studies certainly suggest that such an assumption is warranted. In 1958, Wolfgang studied the police records for all homicides occurring in Philadelphia between 1948 and 1952, and found that 82% of the perpetrators were male. That study, considered a classic, is nevertheless several decades old; do more modern statistics continue to follow this pattern? They seem to. The UCR, compiled each year by the FBI, also finds that about 9 out of every 10 murderers are male (Federal Bureau of Investigation, 1989). Similarly, perpetrators of assault and rape are primarily (if not exclusively) male, when official statistics are examined; in fact, the gender difference is presumed to be so marked that many researchers do not even bother to include women as subjects in their studies of violence (Cervi, 1991; Huesmann, Eron, Lefkowitz, & Walder, 1984; Olweus, 1979; Rosenbaum & Hoge, 1989; Spellacy, 1978).

Once again, however, we see that there may be an important distinction between family violence and street violence, and between official and self-report statistics. Most official statistics, as we know, reflect street crime and do not accurately reflect domestic violence. However, as we have seen, most violence in the United States appears to occur in the domestic domain, rather than in the community (Hotaling et al., 1989; Kandel-Englander, 1992). Therefore, as we attempt to understand the male to female ratio, it is very important to examine both self-report research and research on family violence. When we do so, the picture changes somewhat. For example, both men and women engage in child abuse; in fact, the 1975 National Family Violence Survey found that 71% of mothers and 58% of fathers reported some violence against their children (Straus et al., 1980). Does this study suggest that, given the appropriate victim, a woman is just as likely to be violent as a man? Not really. Although women abused children at least as often as men in this study, the men used significantly more severe violence. In addition, the comparison is probably not a fair one; after all, women have much more opportunity to abuse children than do men because they are typically the primary caretakers. A truly informative study that sought to compare rates of male- versus female-perpetrated child abuse would have to compare men who are primary caregivers with women who are primary caregivers. Unfortunately, no such study has yet been conducted.

The data on spouse abuse present another interesting challenge to the notion that violence is primarily male. Although the government, via the NCS, has estimated that the husband is the perpetrator in 70% of violent assaults between spouses (Langan & Innes, 1986), self-report surveys suggest otherwise. In the 1975 NFVS, approximately 12% of both men and women admitted using some form of violence against their spouses (Straus et al., 1980). More recent surveys, including the 1985 NFVS, also suggest approximately equal rates of male- and female-perpetrated spousal violence (O'Leary et al., 1989; Straus & Gelles, 1986). However, as with child abuse, the type of violence and the motive for the violence may still differ dramatically between the sexes. For example, men are more likely to use severe violence (e.g., punching and kicking), whereas women are more likely to use minor violence (such as throwing things or slapping; Straus &

Gelles, 1990; Straus et al., 1980). In addition, men use violence against their wives in order to establish control or to get them to do something, whereas women use violence against their husbands in self-defense or retaliation, or to reduce their own tension, or in an attempt to convince their husbands to talk (Adler, 1991; Straus & Gelles, 1990).

In summary, therefore, men perpetrate street violence in numbers overwhelmingly larger than women. In contrast, women seem to perpetrate family violence as often as men do, although their aggression is generally significantly less severe, is much less often fatal, and is more likely to result from self-defense.

There are two major approaches to explaining these differences—one emphasizing biological factors, and one emphasizing sociopsychological ones.

Biological Explanations

Biological explanations emphasize the role of male biology in the gender gap in aggressive behavior. Although the presence of the Y gene on the 23rd pair of chromosomes is known to make males more vulnerable to many physical disorders (e.g., heart disease), genetic influences do not appear to be critical in the etiology of violence (Mednick et al., 1984; see chapter 4). However, several biological markers of violence are found more often in men than women. For example, minimal brain dysfunction has been found to occur more frequently in men (Nichols, 1987); similarly, perinatal complications are more common in men (Kandel, 1989; Pasamanick, Rodgers, & Lilienfield, 1956).

A fruitful area of research, explored in chapter 4, is the role of androgens in violence. Recall that androgens are male sex hormones, secreted by both males and females, but much more abundant in males. Androgens have certainly been linked to criminal violence (L. Ellis, 1990), albeit in indirect ways (e.g., prenatally), as well as to other sex-typed "male" behaviors (Berenbaum & Hines, 1992). One study of girls with congenital adrenal hyperplasia, a disorder in which they are exposed to high levels of androgens in utero, found a marked preference for boys' toys (Berenbaum & Hines, 1992). Although androgens probably only play an indirect role in aggression, it seems likely that the fact that males are exposed to more androgens in utero is one reason why males are more prone to behave violently.

Another biological factor that has been linked both to males and to violence is MAO (monoamine oxidase, an enzyme). Blood levels of MAO have been related to a number of behavioral patterns, including level of motor activity and infant fussiness (L. Ellis, 1991). Low levels of MAO in the blood of infants is associated with problems such as nail-biting and enuresis (bedwetting; L. Ellis, 1991). Statistically, men have lower MAO levels than women. They drop especially low during a person's 20s and 30s (coincidentally, when aggressive behavior peaks). Lower MAO levels are associated with aggressiveness in general, sudden feelings of anger and frustration, and especially to impulsiveness (L. Ellis, 1991). MAO levels vary with levels of testosterone, one of the androgens (L. Ellis, 1990). One case study of a family with a high number of aggressive men found a defect on the chromosome that regulates MAO (Morell, 1993). All in all, MAO seems to constitute one more piece of the gender discrepancy puzzle.

Sociopsychological Explanations

Biology aside, there are clearly important differences in the manner in which boys and girls are socialized that are relevant to the gender gap in violence. Girls are much more likely to be taught to be expressive caregivers in preparation for their role as the central parent of children. They are also taught to be the spouse who is the emotional watchdog in marital relationships. Individuals who are socialized in this way are undoubtedly less likely to be violent and assaultive. Male socialization, by contrast, typically involves emphasis on the role of competition with others and the importance of being dominant and powerful; much adult violence is, in fact, in pursuit of these goals.

Parents treat boys and girls differently; boys are generally encouraged to be independent, exploratory, assertive, and sometimes even openly aggressive; girls, to be dependent on their families and nurturing of others. After the preschool years, parents are much more likely to use physical punishment with boys than with girls (J. Anderson, 1972). The different ways that parents and society raise boys and girls undoubtedly result in different behavioral styles and tendencies.

Apart from the way in which they are treated, some differences in childhood behavior between boys and girls undoubtedly lead into different emotional landscapes. Developmentally, boys are prone to more behavioral disorders, including those that are linked to aggression and violence. For example, hyperactivity is more common in boys, as are CDs (G. Weiss, 1990; Zagar et al., 1989). Because we know that developmentally, a child who is hyperactive or conduct disordered is at greater risk of becoming violent, the fact that boys have higher rates of these childhood disorders makes them one more part of the causal equation explaining the male–female discrepancy in violent behavior.

Even a child's reaction to violent victimization may depend, at least to some extent, on his or her gender. Faced with psychological trauma in general, girls are more apt to withdraw, whereas boys are more apt to act out aggressively. When girls and boys who had been violently abused were compared, one study found that although girls had significant adolescent problems, it was the boys who were violently abused as children who were more likely to commit crimes (Rivera & Spatz Widom, 1990). In general, men are freer to react aggressively to stressors because society forgives violence more readily in men and even applauds it at times.

EDUCATION AND VIOLENCE

A person's educational achievement is strongly affected by both external and internal factors, including the quality of the school they attend, the family's attitude toward education, social investment in education, and the child's inherent abilities that can make school success easier or more difficult. The evidence regarding school achievement and violent and criminal behavior is monotonous in its uniformly positive findings of an important relationship between school failure and antisocial behavior.

A number of studies have examined school performance and its relationship to criminality or delinquency in general. G. Weiss (1990) found that hyperactivity (a risk factor for criminality) was associated with lowered educational achievement, and that recovery from mild to moderate perinatal complications (a risk factor for violence) seems to depend (at least in part) on the quality of a child's educational experiences. L. Ellis (1990) also found that school achievement is important in combination with other factors in leading to criminality. Kirkegaard-Sorenson and Mednick (1977) noted that school behavior in general is a good predictor of criminality, and Denno's (1990) study of Philadelphia delinquents found that language achievement and maternal educational levels were good discriminators between delinquents and nondelinquents. Finally, one study found that children who are at high risk for delinquency but do not become delinquent may be protected by factors, such as high IQ, that make it easy for them to succeed in school (Kandel, 1987; Kandel et al., 1988).

Other research has examined school achievement in relation to violent behavior, rather than criminal behavior in general. One report focused on family violence specifically, and noted that most studies reviewed found evidence for an inverse (opposite) relationship between a man's educational achievement and his risk of being violently abusive toward his wife (Hotaling & Sugarman, 1986). Similarly, a 1986 study of adults on death row for capital crimes found a clear and consistent pattern of childhood and adolescent educational and intellectual difficulties (Lewis et al., 1986). Other research has focused on juveniles, particularly on juveniles who are among the most violent: those convicted of murder. Busch et al. (1990) studied adolescents who had killed both family and nonfamily victims, and compared them to other delinquent teenagers. He found that severe educational difficulties were common in the backgrounds of the homicidal adolescents; he also noted that although intelligence discriminated between adolescent murderers and nonmurderers, it did so to a lesser degree than other factors such as having a violent family member, gang membership, and alcohol abuse. Other research on homicidal adolescents has found essentially the same results: Individuals who kill as adolescents are inevitably marked by "insurmountable" and "severe" educational difficulties (Bender, 1959; Lewis et al., 1988; Zagar, Arbit, Sylvies, Busch, & Hughes, 1990).

The evidence points strongly to an association between school achievement, criminality, and criminal violence. But how does school achievement relate to different types of criminal violence? Does the level of education an individual achieves have an impact on his or her tendency to be violent, either across the board, with family members, or on the street? In other words, do different types of violent offenders show different relationships to education? One approach to this question is to compare the number of years of school completed by violent and nonviolent men. In one study (Kandel-Englander, 1992), I compared educational patterns among different groups of subjects. Violent and nonviolent White subjects, it turned out, did not differ much in years of schooling completed. Violent and nonviolent non-White men did. Education, therefore, may be a more important contributor to violence among non-White than among White men.

As we have seen, there are real differences between those men who are street- and pan-violent, and those who are violent only with their families. These differences were correlated with differences in education. Overall, family-violent men stayed in school as long, or longer, than nonviolent men. The pan- and street-violent attained, on the average, much less education. When only White men are considered, however, education appeared not to differ between the family-, pan- and street-violent males. (Note that this analysis only considers the years in school, not the quality of school experiences.) A very different pattern characterized non-White violent men. The family-violent and nonviolent had completed a similar number of years in school; the street- and pan-violent had completed significantly fewer years.

To summarize, the number of years a child goes to school may be important in determining whether or not that child will become violent, but if this is the case, it is less true for White men than for non-White men. Among Whites, there were no differences among street-, pan-, family-violent, and nonviolent offenders. Among non-Whites, family-violent and nonviolent offenders were similarly highly educated, whereas pan-violent and street-violent offenders were less educated.

It is interesting to note that although non-White subjects in the study achieved less education than White subjects, they were similar to the U.S. population as a whole. For example, 12% of the U.S. population drops out of school before high school; this is in comparison to 14% of the non-White study sample, and only 5% of the White study sample. Thus, non-White subjects were not characterized by extremely low educational achievement; rather, White subjects were characterized by higher educational achievement. Other research has suggested that longer stays in school may actually protect otherwise high-risk children from developing antisocial behavior (Kandel et al., 1988).

Why would family-violent offenders be as highly educated as nonviolent men? One possibility is that violent men who are as highly educated as nonviolent men may be "protected" from involvement in street violence by their investment in their status. Thus, if they stayed in school, they choose only family victims because doing so is less risky than choosing outside victims. This interpretation rests on the social truism, well documented, that violence against the family is less often regarded as a "crime" than is violence in the streets. It certainly seems very likely that battering is seen as more socially acceptable (and thus is less socially controlled) than street violence (Straus, 1976). Because of such cultural beliefs, men may perceive that street violence carries much more risk of official detection and punishment than does the commission of family violence. Those men who have managed to stay in school and achieve a higher social class may not wish to jeopardize their gains by assaulting outsiders, when they feel able to assault family members more easily and with relatively greater impunity.

More generally, how might educational achievement help protect children against delinquency and violence? High achievement in school seems to increase children's self-esteem, which may protect them against becoming involved in delinquent or aggressive activities (T. Moeller, 1994). Students who achieve in school rate their own competence and abilities highly; their parents have similarly high expectations for them (Sink, Barnett, & Pool, 1993). High educational achievement is also associated with higher social class, which in turns helps prevent aggressiveness in boys (Moss, Mezzick, Yao, Gavaler, & Martin, 1995). One study found that low educational achievement—but not low IQ—during the early school years predicted later delinquency in both boys and girls (Fergusson & Horwood, 1995). Although low IQ does not predict well to delinquency, high IQ seems to protect children who are at high risk for violent and delinquent behavior—probably because high IQ makes school achievement relatively easy (Kandel, 1987; Kandel et al., 1988). School achievement helps children develop an internal locus of control and a belief in their own power to influence their environment (Ferrari & Parker, 1992). Finally, high achievement during school years is one of the best predictors of college attendance, which undoubtedly rewards children for maintaining good behavior (Wesley, 1994). Thus, school achievement is itself predictive of prosocial behavior, and is related to other variables, such as financial success, high self-esteem, and internal locus of control, which by themselves appear to help protect vulnerable children.

UNDERSTANDING BIOSOCIAL CAUSES
OF EXTREME VIOLENCE

Instead of studying all violent offenders, some researchers focus on only the most violent individuals in our society: those sentenced to execution and thus on death row. Although these individuals, who are highly violent and highly recidivistic, are relatively rare, their propensity for aggression clearly sets them apart. Thus, their characteristics may tell us something about what the most critical determinants of risk for violence are. These determinants seem to be medical history (an internal factor), family history (their external environment), and record of school achievement (an internal factor).

Dorothy Otnow Lewis is a psychiatrist and physician at New York University. With several colleagues, she has studied several groups of inmates on death row for violent offenses. It is her work that gives us most of our knowledge of the psychological functioning of these criminals.

In 1986, Lewis and her colleagues studied 15 condemned adult men (13) and women (2) in five states. Medically, Lewis noted several important points. For example, every single inmate studied had a history of significant head injury. The injuries were severe enough in all cases to lead to possible brain dysfunction. In addition to head injury, 12 of the 15 (80%) inmates had other neurologically abnormal symptoms, such as paralysis, seizures, and blackouts. Intellectually, all but one of the inmates tested in the "average" range on psychoeducational intelligence tests. However, despite their total average scores, subjects generally showed intellectual problems in specific areas. This suggests that although educationally the inmates may not have suffered from global intelligence impairment, they may have had specific learning problems (e.g., an inmate as a child may have had adequate intelligence overall, but great difficulty learning to read). In general, the evidence of medical and neurological problems was somewhat stronger than the evidence of intellectual problems, although the two are typically related and intelligence problems appeared likely in all inmates. Psychologically, 6 (40%) of the inmates were found to be psychotic—so seriously mentally ill that they were out of contact with reality. The presence of these disorders indicates both a probable biological propensity and, often, a disturbed family environment. (Lay people tend to think of *psychotic* as synonymous with *insane,* although the two terms are not necessarily identical technically and legally.) Nine (60%) of the inmates had suffered symptoms of mental disturbance during childhood that were severe enough to require medical attention or to make it impossible for the child to attend school in a normal classroom (Lewis et al., 1986).

Having completed her study of adult condemned inmates, Lewis and her colleagues then began to study juveniles who had committed such serious violent crimes that they had been condemned to death. All 14 boys studied had committed capital offenses before they reached the age of 18, and had been sentenced to death in one of four states that permitted the execution of minors. Of the adults previously studied, all had had histories of significant head injuries. Of these 14 juveniles, 8 (57%) had a history of head injuries that were severe enough that hospitalization was required, or that a permanent skull indentation resulted. In addition, 9 (64%) of the juveniles had "serious neurological abnormalities" that could be documented by a history of seizures or abnormal EEG findings, suggesting that the difference in rates of neurological abnormalities between the adults and the children could have occurred by chance alone; after all, only 15 and 14 cases were examined in each study, respectively. Another possibility is that the juveniles had less time to acquire neurological abnormalities, relative to the adult offenders (e.g., a juvenile offender may have had only 15 years to injure his head prior to incarceration, whereas an adult offender may have had 25 years to do so). In any case, it seems clear that abnormalities in the way the brain functions are more common than not among the most violent offenders.

Psychologically, 7 of the 14 juvenile inmates were psychotic at the time of the study, or had been diagnosed as psychotic earlier in their lives. Four others (for a total of 11 juveniles or 79%) had evidence of severe mood disorders, which can be as severe as psychosis but involve very extreme mood swings rather than impairments of cognition. Psychologically, therefore, it was even more common for the violent juveniles than for the violent adults to have severe psychological disorders.

Although almost all adult violent death row inmates had normal intelligence, 12 (86%) of the juvenile inmates had IQs below the "average" range, and almost all of them failed to read at their appropriate grade level.

The researchers took a family history of each juvenile, and paid particular attention to any episode of physical or sexual abuse. Not surprisingly, 12 (86%) of the juveniles had been "brutally" physically abused, and 5 (36%) had been sexually abused (sodomized) by an adult male relative during childhood. In addition, again not surprisingly, the families of these very violent juveniles showed very high rates of a multitude of serious problems, such as alcoholism and drug abuse and histories of psychiatric treatment and hospitalization (Lewis et al., 1988).

Clearly, very violent and recidivistic individuals frequently have a multitude of handicaps, including neurological and medical disorders, profound psychological disorders, and intellectual and familial dysfunction. Noting these, we realize just how important it is to intervene in their lives early on, to minimize the incidence of the kind of predatory and relentless violence committed by most death row inmates.[1]

The causes of violence can be controversial and disturbing to study. It is difficult and painful to contemplate the ways in which we may be damaging, or damaged by, our children. But scientists seek not what is pleasant to know, but what is true.

It is easy to confuse the study of very violent criminals with a desire to treat them leniently. The first priority of every psychocriminologist is public safety and preservation of the basic rights of all not to be victimized. However, unless we learn the truth about what makes very violent people tick, prevention is an impossible goal.

---

[1]The understanding that extremely violent people frequently have problems that predispose them to aggressive behavior does not necessarily imply any political stand on how they should be treated (e.g., support for or criticism of the death penalty or "three-strikes" laws).

Part II

SPECIAL ISSUES

Chapter 8

Substance Abuse and Violent Behavior

Personality, biology, and socioenvironmental variables may generally predispose individuals to violence, but other, more immediate influences can place a particular individual at a particular point in time at high risk. Why might a man be violent today, and not yesterday? One frequently cited reason and a focus of public concern is the relationship between substance abuse and aggressive behavior (Bakan, 1971; Busch et al., 1990; Jackson, 1958; Rosenbaum & Hoge, 1989; Snell, 1992; Stephens, 1994; Taylor & Sears, 1988; U.S. Department of Justice, 1990; Zagar et al., 1990). Can intoxication cause an otherwise nonaggressive individual to become violent? Do different types of substances cause different degrees of behavioral change?

SUBSTANCE ABUSE (DRUGS AND ALCOHOL) AND VIOLENCE

The proliferation of drug abuse grabbed the spotlight during the 1980s in the United States. The number of persons arrested, convicted, and imprisoned for drug offenses has skyrocketed in the last decade. For example, the fastest growing group of female prison inmates are those convicted of a drug offense (Snell, 1992). One of the most compelling arguments in favor of strict enforcement of drug laws is the presumed association between substance abuse and violence.

Background

The U.S. Department of Justice (1990) conducted a comprehensive survey of drugs and crime. The results were as expected. By 1989, 38% of Americans who responded to the Gallup Poll indicated that drug abuse was the most serious problem facing our country. This was in comparison to 2% in January 1985. In addition, 58% of these Americans felt that drugs were the factor most responsible for crime in the United States (vs. 13% in 1981). In 1992, President George Bush called for a renewed effort to fight drugs and crime (Dillingham, 1992). How bad was (and is) the problem? Only 9% of public school students stated that it was "impossible" to obtain drugs at their schools (Bastian & Taylor, 1991).

When victims of violent crimes were surveyed in the 1990 study, the results were equally compelling. Victims reported that they believed their assailants were under the influence of drugs or alcohol in about 36% of the incidents of rape, robbery, and assault, taken together (U.S. Department of Justice, 1990). In 43% of the violent incidents, victims did not know if their assailants were under the influence of a substance. In only 20% did they feel certain that the offender was not under the influence.

Another part of the same study surveyed criminals themselves. Nearly two thirds (64%) of state prison inmates serving time for a violent offense reported that either they or their victims (or both) were under the influence of drugs or alcohol at the time of the offense. Fifty-four percent reported that they themselves were using drugs or alcohol, whereas nearly 30% of the victims were perceived by the perpetrator to be using drugs or alcohol at the time of the assault.

Interestingly, drug use appeared to be highest among violent offenders who victimized strangers (as opposed to family). Manslaughter was the crime that most often involved drug or alcohol use by the offender, victim, or both (76% of manslaughter convictions involved such use). Sexual assault other than rape was, relatively speaking, the least likely to involve drug or alcohol use, although 50% of such assaults still involved substance abuse.

Substances can have a variety of effects on human behavior. These include either stimulation or depression of the central nervous system (CNS) and alteration of basic thought processes. The effect a drug has on any given person depends both on the drug chosen and the dose taken, as well as on psychological and emotional factors. A drug can worsen psychological symptoms in already disturbed individuals; for example, slightly paranoid individuals may become extremely paranoid when they ingest alcohol, and thus may commit crime in the belief that they are defending themselves against imaginary evil. Individuals' expectations about how the drug will affect them also have profound effects; people can, for example, even become "drunk" on flavored water when they believe it is alcohol!

There are three mechanisms whereby a substance might increase a person's tendency to be violent. First, drugs might change a person's behavior from nonviolent to violent—for example, cause extreme paranoia in a person who, when sober, was only mildly paranoid. Second, a person might commit a violent crime in order to obtain drugs (or money for drugs), especially if he or she was addicted, although it is true that most violent crime is not committed strictly for material or financial gain (Vince, 1989). Finally, substance abuse and violence might be linked through a third factor: for example, alcohol abuse is associated with a high level of head injury from accidents (Rosenbaum & Hoge, 1989). Head injury is associated in turn with violence (Lewis et al., 1979). At least in some cases, the drugs-and-violence link may have more to do with brain dysfunction than with the effects of drugs per se.

"Addiction" to drugs, also called *dependency,* can be either physical or psychological. Physical dependency is more acute and painful, because it involves a physical need for the drug. Not having the substance results in real physical pain, which can be a powerful motive for committing instrumental violence. Psychological dependency is generally less serious although it may also be a motivation for crime because a person who is psychologically dependent on a substance generally believes that he or she must have that substance in order to function. Not having the substance, the psychological addict believes, could lead to devastating consequences. Such a belief might be motive enough to do anything necessary to obtain a "fix."

Alcohol and Violence

What drugs are most likely to increase the possibility of violence? Alcohol is one drug that has certainly been linked to aggressive behavior. Because it is legal, widely available, and socially acceptable (even desirable), alcohol is the drug most commonly used and abused in the United States. It is consumed "socially" (i.e., in at least occasional small quantities) by a majority of Americans (Bassuk, Schoonover, & Gelenberg, 1983). About one third of all U.S. families include at least one person who has, or has had, a problem with alcohol, on a continuum from heavy drinking without addiction to full-blown alcoholism (Peele, 1984). In addition to high levels of consumption, Americans tend to have different consumption patterns than members of other Western societies. They tend to drink heavily during short periods of time, whereas others tend to spread out their drinking throughout the day (Bartol, 1991). For example, a French individual may have several glasses of wine with both lunch and dinner, whereas an American is more likely to consume his or her daily alcohol in stronger liquor or in a compressed period of time (e.g., during a "happy hour" after work).

Alcohol certainly has some strong effects. Its most marked effect is on the brain (Bassuk et al., 1983), where it impairs nearly every aspect of information processing (National Institute on Alcohol Abuse and Alcoholism, 1994). Perhaps most notably, it is the third leading cause of death in the United States, and is responsible for more deaths than all other drugs combined (Bartol, 1991). Forty percent of all deaths from traffic accidents are alcohol-related, and traffic accidents are the leading cause of death in the United States (Zobeck, Stinson, Grant, & Bertolucci, 1993). People can become dependent on (or addicted to) alcohol, both psychologically and physically. Whether alcohol causes an increase in violence is a less simple question. As stated previously, some research has suggested that alcohol has been involved in the crimes of about half of the violent inmates in prisons. Alcohol seems to have the strongest impact on violence when both offender and victim are not sober; possibly a sober potential victim is more able than an intoxicated one to defend him or herself or otherwise avoid victimization. Laboratory studies have found that subjects who are given alcohol are consistently more willing to be aggressive than sober subjects (Taylor & Sears, 1988). Among college students, alcohol was one of the factors related to sexual aggression on campus (Koss & Gaines, 1993). In the case of family violence, treatment programs for abusive husbands have noted that alcohol use after treatment helps to predict violent recidivism (Hamberger & Hastings, 1990).

This evidence seems overwhelming. However, some caveats are in order. As hypothesized earlier, alcohol may be related to violence through a third factor. One study, which examined the relationship between alcohol use and violence in teenagers, went to special trouble to control for confounding factors. This survey of more than 12,000 Norwegian adolescents (Rossow, Pape, & Wichstrom, 1999) examined violent behavior, alcohol use, and other factors likely to be confounds in the relationship between the two (such as a pattern of problem behaviors, or gender role orientation). They found that once such confounds are controlled for, a significant but distinctly modest relationship existed between drinking and violence. This relationship was much more apparent in males and in younger teens (those 12 to 14 years old). Another study, examining the potential of biological confounds, showed an association between accidental head injury and high levels of alcohol use (Rosenbaum & Hoge, 1989); and as outlined in chapter 4, head injury is one of the biological markers of a predisposition to violence in at least some cases. Thus, alcohol may not always directly increase aggression. In some men, high levels of alcohol use may be related to high-risk activities (such as fast driving or dangerous sports), which in turn increase their risk of head injury and violence. In addition, alcohol abuse and violence may develop independently and thus be correlated but not always causally related—as in theories that emphasize that both problem drinking and problem violence behavior can be learned through modeling (Rossow et al., 1999). In any case, the studies in this area suggest that both scenarios are plausible—that alcohol is spuriously related to violence, and also that it can cause an increase in violence.

To further complicate the matter, however, in low doses alcohol may actually inhibit violent behavior. There seems to be a direct relationship between the amount of alcohol ingested and the tendency to be aggressive (Taylor & Sears, 1988). Lower doses of alcohol do not seem to have the same effect as higher doses; studies comparing individuals who had ingested low versus higher amounts of alcohol found that it was only the higher amounts that increased the subject's tendency to be aggressive (Taylor, Schmutte, Leonard, & Cranston, 1979).

Finally, social expectations may be critical in mediating the alcohol–aggression relationship. People expect to become "drunk" when they drink, and drinking is an at least marginally socially acceptable excuse for what might otherwise be inexcusable behavior. Although violent offenders (and others) tend to believe that alcohol is disinhibiting, at least some studies failed to find that this is so (Ullman, Karabatsos, & Koss, 1999). Many researchers now believe that individuals' expectations strongly influence the effects of alcohol on their behavior in general and their aggressive behavior in particular (Koss & Gaines, 1993). In addition, subjects in one study, given alcohol, appeared to become more aggressive at least in part because they were frustrated or provoked while intoxicated (Taylor et al., 1979). Thus, it has been suggested that alcohol must be combined with provoking or inciting experiences in order to produce an increase in violence or aggression (Bartol, 1991).

CNS Stimulants and Violence

The CNS stimulants most commonly associated with violence are cocaine and crack cocaine. Toward the end of the 1970s, cocaine and crack cocaine use in the United States sharply increased. Cocaine has been used in the United States since the 19th century, and was once legal; it was not criminalized until the early years of the 20th century, when social policymakers became concerned about the epidemic of individuals addicted to cocaine-laced "tonics" and "medicines." As the popularity of illegal cocaine rose in the 1970s, massive amounts of the drug began to be smuggled into the United States from South America, where the drug grows as a shrub. Crack cocaine has been so named because of the "crackling" sound it gives off when smoked. It is not really purified cocaine but a product made of cocaine, baking soda, water, and various other products. Crack cocaine results in euphoric "highs" and "crashes"; addicts continually crave more and more crack, and will go to any lengths to obtain it. Crack may be the most addictive drug currently available (Bartol, 1991).

The rise in violent crime during the same decade as the rise in cocaine and crack cocaine use suggested to many that the two are related (Fagan & Chin, 1989; "The Wages of Crack," 1994). Some research found an association between crack cocaine use and number of arrests, as well as other multiple risk factors, such as a history of sexual molestation (Kang, Magura, & Shapiro, 1994). However, such research is limited because cocaine use is typically only one of many risk factors found in crime-prone individuals, leaving open the possibility that other risk factors are more important (Kang et al., 1994). In addition, the impact of cocaine on antisocial behavior may depend on how the drug is used (e.g., sniffed vs. injected; Giannini, Miller, Loiselle, & Turner, 1993) or on the gender of the user (P. Goldstein, Bellucci, Spunt, & Miller, 1991). In fact, a substantial body of research suggests that there is no simple, direct relationship between cocaine use and an increase in violent crime. Studies noting correlations between aggression and cocaine, and aggression in cocaine-ingesting rats, may lend credence to the belief that cocaine causes an increase in aggression (Wood & Spear,

1998). However, studies examining aggressive behavior in psychiatric emergency-room samples in more depth have found that there is little or no association between cocaine use and violence in these clinical samples; rather, past psychopathology seems to be a much stronger predictor of aggression (Dhossche, 1999; F. Moeller et al., 1997). One study of 427 New York City male adolescents found that although cocaine or crack use and rates of crime were similarly high, use of cocaine or crack was not related to any particular type of crime, including violent crime (Kang et al., 1994). Another study in Miami found that crack use was related primarily to the crime of drug sales (Inciardi & Pottieger, 1994). Even parental use of crack, while placing children at higher risk of behavioral problems, did not predict the number of children's arrests before age 18 (Caudill, Hoffman, Hubbard, Flynn, & Luckey, 1994). Thus, despite the widespread belief that crack directly causes violence, there is no definitive evidence that cocaine causes a general increase in violent crime, although in high doses, via certain routes of administration, and when given to people who already tend to be aggressive, it may increase levels of aggression.

Chapter 9

Youth Violence

At 2:00 P.M. on February 2, 1996, a 14-year-old named Barry Loukaitis walked into Frontier Junior High School in Moses Lake, Washington, and ignited a renewed national concern with the problem of youth violence. That school shooting was only the first of a string of school shootings, lasting until the time of this writing, that engulfed the American consciousness and convinced most Americans that youth violence was a serious problem that was only becoming more serious.

In reality, the violent crime arrest rate for youths under 15 years old peaked in 1994 and has been declining since then (Puzzanchera, 1998). Senator Joseph Biden did point out a fact that has concerned criminologists—the fact that there are currently almost 40 million children who "stand on the edge of their teen years" and thus are likely to fuel another increase in youth crime in the coming decade (Biden, 1998). Currently, however, violent crime among younger teens (who are still primarily tried as children in juvenile court) is on the decrease, not on the increase.

Despite this fact, two areas of youth violence continue to be a major source of social concern. One of these, gang violence, has been a social problem for half a century, although it became increasingly visible during the 1980s. The other area has only appeared in the last decade: "copycat" school shootings, primarily involving rural and suburban middle-class children who attack schoolmates with firearms and wound and/or kill multiple victims.

In general, the age of first offense appears to be an important predictor of the probability that an offender will continue to become a multiple offender (Denno, 1990). For this reason the data on the youngest offenders is of particular interest in the study of youth violence. For most of the 1980s, the violent crime arrest rate for children 15 and younger remained stable. A dramatic increase in this arrest rate occurred between 1988 and 1994, after which the arrest rate leveled off (Puzzanchera, 1998). This increase coincided with a general crime wave in the United States during the late 1980s. Although the subsequent decline after 1994 was significant, it did not return youth violence to the pre-1980s level. In fact, the youth arrest rate for violent crimes in 1996 was still 60% higher than the rate in 1980. The youth homicide rate was similarly 67% higher in 1996, relative to 1980 (Puzzanchera, 1998).

The property crime arrest rate for juveniles followed a similar pattern, although it peaked somewhat earlier, in 1991 instead of in 1994. The general increase in youth crime after 1988 fueled a 50% increase in the number of cases handled by juvenile court involving youths under 15 years old. Indeed, the proportion of cases involving such very young offenders is now almost 40% of the cases in juvenile court, suggesting that very young offenders may be a growing problem. Some have pointed out that juvenile courts across the nation have become so burdened with large caseloads that they suffer from ineffectiveness (Biden, 1998). These overloaded courts may actually contribute to youth crime by teaching youngsters that only the most serious offenses will be closely examined. Congressional legislation has been criticized for failing to address these legal needs and for ignoring the role that easy access to guns plays in the commission of juvenile violence (Biden, 1998).

CAUSES OF YOUTH VIOLENCE

All of the causes of violence in general contribute to youth violence as well. These risk factors include the biological factors such as perinatal problems (Kandel, 1989; Kandel & Mednick, 1991; Lewis et al., 1979; Mednick, Mura, Schulsinger, & Mednick, 1971), head injuries (Lewis et al., 1986; Lewis et al., 1979; Rosenbaum & Hoge, 1989), and childhood disorders such as Attention-Deficit/ Hyperactivity Disorder (Ellis, 1991; Fergusson & Horwood, 1995; Halperin & Newcorn, 1997; Hughes, Zagar, et al., 1991; Jacobvitz & Sroufe, 1987; Kandel & Mednick, 1989; Zagar et al., 1989). Social factors are also important contributors, just as they are for adults, and include risk factors such as parenting skills (Baumrind, 1994; Gardner & Timmons-Mitchell, 1990; Haskett, Johnson, & Miller, 1994; Kelley, 1992; Patterson, 1986) and family stability (Campbell, 1994; Dodge, Bates, & Pettit, 1990; Farrington, 1978). As they are with adult offenders, childhood developmental problems are also disproportionately prevalent with juvenile offenders, and include risk factors such as learning disorders (Cornwall & Bawden, 1992; Farnham-Diggory, 1978; Zagar et al., 1989) and conduct disorders (August et al., 1983; Haddad et al., 1991; Miller & Prinz, 1990; Vitaro et al., 1998; Webster-Stratton, 2000).

The interesting question, when it comes to youth violence, is the following: What are the differences between those individuals who begin criminal violence as an adult versus those who begin during their adolescence? Study of many adult offenders suggests, in fact, that most begin with some form of antisocial behavior during adolescence (Spatz Widom, 1989a). That most probably seeming to be the case, the issue is one of degree. In other words, most offenders probably begin some form of antisocial behavior during adolescence, but some graduate much more quickly than others do to serious criminal violence. What research exists examining the difference between adolescents who commit serious criminal offenses at a very young age versus more typical antisocially behaving teenagers?

Some factors, interestingly, appear to be less important among very young offenders. For example, although drug use is commonly reported in 40% to 60% of youths arrested, the proportion of drug-using arrestees is actually lower among the youngest offenders, relative to the older adolescents (Brennan, 1999). Although drug use is clearly a factor in all violent crime, it may be less important in the case of very young offenders than it is in the case of older offenders. Interestingly, although very young offenders are less likely to be arrested for drug offenses and more likely to be arrested for property offenses, they commit violent offenses in about the same proportion as adult offenders (Catalono, Loeber, & McKinney, 1999).

Kelley, Thornberry, and Smith (1997) examined the different developmental pathways that lead boys to delinquency. As part of their analysis, they attempted to differentiate between boys who begin criminal behavior early in adolescence or even before adolescence, and boys who begin antisocial behavior later in life. Interestingly, they were able to identify different "pathways" to delinquency, which seem to help tease apart these two groups. Kelley et al. (1997) identified "first stages" that seem to occur exclusively among children who enter delinquency early in life. These important first behaviors were identified as (a) perpetual conflicts with authority and (b) consistently stubborn behavior. Children who began delinquency later in life, on the other hand, seemed to show different "first stages": They showed signs of minor aggression or petty property crime as the initial signs of delinquency. This analysis emphasizes that boys at different developmental stages must master different developmental tasks, and failing at one developmental stage or task may place them at high risk for delinquency during that stage and subsequent stages.

Foote (1997) described research by Loeber and Farrington that studied the most violent juvenile offenders. The researchers found that these offenders tend to start their criminal careers earlier and continue them later than other offenders. Furthermore, they found that very young offenders (those under age 12) did at times show signs of becoming very violent; however, despite these "warning signs," these children were typically not processed through the criminal juvenile justice system and were frequently not given any type of intervention that might prevent future violent criminal careers. The researchers emphasized the need to use currently-recognized risk factors to identify high-risk children, and continue research on these risk factors to aid understanding of why some children begin criminal careers so early in life.

Apart from research on youth violence in general, two specific topics are of interest: (a) the recent spate of school shootings across the United States; and (b) juvenile gangs and the crimes they commit.

SCHOOL SHOOTINGS

Although not much empirical research exists about school shootings, one study of 110 middle- and high school students does exist (Lockwood, 1997). This study examined the reasons for, and circumstances of, violence at school in this age group. The first finding revealed that most violence was the result of a minor insult or altercation that escalated until it resulted in extreme violence. In addition, the major goal of the violence was revenge or retribution for the insult. Most students revealed in this study that such use of violence for retribution was considered morally acceptable and was not an indication that the violent student had an absence of values. Interestingly, although much of the findings of this study seem applicable to the spate of White, middle-class, rural and suburban school shootings, Lockwood's research was conducted on minority, urban adolescents. This suggests that the differences between violence in urban versus rural/suburban schools may be fewer than has generally been thought likely.

Examining all school shootings between 1996 and 1999 reveals some consistencies. They appear to be as follows: The shooters are all male. This is not inconsistent with the majority of violent offenders, who are in fact predominately male. It is probable that there have not been female shooters simply because school shootings are still relatively rare violent crimes. The shooters have all had interests in violent media and/or violent video games. These included games such as Mortal Kombat, Doom, and Quake, books by Adolf Hitler and Stephen King, and musicians who emphasize anarchy and violence. The shooters had all experienced some form of social humiliation or rejection prior to the shooting, including being called "gay" or "fat," or being rejected by girlfriends or teased by high-status adolescents (such as athletes). Most shooters came from intact families, although a few of these boys came from families where mental illness or divorce was present. There was no clear familial pattern that indicated serious issues with family stability. All shooters indicated some mental health problems, and difficulties such as depression, poor coping skills, and aggression were common. However, no mental health pattern was universal among the shooters, which suggests that any of several emotional difficulties may contribute to such shootings, rather than one particular type of emotional difficulty. Clearly, despite media reports, these shootings do not simply "appear" in children who evidence perfect mental health and perfect adjustment prior to the shootings. On the contrary, shooters are children who evidence emotional and behavioral problems, troubled social status, social humiliation and/or rejection, and who may be avenging what they perceive as insults or degradation. Their anger at these slights may be encouraged or given a form of expression by their continual exposure to violent mass media and violent video games (which begin them on the road to acting out their fantasies of revenge).

The absence of a clear pattern of family problems suggests one of two hypotheses: First, it may be that the types of family problems that lead to such violence are not easily apparent to the public. For example, whereas divorce is an easily observable indicator of family problems, emotional dysfunction is not. A second hypothesis is that these adolescents are less affected by problems with their families than they are by problems with their peers. In other words, the immediate factors that influence violence during adolescence may be social factors rather than familial ones.

GANGS

Adolescent criminal "gang" activity has become a significant threat to public safety, both in the United States and abroad. Although the United States has seen gang activity of one form or another since World War II, western Europe has begun to see gang formation in response to an increased drug trade (Kroeker & Haut, 1995). What currently alarms communities is not the existence of gangs, but rather disturbing trends toward increasingly violent behavior (Gaustad, 1990). Previously unheard-of gang behavior, such as drive-by shootings, now occurs across many different types of communities, and studies suggest that violent gang behavior has increased dramatically in recent years (R. Davis, 1995). Once confined to inner cities, gangs are now seen even on Native American reservations (Mydans, 1995).

President Bill Clinton declared September 12th to September 16th, 1994, "National Gang Violence Prevention Week." He expressed concern about the rise in gang-related violence and especially about the increasing involvement of preadolescent children in gangs (Clinton, 1994). In Chicago, an 11-year-old child (Robert Sandifer), already a member of the "Black Disciples" gang, fired a gun that hit and killed a 14-year-old boy. He was later executed by other gang members (Grace, 1994). The average age of gang members is dropping; in 1984 it was 15, but by 1987 it was only 13½ (McKinney, 1988). Despite this trend, the composition of what we call gangs varies enormously, both in membership and in activities. Gangs can have a few members or a few hundred. They are usually male, but some gangs are female (Moore, Vigil, & Levy, 1995). They may belong to one race or be interracial, and come together for the express purpose of behaving violently or criminally—or just to socialize (Spergel, 1986). Members typically advertise membership through distinctive dress, behaviors, or the guarding of territory ("turf"; Gaustad, 1990). Gangs that do have territory will frequently mark it as theirs with graffiti and meaningful symbols.

There is no doubt that during the 1980s and 1990s violent gang activity increased; gang-related homicides have risen in Los Angeles County alone by 250% since the mid-1980s (Brantley & DiRosa, 1994). Despite media portrayals, however, all juvenile offenders are not violent gang members.

What proportion of violent youths commit their crimes while in a gang? In May 1995, the Office of Juvenile Justice and Delinquency Prevention released a summary of juvenile involvement in violent crime (Snyder & Sickmund, 1995). That report noted several important facts about juvenile gang behavior. In 1991, juvenile groups committed 6% of all serious violent crimes; another 8% were committed by a group of offenders that included at least one juvenile and one adult. Adults are less likely to commit crimes in groups; of all the serious violent crime committed by juveniles, fully one half involved a group of offenders (Snyder & Sickmund, 1995).

Most serious violent crime involves assaults; when one examines homicide alone, the picture presented is different. Although a great deal of juvenile assault may be committed in gangs, most juvenile homicide is not (contrary to popular belief). In fact, most juvenile murderers commit homicide alone. Furthermore, the percentages of murders committed decreases as the number of involved offenders increases. For example, 14% of juvenile homicides involved two offenders, 6% involved three offenders, and only 3% involved four or more offenders. Gang murders, when they do happen, occur as often as not during the commission of other felonies (e.g., armed robbery, forcible rape). Almost all group offenders are male (92%) and about half are Black (52%). By 1990, criminally oriented groups or "gangs" were located in almost every state throughout the United States (Spergel, 1989).

One interesting difference between group homicides and individual homicides is the crossing of racial lines. Individual homicides are committed intraracially when the offender is White; 95% of White juveniles choose White victims. When the single offender is Black, the choice of victim *is* mixed: 57% were White and 37% were Black (Snyder & Sickmund, 1995). Overall, only 11% of single-offender killings by juveniles were interracial compared with 25% of group killings. Group killings are predominately Black offenders killing White victims (71%), usually during the commission of a robbery (60%).

Developmental predecessors of adolescent gang formation can be seen in preadolescent "friendship networks," as reviewed in chapter 4 (see the section on the Developmental Model). Certainly, male preadolescent friendship groups tend to display many of the hallmarks of later adolescent gangs, including an emphasis on competition, loyalty, and a rigid status hierarchy. They also deemphasize emotional intimacy and emphasize shared activities instead. Rules are clearly laid out and rigidly enforced (Los Solidos Natim, 1995). Despite these similarities, gangs are not always mere social networks. For example, some gangs specialize in a particular type of crime, and surveys of incarcerated teenage boys who claim to belong to gangs reveal that at least some gangs form particular friendship networks specifically to commit crimes (Sheley, Zhang, Brody, & Wright, 1995). Nor is all criminal behavior by gangs local or relatively unimportant. One gang, before being stopped by federal authorities, had a cocaine distribution network that stretched across five states (Bonfante, 1995). Others are similar to organized crime groups, gleaning large profits from larceny, robbery, and burglary (Sccente, 1993). However, most boys who engage in preadolescent networks do not become involved in criminal behavior as a part of an adolescent gang. How do such criminal networks develop? Many years ago, Tuckman (1965) suggested that gangs are groups that establish roles and relationships and focus on achievements and tasks, and reward productivity. Indeed, although many might not consider criminal activities to be "achievements," this description might fit some modern gang involvement. Certainly not all teenage gangs engage in criminal behavior (Clay & Aquila, 1994); the purpose of such a group might be shared activities, socializing, or merely demographic convenience (e.g., living close together). Teenage gangs that do specialize in criminal behavior might do so actively or only sporadically (Clay & Aquila, 1994). Some researchers have suggested that the increase in gang involvement among U.S. youth is due primarily to the lucrative nature of the narcotics trade (Sccente, 1993), but others dismiss this explanation and point out that many children join gangs for protection from increasingly dangerous neighborhoods ("The Wages of Crack," 1994). Indeed, one study of gangs in Milwaukee found that the more hierarchical a gang is, the less likely it is to be involved in selling drugs, suggesting that larger, more complexly organized gangs are not joined primarily for the potential profits from narcotics trade (Hagedorn, 1994). Another study found that most gang members were engaged in the drug trade only sporadically, moving in and out of the conventional labor market (Hagedorn, 1994). If the drug trade is not always the motive for joining a gang, what other motives are feasible? Some answers emerge from research on the differences between adolescents who join gangs and those who do not. One study compared 36 high school students who were in gangs with 65 students who were not. The two groups similarly held negative racial stereotypes, but gang members had much lower self-esteem and were significantly less likely to name a parent or teacher as a role model. This study suggested that an absence of parental or teacher role models may result in lower self-esteem, which in turn may help explain why some high school students join gangs (Wang, 1994). Other research has suggested that adolescents become gang members because they need a family structure and are already familiar with violence (J. W. Williams, 1992). Poorer communities, which have higher rates of both family breakdown and street violence, may thus provide fertile ground for the formation of gangs. Gangs may offer kids a boost in their status and self-esteem, which may be particularly important if they believe they are worthless and powerless (Stover, 1986). Although the drug trade may not be the most important reason for joining a gang for all children, at least for some prospective members the lure of financial gain must be very tempting, especially for youths with no education and no hope of lucrative employment. There certainly are vast sums of money available through the drug trade, although most gang members do not become vastly rich; perhaps psychologically the mere possibility of money is enough to lure youngsters with no other prospects into gang membership (McKinney, 1988). As previously stated, gang-committed homicides usually involve Black perpetrators, predominately young and male. The young Black male in North America today faces a multitude of difficulties that increase his vulnerability to joining a gang (Ascher, 1991). African-American young males suffer from too few prosocial adult male models; on the other hand, they are bombarded with negative images of Black men. Similarly, their self-esteem in general may suffer from pervasive negative images of African-Americans, and inner city ghettos typically lack the resources necessary to sustain academic achievement (which could protect such at-risk boys from joining gangs). Single-parent, low-income homes make enormous demands on stressed parents who may be unable to control their adolescent offspring, and fatherless households may make the transition to manhood particularly difficult. These boys are exposed to violent communities, given little supervision by adults who are struggling to make ends meet, and placed in schools that are chronically underfunded and that unfortunately lack Black male teachers who could serve as positive role models (Ascher, 1991). Given the situation in many U.S. inner cities today, it is hardly surprising that many young African-American males choose to increase their status and prospects by rejecting the mainstream culture and joining gangs. Although the mass media popularly depicts gang violence as occurring primarily in the streets, schools often become the focus of gangs. Although some types of school crime and violence have remained level or even diminished, violence in the schools—particularly between gangs—has been increasing since the early 1970s (Gaustad, 1991). The U.S. Department of Education reported in 1989 that assaults and weapon possession in schools increased by 16% and 28%, respectively, between 1985 and 1989. In addition, the National School Safety Center estimated that in 1987, 135,000 boys carried guns to school daily. Many of these weapons and these assaults occurred between children who were members of gangs.

Why has the rate of school crime and violence increased so dramatically so quickly? Increased gang membership and gang violence is one reason. Battles between gangs often occur on school grounds and during school hours (Gaustad, 1991). Gangs even increase violence in schools among students who do not belong to their groups; nongang members often carry weapons to school because they fear being targeted by gangs or becoming involved in a fight with a gang member, and even gang members themselves note that if a student has a weapon, when challenged he or she is extremely likely to use it (Barrett, 1991).

Easy access to weapons is no longer a problem in the United States. Earlier this decade, the Center to Prevent Handgun Violence noted that every household in the United States now has, on the average, two guns owned by private citizens, and in major U.S. cities guns, can even be "rented" for temporary use (Barrett, 1991).

The problem of gang violence in schools is complicated by the fact that other students may not want to "tattle" on their peers and that school personnel may erroneously see gang activity as a stage "all kids go through" (Gaustad, 1991). Admitting to gang activity is also humiliating for many schools that may like to pride themselves on being better achieving schools. Despite this, many schools have openly admitted that they are struggling with gang violence and have begun programs designed to combat the problem. School administrators have noted that teenage gang members often need to be taught not simply to be nonviolent, but also what alternative prosocial behaviors exist to resolve disputes. Several states are experimenting with programs designed to teach high school students how to identify emotions and resolve confrontational situations. The Bureau of Alcohol, Tobacco, and Firearms has even initiated programs with seventh graders, entitled Gang Resistance Education and Training (GREAT; Magaw, 1995). What impact such programs can have, in the face of such significant social catalysts to gang violence, remains to be seen.

Chapter 10

Sexual Assault

Few researchers disagree with the characterization of sexual assault as a violent crime (Roberts, 1995), both in a legal and a psychological sense. As such, perpetrators of sexual assault frequently suffer from the same general causes of violence as perpetrators of other violent crimes (see chapters 3, 4, and 5). However, there are other causes specifically associated with the crime of sexual assault, against both domestic partners and strangers. Although sexual assault is frequently studied as a street crime, it also occurs domestically (Finkelhor & Yllo, 1985). Like other interpersonal violent crimes, sexual assault involves a perpetrator, a victim, and a set of circumstances. All three of these variables must be considered in the search for the causes of rape.

PERPETRATOR CHARACTERISTICS

Anger and violence are clearly associated with some incidents of sexual assault, whereas others are committed with a minimum of violence and injury (Finkelhor & Yllo, 1985; Groth, 1979). This is not to minimize the violence inherent in any sexual assault, but rather to point out that in understanding what causes such a crime, it may be important to recognize that some offenders engage in violence *apart* from the sexual assault whereas others do not. Several writers, in forming typologies of rapists, suggest that the distinction between violent and nonviolent rape is an important one.

The Violent Rapist

Groth is a psychologist who bases his types of rapists on his interviews with convicted felons. Like Finkelhor and Yllo (1985), he characterized the *angry* or *violent* rapist as an offender who uses sexual assault as an expression of hostility and rage. This perpetrator typically does not confine his violence to the sexual assault and beats his victim brutally, usually causing significant injury. Such an offender consciously experiences "bad" feelings and frequently knows that he is attacking because he is angry, enraged, and/or depressed. As Groth (1979) described it, this offender uses sexual assault in addition to physical assault because he believes that rape is especially hurtful to his victim. Sexuality is secondary to this offender, and he typically does not find the attack "sexy" or arousing; in fact, he may have difficulty achieving an erection or ejaculating.

Violent and brutal rape also occurs between spouses or partners. Finkelhor and Yllo (1985) described the case of "Gretchen," whose husband frequently raped her after beating her. He went so far as to beat and rape her 2 days before she was expecting a child, and again 2 days after the baby was born. He ripped her vagina with his hand and liked to "play rape" (p. 32). Although this case occurred between spouses, it is no less violent than angry rape that occurs between strangers. A case described by Groth (1979), which occurred between strangers, portrayed a rapist who randomly victimizes a woman who has driven up in a car; the offender beats her and rapes her brutally, never even sure why he did it (pp. 15–16). Finkelhor and Yllo found that when violent rapes occurred between spouses, it was not because of sexual difficulties in the marriage but rather as a way for the husband to punish, dominate, and humiliate his wife. Groth pointed out that such offenders are typically very conflicted and perpetually angry and displace their anger onto anyone available—either a partner or a stranger.

The Power Rapist

In contrast to violent rape, both Groth and Finkelhor described a second type of sexual assault called *power rape,* which involves only enough force to complete the offense. Power rapes are not characterized by excessive violence and typically do not involve brutal beatings or other physical injury. Finkelhor and Yllo (1985) found that power rapes between spouses were more typically committed by middle-class, relatively educated offenders whose conflicts with their wives often revolved around sexual difficulties. A husband who committed power rape did so to demonstrate his dominance over his wife and to show her that he held ultimate power over when they had intercourse. Among strangers, Groth pointed to underlying feelings of inadequacy as the motive for power rape. Like violent rape, power rape can occur either between an established couple (as a demonstration of the man's power in the sexual relationship) or between strangers (as a reassurance to the perpetrator of his own power). The assault may not live up to the man's sexual fantasies, but it succeeds in the sense that it establishes that he is powerful and, in the case of marital rape, that he is in charge of the relationship—or at least in charge of the sexual relationship.

Psychological Characteristics of Rapists

Apart from the distinction between power and anger rape, there are other characteristics that sexual offenders tend to have in common. One of these is a *lack of empathy* (empathy is the ability to feel for another person, to place oneself in another person's shoes, so to speak, and feel what they feel). Most research has noted that sexual arousal is frequently inhibited in men when they are presented with descriptions of violence during a sexual encounter (i.e., rape; Malamuth, 1992). However, men who commit sexual assault may differ in this respect from other men. One study examined this issue directly by hypothesizing that although a nonrapist male would feel empathy for a rape victim, and thus not feel sexually aroused by her rape, a rapist might not experience such empathy. Indeed, when presented with an account of a rape with the victim suffering, 14 nonrapists displayed significantly more empathy for the victim in comparison to 14 heterosexual rapists (Rice, Chaplin, Harris, & Coutts, 1994). The rapists' lack of empathy, particularly in association with victim distress and violence during rape, appears to increase their sexual arousal in response to the accounts of rape.

Although lack of empathy is an emotional issue, cognitive issues have also been examined in rapists (and in other samples). One of the most important cognitive factors associated with sexual assault is the belief in, and acceptance of, rape myths (Lonsway & Fitzgerald, 1994). Examples of rape myths include:

1. Those that justify sexual violence ("She asked for it"; "He got drunk or carried away and couldn't help himself").
2. Those that deny the existence of sexual violence ("Rape is a crime that only occurs between strangers"; "No woman can be raped against her will"; "All women secretly want to be raped and enjoy rape").
3. Those that deny the importance of sexual assault ("She's making a big fuss over nothing"; "Rape doesn't really hurt women").

This body of research has been criticized for its lack of precise definitions (Lonsway & Fitzgerald, 1994), but it nevertheless reveals the breadth and depth of the myths about sexual violence that our society holds. Belief in rape myths has been found in both males and females as young as eighth grade students (Boxley, Lawrance, & Gruchow, 1995). Although most children in this study did not believe in rape myths, 10% of the girls and fully 30% of the boys did tend to accept such myths. Another study conducted on 315 male and female college students at a midwestern university found similarly that men were more likely to accept rape myths than were women (Struckman-Johnson & Struckman-

Johnson, 1992). Both studies found that despite a substantial minority of subjects who accepted rape myths, most subjects tended to reject such myths (Boxley et al., 1995; Struckman-Johnson & Struckman-Johnson, 1992). However, in the minority of subjects who do tend to believe in such myths, how might such beliefs be related to tolerance of, or even perpetration of, sexual assault?

A tendency to believe in rape myths has been associated with a variety of risk factors for sexual assault, including: (a) the sex-role stereotyping of women (associated in turn with tolerance of sexual violence; Boxley et al., 1995); (b) the heightened perception that female targets of sexual assault behave sexually (Abbey & Harnish, 1995); (c) a weak association with viewing nonviolent pornography, and a stronger association with the viewing of violent pornography (Allen, Emmers, & Giery, 1995); (d) the use of pornography for sexual enhancement, versus its use for sexual release (Perse, 1994); (e) the belief that forced, nonconsensual sexual intercourse with an acquaintance does not constitute rape (Kahn, Mathie, & Torgler, 1994); and (f) a history of violent sexual victimization (Kalof, 1993). Perhaps the most interesting among these is the tendency to interpret "neutral" female behavior as "sexualized." Such a distorted perception brings to mind the research on cognitive biases, which seem to be an important factor in violence in general (see chapter 4). It is possible that one reason that some violent offenders choose to rape (versus choosing physical assault, for example) is because their cognitive biases focus on sexualized interpretations, rather than on hostile interpretations per se.

Apart from personality types, emotional factors, and cognitive factors, Thornhill and Thornhill (1992) proposed that rape might have evolved in much the same way that other human characteristics have evolved. That is, they hypothesized that rape has evolved because males who commit rape have been more successful at passing on their genes. The result is that men may respond positively to rape (be sexually aroused by it) or commit rape because they are descended from males who have successfully committed sexual assault in the past. At first glance there appears to be some merit in this theory. However, it makes several assumptions. First, it assumes that males who commit rape would almost always ejaculate semen into their female victim. Second, it assumes that males pick fertile females as victims—not children, or elderly females, or other males. Finally, it assumes that rape is a behavior that is heavily influenced by, if not dictated by, genetic influences.

Needless to say, the response to the Thornhills' proposed theory has been vocal and adamant. The criticism has centered on several counterarguments. First, human sexual behavior is much more complex than a simplistic evolutionary analysis suggests, as it always occurs in the context of complex social interactions (Akins & Windham, 1992; Futterman & Zirkel, 1992). A complex, social, and violent behavior is unlikely to be primarily dictated by genetics, particularly in light of the weak association between genetic influences and violence in general (see chapter 4). There is no compelling reason to think that rape is utterly unlike other violent behaviors in this sense. Second, although it was once believed that males predominately rape women in their child-bearing years, we now know that children are frequently the victims of sexual assault, as well as the elderly and other males—and the Thornhills' theory makes no allowance for such victims. Third, most studies find that men are more sexually aroused by willing females than by rape victims, which directly contradicts the Thornhills' theory (Allgeier & Wiederman, 1992; Malamuth, 1992). Finally, many sexual assaults do not involve an ejaculation inside a female victim, for a variety of reasons (e.g., lack of sexual arousal; Groth, 1979). Despite the validity of these criticisms, research has not ruled out the possibility that a tendency to behave in a sexually coercive or violent manner may be at least partly inherited or adaptive. At present, it remains an intriguing but largely unsubstantiated theory.

VICTIM CHARACTERISTICS

As with any interpersonal violence, certain individuals are at higher risk than others of being vulnerable to sexual victimization. Which factors determine an individual's vulnerability? A number of recent studies suggested that prior sexual victimization may increase vulnerability to future victimization. Prospective research, following 857 college women, found that earlier victimization experiences were a risk factor for later victimization (Gidycz, Coble, Latham, & Layman, 1993), possibly because earlier victimization experiences change a woman's cognitive and emotional resources and thus limit her ability to protect herself. A follow-up of this study also found that the severity of prior sexual victimization was related to the likelihood of current sexual victimization; the more severe the earlier victimization, the greater the chance of current victimization (Gidycz, Hanson, & Layman, 1995). Another study found a statistical relationship between childhood sexual victimization and sexual victimization with dating partners (Himelein, Vogel, & Wachowiak, 1994). One researcher, who compared sorority to nonsorority women, found that sorority women were more likely to have been both violently sexually victimized and to have rape-supportive attitudes (Kalof, 1993). Finally, a prior history of rape or incest was found to be a risk factor for sexual assault in a study that examined a wide variety of ethnic groups of women (Scott, Lefley, & Hicks, 1993).

Apart from personal history, some studies suggest that certain groups of women are more vulnerable than other groups. For example, two studies found particularly low rates of sexual victimization among Hispanic women (Scott et al., 1993; Sorenson & Siegel, 1992), although this may be partly due to less willingness to report. Women with psychiatric or developmental difficulties appear to be at particular risk of sexual victimization (Scott et al., 1993; Sorenson & Siegel, 1992), as do women who are tourists and thus unfamiliar with their surroundings (Scott et al., 1993). Homeless women are, of course, at higher risk for all sorts of victimization, including sexual assault (Scott et al., 1993).

SOCIAL CONDITIONS

Apart from factors related to the perpetrator and to the vulnerability of some potential victims, situational factors can contribute to sexual assault. One such factor that appears to be very important is alcohol. Several studies found that alcohol use affects both the incidence and the severity of sexual assault; in fact, one study found that alcohol was the "most significant predictor of the level of sexual aggression" (Koss & Gaines, 1993). Furthermore, alcohol appears to be even more potent when consumed by both perpetrator and victim; in that case, it affects not only the likelihood of assault, but also others' perception of sexual suggestiveness of both perpetrator and victim (Abbey & Harnish, 1995). Groth (1979) found that more than 40% of the rapists he interviewed had a history of problem drinking, and half of their sexual offenses were committed after having used some substance, usually alcohol. He reasoned that although alcohol appears to reduce the offender's inhibitions, reasoning, and judgment, by itself it cannot fully account for the assault. Nevertheless, as with all violent crime, alcohol and other drugs appear to substantially contribute to the crime of sexual assault, particularly when used by both the perpetrator and the victim (see chapter 8).

Although a great deal of research has pointed to victim and perpetrator behavior and other factors as important causes of sexual assault, several researchers have suggested that such an approach misses a critical point in understanding why and how sexual assault occurs. It is possible that although individual factors contribute to sexual assault, the most critical variables may be larger social circumstances, such as poverty, racism, and sexism (Sorenson & White, 1992). It appears probable that there is some evidence of racism in how the criminal justice system handles sexual assault: One study of 206 convicted sex offenders found that a disproportionate number of rapists were Black, and other studies have noted that African-American males are more likely to be targets of arrest and conviction than are White males (West & Templer, 1994). Thus, racism may account for some of the arrests and convictions for sexual assault.

Other researchers have pointed to sexism as the social evil responsible for rape. Several researchers have suggested that the link between pornography and sexual assault implies that the root cause of sexual assault is sexism; however, one intriguing study found that all pornography use is not equal (Perse, 1994). That is, Perse found that individuals who used pornography for sexual enhancement did indeed demonstrate a link between sexism and acceptance of rape myths, whereas individuals who used pornography for sexual release did not. Thus, for some individuals, pornographic environments do seem to encourage sexism, which in turn is linked to acceptance of rape myths. Sexism may also be important in the commission of sexual assault via the subordinate position of women in the economic and social systems (Peterson & Baily, 1992). The income differential between males and females is statistically linked to sexual assault rates, although occupational status does not appear to be a contributor (Peterson & Baily, 1992). Such an analysis points out the importance of controlling for economic factors in trying to assess any individual's vulnerability to sexual assault.

Chapter 11

Spouse Homicide

One of the most common questions regarding domestic violence is "How frequently does it occur?" Another, equally important, is "How serious is it when it does happen?" This chapter looks at the severity of spousal violence in general, and considers in detail one of the most severe types of partner violence—the homicide or murder of one partner.

It is not rare, in the United States, for couples to be violent. In both 1975 and 1985, the NFVS was conducted. The 1985 NFVS found that approximately 16% of U.S. couples—one out of every six—experienced at least one incident over the past year in which one spouse physically assaulted the other spouse (Straus & Gelles, 1988). Most of the incidents were "minor" (i.e., they only involved one partner pushing, slapping, shoving, or throwing things at the other partner). However, approximately 40% were potentially injury causing (e.g., ones in which the violent partner kicked, punched, or stabbed the victim partner). Furthermore, one quarter of the homicides in the United States are perpetrated against domestic victims (Straus, 1992b).

Most individuals think of spousal violence as husband-on-wife attacks. Indeed, husband-on-wife attacks tend to draw much more attention than wife-on-husband attacks, both because men's relatively larger physical sizes imply a much greater potential for injury (Straus & Gelles, 1988), and because men tend to use violence to dominate and control, whereas women tend to use violence in self-defense or as retaliation after a beating (Adler, 1991). Additionally, men tend to be perceived as more violent and aggressive in general, probably because they are so much more violent in the streets and outside the home, and account for an overwhelming number of arrests for violent offenses (Stephan & Jankowski, 1991).

The perception of the seriousness of husband-on-wife violence is not a mistaken one. However, wives also sometimes perpetrate serious violence on husbands. One purpose of this chapter is to compare spousal homicides committed by husbands with spousal homicides committed by wives. Women commit almost as many spousal murders as men do, albeit for very different reasons (Straus & Gelles, 1988). What are the differences between men and women who kill their spouses? In addition, how can we identify and characterize women who kill abusive spouses from more "typical" female murderers?

RATES OF SEVERE VIOLENCE BY HUSBANDS AND WIVES

How frequently are men extremely violent with their wives? The results of studies vary, but most suggest that approximately 5% of U.S. men resort to severe violence against their wives. Interestingly, although the NCS estimates that the husband is the perpetrator in 70% of spousal attacks (Langan & Innes, 1986), other surveys and longitudinal studies find that husbands and wives aggress almost equally (O'Leary et al., 1989; Straus & Gelles, 1988). However, it should be noted that men appear to underreport their own severe violence in surveys, whereas women do not (Stets & Straus, 1990b).

How frequently are women extremely violent with their husbands? Again, the results of studies vary, but most suggest that approximately 5% to 6% of U.S. women resort to severe violence against their husbands at some point (Makepeace, 1981; Meredith, Abbott, & Adams, 1986; Straus, Gelles, & Steinmetz, 1980). Furthermore, when the 1985 NFVS asked who had initiated or started the hitting during those conflicts, it appeared that men and women report about equal rates of hitting first (Straus & Gelles, 1988). In other words, when only the conflicts in which women hit are examined, about half the time men hit first and then women hit; in the other half, women initiate the violence. What this survey did not examine, however, was how often women hit first when they use severe violence. Other research, discussed later, examines that question. In all such research, however, it should be remembered that, as stated previously, women are less likely to underreport their own use of severe violence (Stets & Straus, 1990b).

MALE- VERSUS FEMALE-PERPETRATED DOMESTIC HOMICIDE

Some research has compared male- and female-perpetrated domestic homicide. Cazenave and Zahn (1992) conducted a unique study in which some of the differences in spousal homicides by men and women in 1985 in the cities of

Philadelphia and Chicago were described. They examined 83 cases of homicide: 42 cases involved husbands who had killed their wives; 41 cases involved wives who had killed their husbands.

Several differences between male and female perpetrators of domestic homicide were immediately apparent. First, female killers picked only victims with whom they were living; male killers were much more likely to kill estranged spouses from whom they were separated. Once out of the relationship, potential male victims were safe; however, potential female victims remained at risk regardless of whether or not they had left the relationship.

In addition, men and women showed very different "styles" of killing. Men were much more likely to use guns, to kill their spouses by beating them to death, or to strangle them. Women tended to use knives or other kitchen implements. Part of the reason is undoubtedly a matter of opportunity (e.g., men typically have more access to guns than do women), although part of it is probably also related to the fact that men tended to kill more violently in general. Although other research (Straus & Gelles, 1988) concluded that when women are ultimately violent in a relationship, men and women initiate violence equally, Cazenave and Zahn (1992) found that when domestic homicide occurs, the man was the initiator of violence more than 90% of the time. This was true regardless of whether the man was ultimately the victim or the killer. Therefore, there appears to be a substantial difference between couples who are violent with each other and couples who kill each other. When couples are "only" violent with each other, either partner may have initiated the violence; when couples kill each other, however, the male initiates the violence 90% of the time. This is in accord with Browne's (1987) findings that when battered women kill their abusive spouses, they are typically too terrified of them to initiate violence.

An examination of the type of killing also supported Cazenave and Zahn's finding that men are more violent when they kill their spouses. In 18 of the 42 male-perpetrated homicides (43%), the killing involved multiple blows to the wife. In many cases, the husbands inflicted more blows than were needed to kill their wives. In contrast, only 5 of the 41 female-perpetrated homicides (12%) involved multiple blows to the husband-victim.

MOTIVE IN MALE- VERSUS FEMALE-PERPETRATED DOMESTIC HOMICIDE

Men and women also tended to differ in the reasons why they killed their spouses. These differences tended to mirror differences in the reasons why women and men use violence in the first place—specifically, that women tend to use violence in self-defense and men tend to use it to control and dominate their partners (Adler, 1991). Cazenave and Zahn (1992) found similar distinctions between male and female homicide. In their study, the largest class of female killers were those who had used lethal violence against their spouses in self-defense. In contrast, the largest class of male killers were those who killed their wives in response to the victim's attempt to leave the relationship.

Eighteen of their 83 cases involved killing in self-defense—all of men by women. In two thirds of these cases, it was confirmed that the female killer had been beaten by the victim prior to the killing. Furthermore, alcohol was found to be used by either the victim or the killer in 39% of these cases.

There were 14 cases of homicide because the woman was trying to leave the relationship—12 of women being killed by men. In contrast to the self-defense killings, these killings did not occur immediately after a beating had taken place. Apparently, women may kill their husbands when they fear a beating is becoming so dangerous that they may be killed themselves, but when a husband decides to kill his wife for attempting to leave the relationship, he does not beat her first; he simply kills her.

Another difference between self-defense killings and attempts-to-terminate-the-relationship killings is the use of alcohol. As was just mentioned, alcohol seems to be frequently involved in self-defense killings, but it was involved in none of the killings of wives who wanted to leave the relationship by husbands. As Cazenave and Zahn noted, in contrast to the self-defense killings, these killings appear to be much more carefully planned and not a spontaneous reaction to ongoing violence.

Although the two largest categories of murder by far were self-defense and killing in response to an attempt to leave, other motives were noted. The next most common motive (a distant third) was jealousy. These killings typically involved the man's jealousy about the woman's seeing or expressing a desire to see other men. Most jealousy killings (83%) involved men killing their spouses; there were no cases in which a woman killed a man because she was jealous of the possibility that he was seeing other women, although in one case a woman killed her husband after he had initiated an argument over her seeing other men.

These studies noted important differences between men and women who are involved in the most severe form of domestic violence: domestic homicide. Browne (1987), however, conducted the definitive study on women who kill domestically in her groundbreaking study of women who killed abusive spouses.

BATTERED WOMEN WHO KILL
ABUSIVE SPOUSES

What are homicidally violent couples like? What are their marriages like? Browne set out to discover this in her research, conducted on and comparing couples who abused, couples who did not abuse, and couples whose abuse had led to the killing of the husband by the wife. Browne's (1987) study included 42 couples in which the wife had killed or seriously wounded the husband and had subsequently been charged with a crime. Almost all were charged with murder, although a few were charged with conspiracy to commit murder or attempted murder. The average age of these women was 36 years; they had an average of two children each. More than 50% were White; the remaining 33% were Black and Hispanic. Of these women, 46% were from working-class homes, 25% were middle-class, and 25% were from lower class backgrounds. Only 1 in 5 had attended college, but more than 66% had finished high school. Approximately 50% of the women were employed. One point that is evident from this description of Browne's sample is that the problem of severe abuse, and domestic homicide, cuts across social and ethnic lines and affects nearly every group of Americans. Although poor and minority women were more likely to receive jail terms for their killings (Browne, 1987), they were by no means the only domestic killers.

A conclusion that became apparent early on in the study is that the nature of violence was fundamentally different in couples in which the husband was eventually killed. It is not merely that these wives were battered, but that they were extremely severely battered, in prolonged sessions of physical torture and sexual assault that culminated in serious injuries. Browne (1987) described wife-beating sessions in which the victim was dragged through the house by her hair, kicked and punched; had her eyes blackened, her ribs broken; her hair hacked off, and her eyes severely gouged with her broken eyeglasses; and was anally raped. Clearly, the degree to which many of these women are abused is almost unthinkable.

A second conclusion is that the dynamics of the violence were also different. Several researchers found that some domestic violence between spouses is mutual; that is, that although wives are beaten, a substantial number tend to hit their husbands back (typically in self-defense; Adler, 1991; Straus & Gelles, 1990). Browne (1987) noted, however, that this pattern does not hold in couples in which the wife eventually kills the severely abusive husband. In such couples, wives appear too terrified of the potential violence of their husbands to hit back, even in self-defense. Their goal is survival, and rather than risk escalating the already severe violence to lethal levels, they take the extreme abuse and hope to live through it.

Although many of the homicidal women experienced physical and sexual abuse as children, it is interesting to note that they did not differ from nonhomicidal abuse victims in this respect: In both groups, approximately 75% of the women experienced physical abuse and more than 50% were victims of sexual abuse (attempted or completed). Thus, it appears that a history of abusive victimization as a child may be important in determining whether one becomes a victim of spouse abuse—but less, if at all, important in determining whether one kills one's spouse.

One factor that does appear to stand out in the background of domestically homicidal female abuse victims is the behavior of the abuser before the wife abuse began. Specifically: "Women noted that these men were, in the first weeks and months they knew them, the most romantic and attentive lovers they'd ever had" (Browne, 1987, p. 40). This attention appeared, in retrospect, to have an obsessive quality, but during a short courtship it may have been very pleasant. Because violence between couples typically does not develop until the couple is seriously involved, living together, or married (Makepeace, 1981), early stages of these relationships might entail extreme attentiveness without beatings. Eventually, however, it was common for Browne to find that this attentiveness had developed into a paranoid obsession. In several cases, these severely abusive husbands were so obsessed with their wives that they controlled and restricted their movements to an extreme degree; for example, they might remove the telephones, forbid their wives to leave the house without permission, and/or force their wives to sever all relations with their families and friends. Many beatings, in addition, were initiated on the paranoid suspicion that the wives were unfaithful or treasonous—even in the total absence of any justification or evidence.

As in the case of other battered women, the beatings in these severely violent relationships did not begin until after the couple had made some major commitment to each other. Occasionally, one of the women who killed reported some minor isolated incident of violence before marriage, but such incidents were unusual and when they did occur, the violence was less extreme.

Apart from being unusually severe, the wife-beatings in these domestically homicidal couples also appeared to have no precipitating event: that is, the wives reported that they were unable to predict when a beating might occur and thus they were equally unable to anticipate and avoid the violence. Furthermore, after the initial beatings began, most of the severely abused women did not immediately seek help, probably as the result of shock, disbelief, and a general pattern of passive acceptance that came to characterize their behavior and that permitted them to survive living with such an intensely violent husband. Typically, later repeated attempts to get help (from police or other authorities) failed to stop the violence.

Eventually, some patterns in the extremely severe beatings did emerge. For example, many of the beatings seemed to stem from jealousy on the part of the husband, or from his inability to tolerate any hint of his wife's independence (e.g., her being employed or simply talking to other people, even a neighbor over a fence). Any threat or suggestion that the wife might leave the relationship was extremely dangerous for her; in fact, leaving or attempting to leave the relationship provoked a great deal of potentially lethal violence on the part of the husband.

Another pattern that emerged was a steady decrease in contrition. During the early years of the relationship, husbands would often beg forgiveness, cry or sob, and express extreme remorse over their violence. As the relationship progressed, however, and the wives remained despite the beatings, the expressions of remorse generally ceased and the severity of the beatings gradually increased. In the case of the homicidal wives, the severity of the beatings they underwent increased to a very extreme degree. In addition to physically and sexually assaulting, these extremely abusive men commonly threatened to kill their wives, themselves, and/or other people. The frequency of the battering episodes also increased over time; almost half of the women in the homicide group reported that by the end of the relationship, they were being beaten by their husbands more than once a week.

It is in the dynamics of these relationships, in the severity of the abuse, and in the personality adopted by these battered women that the key to their lethal behavior lies. Why did these women kill their abusive husbands? It is simplest to conceptualize the killings in terms of self-defense. These women typically perceived that they were completely in the power of their abusers. In the relationship, they were watched constantly and beaten viciously, with no possibility of defense. They all lacked family or friends who were able or willing to come to their defense effectively. In leaving the relationship, they faced even greater peril. The abuser typically understood his victim's desire to leave the relationship and reminded her frequently that if she did so he would hunt her down and kill her and/or kill their children. When and if she did attempt to leave, these men tended to be as good as their word: Several of Browne's cases involved women who had left the marriage but who were stalked constantly by their ex-husbands, whose homes were repeatedly broken into, and whose lives were continually disrupted by violence that they were not able to escape. The killing incident, therefore, occurred in this context: a victim of abuse who feels totally powerless to escape her abuser, and who knows her abuser to be capable of extreme violence.

Although these batterers had typically threatened to kill before, most of the lethal episodes in which they were killed occurred because they had escalated the threat to some new level; for example, threatened to kill a child for the first time, or given some sign of readiness to act on the past threats of killing the woman. It is this new level of threat that Browne noticed in the histories of women who kill their batterers; although the batterer may have threatened to kill before, for some reason, this time she believed him and decided to kill him first. Even if the danger was not acute (e.g., if the husband was asleep), the wife perceived it as present, ongoing, and real, believed escape impossible, and knew the extreme violence of which the victim was capable—hence, the characterization of the killings as self-defense.

All battered women face the question, "Why don't you just leave?" It may seem particularly perplexing in the case of a woman who is so severely abused that she feels obligated to kill to defend herself and her children. The answer is that she failed to leave the relationship because she was seeking to survive the violence. A woman in a severely abusive relationship often knows clearly that leaving the relationship puts her in even more danger; the batterer might beat her if she stays, but he might very well kill her if she leaves. The desire to survive aside, there are also practical considerations that limit the ability of any battered woman to leave a relationship (discussed in more detail in later chapters). These include financial dependency on the batterer, fear of poverty and homelessness, the belief that the children benefit from having a father in the home, and the belief that marriage is a permanent, never-to-be-abandoned relationship within which all problems should be solved.

Finally, how are battered women who kill different from female murderers who do not kill abusive spouses? Perhaps the most noticeable difference is in past behavior. For example, battered women who kill are typically women with no previous criminal record of any kind. In contrast, female murderers who choose other victims tend to have criminal records, and often records of violent crime. In addition, they may have a history of antisocial behavior in work, relationships, and school. The battered woman who kills is very different. Rather than a history of antisocial behavior, she tends to have a history of prosocial behavior: She loves and cares for her children to the best of her ability and is driven to try to keep her family together despite tremendous odds.

These two types of female killers also differ markedly in their personality styles. Battered women who kill tend, by the time of the homicide, to have developed an extremely passive, obedient personality style. In their attempts to forestall the beatings they receive, they live their lives attempting to please and placate their abusers. They do not pursue their own needs and goals; rather, they hope that by completely subsuming their own needs to those of their abusers, they may end the abuse.[1] This strategy is successful in that the victim survives. On the other hand, it ultimately fails to change the abuser's behavior and it leaves a strong passive streak in the battered woman's psyche. This hypothesis should not be confused with other outmoded theories that battered women actually masochistically enjoy the abuse (Pizzy, 1974); rather, it is clear that in cases of extremely severe abuse, the victim becomes passive not out of enjoyment but out of survival instinct. In this sense, victims of very severe chronic battering have been likened to survivors of other major catastrophes, employing the same type of coping mechanisms (Browne, 1987).

---

[1]For a discussion of why women "tolerate" abuse and the theories of female masochism, see chapter 13.

Chapter 12

Child Abuse and Physical Punishment

CHILD ABUSE

In any interpersonal conflict, there are always three relevant factors: the victim (in this case the child), the perpetrator (in this case the abuser), and environmental factors that increase the probability of the crime occurring.

Of course, in some cases the motive for child abuse may seem obvious. Stanley Kidd, a 28-year-old father in Alabama, asphyxiated his 14-month-old twin daughters, apparently because a child support payment of $806 had been deducted from his paycheck. Astonishingly, the jury rejected the charge of capital murder (Associated Press, 1995, Aug. 1). In most cases of child abuse, however, there is not an obvious monetary motive. So what factors do predict to child abuse?

Factors Associated With the Child

Earlier in this century and historically, it was not unusual for experts to conclude that child abuse occurred because a parent lost control with an exceptionally difficult child. This perspective assumed a "normal" parent and a "deviant" child who was largely to blame. Although we now know that abused children can be either "difficult" or "easy," it does seem true that children with profound health and behavior problems, especially during infancy, are at greater risk of being abused (Berkow, 1987). For example, studies of hearing-impaired children find a higher rate of physical and sexual victimization, relative to the general population of children (Porter, Yuille, & Bent, 1995). Another recent study by the

National Center on Child Abuse and Neglect found that handicapped children were significantly more likely than able-bodied children to become victims of parental abuse (Sargeant, 1994). A child's gender even affects his or her level of risk: Boys are at more risk of abuse than girls, and when boys are abused, their parents are more likely to be particularly aggressive (Hegar, Zuravin, & Orme, 1994; Jouriles & Norwood, 1995). It is important to keep in mind that none of these findings are intended to imply that the child is responsible for his or her own abuse. Rather, these findings suggest an increase in parental stress that may sap emotional, financial, and social resources, and thus contribute to abuse (Berkow, 1987; Burrell, 1990; Sargeant, 1994). Just as it is important not to blame children for their victimization, it is equally important to understand the dynamics of the parent–child relationship that lead violent adults to victimize their own children.

Factors Associated With the Parent and the Situation

Psychologists have long sought evidence that abusive parents suffer from a particular mental illness or personality disorder (Francis, Hughes, & Hitz, 1992; Yanagida & Ching, 1993). However, in one typical study, Minnesota Multiphasic Personality Inventory (MMPI) profiles that were taken on 183 abusive adults found no major abnormalities or consistent personality types (Yanagida & Ching, 1993). Other research noted similar findings, and no one personality type nor major mental illness seems to characterize the child abuser. Of course, it remains possible that there are several different types of child abusers (Francis et al., 1992), but using such information predictively seems unlikely.

Despite this, there are some factors that frequently characterize abusers and that are often associated with their behavior. For example, a good deal of research has been conducted on the association between substance abuse and child abuse. This association is not, as reviewed earlier, unique to child abuse but could theoretically contribute to it, nevertheless. One study found that 40% of child abusers also abused substances (Kelleher, Chaffin, Hollenberg, & Fischer, 1994). This, and similar studies, have led to a general acceptance of the hypothesis that substance abuse and child abuse are linked (Sheridan, 1995). However, the relationship is not presumed to be so simple. Perhaps it is not substance abuse per se causing child abuse, but rather, other problems in family functioning that lead to both substance abuse and child abuse. For example, one study found that the quality of family functioning and criminal offending were inexorably linked to both substance abuse and child abuse, at least among incarcerated individuals (Sheridan, 1995). Mothers who use drugs also experience higher levels of stress, both of which could affect rates of child abuse (Kelley, 1992). On the other hand, research has shown that a relationship between child abuse and substance abuse remains even when confounding factors are controlled for statistically (Kelleher et al., 1994). In summary, the research suggests that substance abuse probably affects the probability of child abuse both directly and via other, related factors. Adolescent mothers have received special attention in the child abuse literature and are perceived as being at relatively higher risk of child abuse than adult mothers. Generally, teenage mothers may be more rigid in their parenting attitudes and are more likely to have inappropriate expectations for their children (Haskett, Johnson, & Miller, 1994). Thus, although most parents may believe that a toddler cries because he or she is hurt, a parent with inappropriate expectations may believe that a 2-year-old is crying deliberately to annoy his or her parents. If this inappropriate perception is rigid, it may result in extreme anger or a parent's perception that the child is crying "to get me mad." Haskett and her colleagues (1994) also pointed out that teenage mothers are generally less happy than older women and readily accept the notion of hitting children as a form of discipline. Although Haskett's conclusions are common, other researchers have pointed out that a teenage mother's likelihood of being abusive may not be due to being an adolescent per se, but rather, may be due to the number of stressors she encounters and the financial and social resources she has (Buchholz & Korn-Bursztyn, 1993). Thus, teenage mothers may only be at risk for increased child abuse because they frequently lack the resources that older parents enjoy. It is possible to conceptualize all of the adolescent parent's increased risk of child abuse as being the result of fewer resources: fewer financial and social supports, of course, but inadequate emotional and cognitive resources, as well.

Similar to research noting stable perceptual biases in some violent individuals (see chapter 4), some studies have found cognitive biases in abusive parents specifically. For example, mothers who are at low risk for child abuse typically display a great deal of empathy when shown a picture of a crying or distressed infant. However, mothers at high risk failed to demonstrate similar empathy when shown the same pictures (D. Jones, 1995; Milner, Halsey, & Fultz, 1995). Such findings suggest that abusive parents, in common with other violent individuals, may perceive the world differently in ways that predispose them to behave aggressively.

> Speak roughly to your little boy
> And beat him when he sneezes;
> He only does it to annoy
> Because he knows it teases.
> —Lewis Carroll (*Alice In Wonderland*)

PHYSICAL PUNISHMENT—DOMESTIC VIOLENCE OR RESPONSIBLE CHILDREARING?

Parental aggression to children is commonly conceptualized on a continuum, ranging from the use of mild corporal or physical punishment to very severe child abuse. The use of physical punishment or spanking by parents is enormously controversial among researchers who study the causes of violence. Some experts are opposed to any parental physical punishment (Maurer, 1974). Their concern is that it will lead to aggressive behavior in children (Straus, 1983). The potential harmfulness of physical punishment has even been acknowledged by the American Psychological Association, which announced its opposition to corporal punishment in schools in 1975 (K. Anderson & D. Anderson, 1976).

On the other hand, some experts believe that spanking can be an effective and useful socialization tool (K. Anderson & D. Anderson, 1976; Leviton, 1976; Lowenstein, 1977; Maurer, 1974). Although other experts worry that physical punishment could cause aggression in children, these professionals point out that even abusive parental violence does not always lead to an increase in children's aggression (Spatz Widom, 1989b). In addition, recent surveys have suggested that almost all U.S. parents resort to physical punishment at one point or another. Despite the psychological controversy, many, if not most, Americans appear to regard physical punishment as an appropriate childrearing technique, at least under certain circumstances.

Apart from the controversy over whether any relationship exists between physical punishment and aggression, the nature of this relationship has been questioned. Briefly, there are three types of relationships that could (theoretically) exist between physical punishment and aggression. First, perhaps any parental aggression (even spanking) causes the child who receives it to become more violent (Maurer, 1974; Steinmetz, 1979). On the other hand, perhaps a lack of physical punishment causes the child, unchecked, to become more violent (DiLalla, Mitchell, Arthur, & Pagliocca, 1988). Finally, perhaps the most violent children are reared not by parents who spank, but by parents who spank either too much or too little (Gelles, 1974; Lefkowitz, Eron, Walder, & Huesmann, 1977).

How much research has actually been done on physical punishment? Not a great deal. Typically, more severe forms of parental violence (e.g., child abuse) are examined and are the subject of comprehensive reviews (Spatz Widom, 1989b). Many studies have strongly suggested that being exposed to abusive parental violence constitutes a significant risk factor for the development of violent behavior (Parke & Slaby, 1983; Spatz Widom, 1989b). Given this justifiable emphasis on extreme forms of parental aggression, fewer researchers have examined the consequences of the most common type of physical aggression by parents—physical punishment. Physical punishment differs significantly from abusive parental violence in many ways, including (but not limited to) the degree of aggression used, the potential for injury, the deviance (atypicality) of the behavior, and the intention of the parent. Because they are so different, the research that examines child abuse cannot really address the issue of physical punishment. The goal of this chapter is to clarify the relationship, if any, between physical punishment and child aggression.

To understand the impact of any variable on any outcome, it is important to understand base rates of the studied phenomenon. In other words, before we can examine the possible link between physical punishment and violence, we need to know how common physical punishment is in our society (Spatz Widom, 1989a).

Frequency of Physical Punishment

Frequency estimates range greatly, depending on how people are questioned. When parents of school age and adolescent children are questioned about their use of physical punishment over short periods (e.g., over the previous month or year), the percentage of parents who admit using such discipline varies between 17% (DiLalla et al., 1988), 57% (Lefkowitz, Walder, & Eron, 1963), and 71% (Gelles, 1978). But when adults are asked about their own exposure to physical punishment over their entire childhood, much higher percentages are reported: For example, Deley (1988) found that 89% of his subjects reported that they had experienced physical punishment; similarly, 95% of J. Bryan and Freed's (1982) subjects recalled experiencing such punishment. Furthermore, studies of very young children almost always show that more than 90% of parents use physical punishment (Sears, Maccoby, & Levin, 1957; Straus & Gelles, 1990). Thus, it seems very likely that the vast majority of Americans are subjected to corporal punishment at one point or another during their lives. The almost-universal nature of physical punishment is similar to the almost-universal exposure to television violence. As in the case of television violence, the near-universal nature of physical punishment seems to convince people of the safety of its use (Killory, 1974; Leviton, 1976; Lowenstein, 1977; Straus, 1983). However, as in the case of media violence, this fact does not, by itself, mean that we should simply dismiss physical punishment as a potentially important cause of violence and domestic violence.

To appreciate the potential contribution of near-universal variables such as physical punishment, it is important to remember that there are many universal or nearly universal events that are necessary conditions for the development of rare events. For example, although sexual intercourse is an almost universal behavior, it is associated with a rare event: cervical cancer. Intercourse alone does not "cause" cervical cancer in any simple sense, but cervical cancer almost never develops in people who do not have sexual intercourse (Skrabanek, 1988). A universal event (intercourse) alone does not cause this rare cancer, but it is a necessary condition for the cancer to develop. Just as not all people who have intercourse get cancer, perhaps not all people who are physically punished become too aggressive.

It is not preposterous to hypothesize that physical punishment could be a "mere" contributing factor to the development of violence, rather than its sole cause. In fact, it seems highly unlikely that any parental aggression could single-handedly cause the development of deviant violence (Curtis, 1963; Spatz Widom, 1989b). There is no doubt that childhood violence experiences interact with other important factors in causing aggression and violence (Miller & Challas, 1981). In fact, this was precisely what Spatz Widom (1989b) found in the case of child abuse and aggression. However, just because it is theoretically possible for physical punishment to be related to violence does not make it so. What is the evidence for a relationship between physical punishment and the development of violence or domestic violence?

Retrospective Research

In six studies, individuals were asked to remember their experiences of physical punishment during childhood. In a nationwide survey of 1,176 adult respondents, Owens and Straus (1975) found that the frequency of physical punishment received as a child was related to adult approval of the use of violence. Owens and Straus asked individuals to remember both spanking and more abusive violence (e.g., punching, choking). They then related these childhood experiences to adult attitudes to violence, rather than to adult violent behavior. In other words, they gave adults scenarios that measured their approval of violence in a variety of settings, rather than measuring violent behavior directly.

In the remaining five studies, people were asked to remember their experiences of physical punishment and to judge themselves on how violent they were. Bryan and Freed (1982) questioned 170 community college students about their history of physical punishment and their self-reported problems with aggression. They found that students who had received a "high" amount of corporal punishment also reported more problems with aggression (among other difficulties). Parke and Collmer (1975) found that child abusers often had memories of "physically punitive childhood experiences" (the remembered violence was usually severe and more similar to abuse than to physical punishment). In 1977, Carroll studied 96 adults and found that 37% of those who had rated their childhood experiences as having "high" physical punishment were violent, compared to only 15% of those who reported experiencing "low" physical punishment.

In a similar study, Caesar (1988) found that a sample of 26 wife batterers recalled more parental use of physical punishment than a sample of 18 nonviolent men (58% vs. 31%). Finally, Gelles (1974) found that respondents who recalled being hit by their parents frequently (six or more times per year) were far more likely to physically fight with their spouses than were respondents who recalled being infrequently hit.

Cross-Sectional Research

Cross-sectional research studies examine children directly and try to find a link between a child's current exposure to physical punishment and aggression in that child. For example, Straus (1983) found, in a nationally representative sample of children, that 76% of physically abused children, 40% of physically punished children, but only 15% of non-physically punished children demonstrated a marked tendency to repeatedly physically attack their sister or brother. Because children change so rapidly as they grow, however, and because children of different ages have different tendencies to be aggressive, it is most useful to separate these studies by the age of the child.

Preschool-Age Children. This age group includes children who are less than 6 years old. Several studies have found that the more often a small child is spanked, the more often that child is aggressive toward his or her siblings and parents, as judged by parents, teachers, and researchers (Larzelere, 1986; Sears et al., 1957; Sears, Whiting, Nowlis, & Sears, 1953). Predictably, however, this relationship between frequency of spanking in small children and frequency of aggression appears to be stronger for boys than for girls (Becker, Peterson, Luria, Shoemaker, & Hellmer, 1962; Sears et al., 1953). Although the results of these studies seem clear, other research found very different results. For example, Yarrow, Campbell, and Burton (1968) found no relationship between parental use of physical punishment and the child's aggression. Other research agreed that the data do not strongly support any relationship between physical punishment and aggression in small children (Schuck, 1974). What conclusions can be drawn when studies differ so much in their findings? The relationship between spanking and aggression in preschool-age children is a good example of "mixed results"—an area in which more research is needed before any specific conclusions can be drawn.

School-Age Children. For children old enough to be in school but not yet adolescents (typically 6- to 12-year-olds), the research is more consistent. Several studies agree that in children this age, the level of aggressive behavior rises in conjunction with the frequency with which they are spanked (Eron, 1982; Larzelere, 1986; Lefkowitz et al., 1963; Straus, 1983).

Adolescent Children. Two studies examined the coexistence of physical punishment and aggression in adolescents, and both found a relationship between physical punishment and aggression. Larzelere (1986) looked at a representative sample of 13- to 17-year-olds (i.e., adolescents from every social class, ethnic background, etc.) and found a positive relationship between the use of physical punishment and aggression toward siblings and parents. R. Welsh (1976) studied 77 aggressive delinquents and found that 97% reported they had undergone either severe physical punishment (e.g., being hit with a belt) or abuse.

To summarize, retrospective studies have all found that violent and aggressive adults recall receiving more physical punishment than nonaggressive adults. When children are examined for the coexistence of spanking and aggressive behavior, the data consistently suggest that in children 6 years and older, there is a significant link between physical punishment and aggression. However, in younger children, the evidence is mixed, and it is less clear that physical punishment is related to aggressive behavior.

Despite the suggestiveness of the research just discussed, a serious problem exists: Retrospective and cross-sectional research cannot tell us causal direction. In other words, studies tell us there is a link between physical punishment and aggression, but leave open three equally possible interpretations:

1. Children who are physically punished become aggressive following the punishment.

2. Children who are aggressive for other reasons provoke more frequent physical punishment (Bell, 1979).

3. Some third variable (e.g., poor parenting skills) is responsible for both an increase in a child's aggression and an increase in his or her parents' use of physical punishment (meaning that the correlation between physical punishment and aggression does not, in fact, mean that one variable causes another).

That is, it may be that the spanking increases aggression, or it may be that aggressive ("naughty") children are spanked more because they are aggressive.

There are other problems with the designs of the studies described. For example, cross-sectional research can only focus on childhood aggression, which is clearly not the same thing as adult violence. Retrospective designs are able to assess adult violence, but rely on the adult's memory of childhood spanking, which might be inaccurate (Eron, 1982).

Because of these problems, a few studies have sought to prospectively examine the association between physical punishment and the later development of aggressive or violent behavior. Prospective studies are longitudinal: Researchers look at a child's experience of physical punishment and then wait until the child grows before examining his or her aggressive behavior. Longitudinal research does not rely on human memory and is not limited to the study of childhood behavior. In addition, because the physical punishment is measured first and the adult aggression is measured years later, we know that the aggression cannot have caused the physical punishment).[1]

Prospective Research

Eleven studies examined parental use of physical punishment and the later development of aggressive or violent behavior. Two of these studies focused on samples of children who were under the care of a physician or psychiatrist for behavior problems such as aggression; they both found that "harsh" physical punishment was common in the clinical histories of violent patients (Nagaraja,

---

[1]One possible confound is that the children in the study may demonstrate adult aggression merely because they were aggressive as children, and not because they were physically punished. However, most longitudinal research included in the sample children who are not initially aggressive in an effort to preclude this possibility.

1984; Rigdon & Tapia, 1977). It is interesting to examine the backgrounds of psychiatric patients and try to uncover the reasons for their violent behavior, but the reports of studies such as these are of limited use because they tend to use vague language (e.g., what does "harsh" mean?) and the researchers do not conduct controlled, systematic analyses.

More important and useful prospective studies have also been conducted, ranging in length from 3 to more than 20 years. Singer, Singer, and Rapaczynski (1984) followed 55 children for 3 years and found a relation between the parents' use of childrearing techniques that emphasized "control and physical punishment" at age 6, and aggression when children were 9 years old, as measured by teacher reports. Lefkowitz et al. (1977) followed children between the ages of 8 and 18, over a 10-year period. They questioned parents about any use of "spanking" or "slapping" as a punishment when the children were 8 years old. Ten years later Lefkowitz and his colleagues found that physical punishment at age 8 was positively related to aggression at age 18, but only for boys. However, this study did not find that the more frequent the spanking, the more frequent the violence; rather, the relation was more complicated. The results suggested that parents who used no punishment, and parents who used very harsh physical punishment, had the most aggressive boys by age 18; the parents who used physical punishment moderately had the least aggressive boys by age 18.

Finally, McCord (1979) followed 253 boys over a 20-year span. At the beginning of the study, parents were classified as "aggressive" or "nonaggressive" with their children. Twenty years later, McCord gathered official correctional records (prison and conviction records) on the men and found that parental aggression 20 years before predicted to so-called "personal" crimes (violent crimes such as rape and murder).

The results of all prospective studies discussed thus far imply that physical punishment during childhood, probably in larger amounts, may contribute to violence and aggression later in life. However, other prospective research has failed to find any relation between physical punishment and later aggression. Sears (1961) followed 160 children over a 7-year period but failed to find any significant relation between physical punishment at age 5 and attitudes toward aggression at age 12. Similarly, Johannesson (1974) studied 212 children and found that nonaggressive children were smacked by their parents just as often as children who were rated as aggressive by their teachers.

In summary, then, five of the seven prospective studies found a relation between earlier use of physical punishment and later aggressive and violent behavior. Of these five, three were high-quality prospective research designs. Two other high-quality designs, however (Johannesson, 1974; Sears, 1961), found no evidence for any relation between physical punishment and aggression.

Again, we are faced with mixed results. However, a close examination of the studies does reveal some consistent trends. For example, different studies examined children at different ages. Johannesson (1974) and Sears (1961) found no link, but only studied the physical punishment of younger children (aged 9 months to 5 years), whereas Lefkowitz et al. (1977); Singer et al. (1984); and Mc-Cord (1979) studied older children and did find a link between spanking and aggression years later. Spanking or slapping older children is certainly more unusual and more deviant (Straus, 1983); this may explain why studies that focused on the physical punishment of school age and older children found a relation between it and later aggressive behavior. In addition, parents who are unusual enough to spank or slap older children may have other unusual parenting practices that could affect the child's tendency to become aggressive or violent. The "mixed" results, thus, do have a consistent thread when they are examined closely. Physical punishment may be linked to violence, but only in children who are school-aged and older.

SUMMARY OF RESEARCH FINDINGS

Most, but not all, of the cross-sectional and retrospective research reviewed here found a positive relation between physical punishment and aggressive behavior. Correlations between physical punishment and aggression in the best-designed studies suggest a moderate relation, with a stronger relation for males. Prospective research examined how well this association is maintained longitudinally, and suggested that when physically aggressive behavior is directly measured in older children (over 5 years old), corporal punishment may be included in the group of variables that potentially contribute to aggressive behavior.

The Relation between Low Physical Punishment and Aggression

Let us examine more closely different types of physical punishment and their relations to aggressive behavior. One important issue is the relation between low (or no) use of physical punishment and aggression in children. For example, are children who are rarely or never spanked the least aggressive of all? Perhaps, in contrast, children who are rarely or never spanked are among the most aggressive.

Most studies agreed that severely punished children were among the most aggressive (J. Bryan & Freed, 1982; Eron, 1982; Gelles, 1974; Larzelere, 1986; Lefkowitz et al., 1977; Lefkowitz et al., 1963; Sears, 1961; Straus, 1983). However, some studies found that "low" physical punishment was associated with higher aggression (Gelles, 1974; Lefkowitz et al., 1977; Sears, 1961), whereas in other studies, "low" physical punishment was associated with lower aggression (J. Bryan & Freed, 1982; Eron, 1982; Larzelere, 1986; Lefkowitz et al., 1963; Straus, 1983). Why would studies reveal such mixed results?

One problem is the way the different researchers defined *low* punishment. In some studies, the low punishment condition consisted of parents who literally used no physical punishment (Straus, 1983), whereas in other studies, the low punishment condition included parents who used some physical punishment (usually to an imprecise extent; J. Bryan & Freed, 1982). Other studies do not report what the criteria were (Eron, 1982; Sears, 1961), and Lefkowitz et al. (1963) based their comparison groups on the number of types of physical punishments used, rather than on their frequency. Another difficulty in studying the impact of low or no physical punishment is accuracy. Given that almost the entire population uses physical punishment to some degree, the possibility of any researcher locating a group of parents who literally utilize no physical punishment at all seems low. It is very plausible that parents often use mild physical punishment that they later fail to remember (e.g., slapping the hand of a toddler). Because of these problems, it is very difficult to draw any conclusions about "low" or "no" use of physical punishment, and whether it is harmful or helpful to a child's development.

Child Abuse and Physical Punishment

As noted earlier, parental aggression may be thought of as occurring on a continuum from abusive violence to very mild physical punishment. One of the greatest difficulties in studying physical punishment is the "teasing apart" of the effects of abusive violence versus the effects of more common and mild aggressive responses to a child's behavior.

It is difficult to separate these two parental behaviors because they may be related to one another. Parents who regularly use physical punishment are also more likely to abuse (Kosky, 1983; Maurer, 1974), although the two do not necessarily go together. Because of this relation between physical punishment and child abuse, Sweden passed a 1979 civil law that forbids parental use of physical punishment (Feshbach, 1980), in an attempt to lower the frequency of child abuse.

Because child abuse and physical punishment are related, and because any large, representative sample of Americans is bound to include some child abusers (Straus & Gelles, 1990), it is probable that child abusers were included among the parents studied by the investigators of the effects of physical punishment. We know that abuse is causally related to aggression (Spatz Widom, 1989a), so the parents who are abusers (rather than the parents who are only spankers) may be responsible for the relations with aggression previously noted. Thus, one important factor to control for, in the study of physical punishment and aggression, is child abuse. The critical question is this: When the presence of child abuse is controlled for, does the association between physical punishment and aggression remain? Does parental violence have to be extreme (i.e., abusive) before it is associated with the development of violence in the child?

Unfortunately, only two studies directly address this issue by controlling for child abuse. In one study of a clinical sample comparing wife batterers to nonbatterers, Caesar (1988) questioned subjects about their exposure to parental violence in their families of origin. They rated the batterers' and nonbatterers' parents as being aggressive at three levels: spanking; use of a switch, belt, razor strap, paddle, etc.; and beating. Batterers, in comparison to nonbatterers, had experienced more parental use of a switch, belt, razor strap, paddle, and so forth. Importantly, however, batterers and nonbatterers were no different in their exposure to spanking. Whether or not one considers use of a razor strap or belt abusive, the important point is that spanking alone was not associated with wife-battering specifically.

The different effects of child abuse and physical punishment have also been investigated in a nationally representative sample. Straus (1983) studied a group of several thousand children and interviewed their parents, asking about both the parents' use of physical punishment (e.g., slapping) and child abuse (e.g., hitting with a closed fist). He then compared how aggressive two groups of children were: those whose parents had only used physical punishment versus those children whose parents had used physical punishment and abusive violence. The study found that aggression was much more common in abused children, when compared to only physically punished children. Although physically punished children were not as aggressive as abused children, they were more aggressive than children whose parents used neither physical punishment nor abusive violence. This second study is stronger because it uses a nationally representative sample, rather than a sample from a clinical setting. However, it does assess childhood aggression, which is not the same thing as adult violence.

Another way of examining the impact of child abuse is to ask whether only moderate physical punishment increases aggression. If the answer is no, then it remains possible that abuse accounts for the relation between physical punishment and aggression. If the answer is yes, then it is more likely that physical punishment may be related to aggression independently of abuse.

Lefkowitz et al. (1963) separated children into "none," "once a year," and "more than once a year" recipients of physical punishment. He found that the crucial distinction in aggression lay between the "no-spanking" children and the other children, implying that any (even very infrequent) use of physical punishment serves to increase aggression in children. Another study also found that even moderate use of physical punishment increased aggression in children (Eron, 1982). As we have come to expect, however, other studies found the opposite: namely, that moderate punishment does not serve to increase aggression in children. In fact, a number of studies have found that children of parents who use physical punishment moderately were the least aggressive (Gelles, 1974; Lefkowitz et al., 1977; Sears, 1961). Others noted that children exposed to "low" and "moderate" physical punishment were similarly low in aggression (J. Bryan & Freed, 1982; Larzelere, 1986).

In summary, then, nine studies addressed the issue of moderate or low use of physical punishment versus child abuse by accounting for severity and/or frequency of use of parental physical punishment. Of these nine, six found that moderate use of spanking produced either the least aggressive children or children who were no more aggressive than the children of low physical punishment parents. The other three studies (Eron, 1982; Lefkowitz et al., 1963; Straus, 1983) found that moderate use of spanking did increase aggression in children (over low/no physical punishment). These results are clearly mixed but lean in favor of the hypothesis that low and moderate use of physical punishment does not result in increased aggression and violence in children.[2]

Males Versus Females

Here, results are consistent. Five studies compared male–female differences in correlations between experience of physical punishment and aggressive behavior; four of these found that the correlations for male subjects were stronger (Becker et al., 1962; Eron, 1982; Lefkowitz et al., 1977; Owens & Straus, 1975). It appears that the relation between severe physical punishment and increased aggression is much stronger for male than for female children.

Physical Punishment and Other Parenting Behaviors

Another issue that is important in evaluating the strength of the connection between physical punishment and the development of aggression was raised by Parke and Slaby (1983), who noted that parents who use physical punishment (especially severe physical punishment) may also have other detrimental parenting behaviors. Perhaps it is these other parenting behaviors that are responsible for the increase in aggression (rather than the use of spanking per se).

For example, some studies have suggested that people who choose to spank children may be different from people who prefer other methods of punishment. One of these found that "close-mindedness" and "neuroticism" were highly related to the use of corporal punishment by public school teachers (Rust & Kinnard, 1983). Another study found that parental anger-proneness was related to the use of "harsh" parental punishment (Engfer & Schneewind, 1982). Becker et al. (1962) found that "hostile" parents tended to use more physical punishment than less hostile parents.

Family factors have also been tentatively related to the use of spanking; such factors include socioeconomic status (Magmer & Ipfling, 1973), cultural values (Escovar & Escovar, 1985), size of family (Wagner et al., 1985), a high degree of family conflict (Engfer & Schneewind, 1982), and marital satisfaction (Kemper & Reichler, 1976).

---

[2]One possible interpretation of this is that moderate physical punishment may tend to be logically related to a child's behavior, whereas more severe punishment may seem irrational from the child's perspective and may be more related to the parents' needs than the child's misbehaviors.

Physical Punishment and Other Parenting Factors

The relation between personality and parenting styles and parental choice of punishment method must be very complex; these few studies can only be suggestive. Before we can definitively tease apart the impact of physical punishment from the impact of other parental and family factors, we must have a much clearer idea of what factors are most strongly associated with the use of physical punishment. Very little research has actually been conducted on other differences in parenting styles between parents who choose to spank and those who choose not to spank. Nevertheless, a few studies have been completed.

One retrospective study (Carroll, 1977) investigated the relation between parental "warmth," use of physical punishment, and the development of aggression. Interestingly, Carroll found that when parental warmth was accounted for, physical punishment was not related to the level of aggression in the children. This finding implies that it is parental warmth, and not the use of spanking per se, that is related to the child's aggressiveness. Larzelere (1986) also found that when parents frequently talked things over with their children, no relation remained between physical punishment and aggression. He did note, however, in preadolescents and adolescents, a particular increase in aggression among those children whose parents used both frequent spanking and minimal discussion.

Finally, Eron and his colleagues noted that physical punishment increased aggression only in boys who lacked close identification with their fathers. When boys were closely identified with their fathers, spanking appeared actually to decrease aggression (Eron, 1982). Lefkowitz et al. (1977) noted the same result. These few studies, although only suggestive, imply that such factors as the warmth and intimacy of the relationship between children and their punishers may be very important when considering the impact of physical punishment on children's aggressive (or lack of aggressive) behavior. In the context of affectionate and effective parenting, physical punishment may not increase a child's risk of aggressive behavior.

CONCLUSION

Whether or not to spank children is one of the most controversial issues in child psychology today. The claim is frequently made that physical punishment, or spanking, increases the likelihood that a child will grow up to be aggressive or violent (Caesar, 1988; Deley, 1988; Maurer, 1974; McCord, 1979; Straus, 1983). However, as we have seen, it is very difficult to make such a simple claim.

First, many studies only examine children and childhood aggression, or they rely on the memory of adults. Second, it seems very possible that different degrees of physical punishment have different effects. Harsh and frequent use of hitting and spanking in older children does seem to increase their aggression, although whether they remain aggressive through adulthood is uncertain. Low and/or moderate use of physical punishment does not appear to increase a younger child's aggression, although the evidence is clearly mixed. Finally, a few studies tentatively suggest that for a child who has a warm, close relationship with parents who frequently discuss as well as punish, spanking or other types of physical punishment may have no deleterious effects at all.

Chapter 13

Victims: The Consequences of Family Violence

So far, we have discussed several important issues: the definition of violence in general and family violence in particular, the frequency of violence, the types of behaviors that may or may not be called violent, and finally, the characteristics of perpetrators of violence and the possible causes of their violence. In this chapter, the focus shifts to victims and considers the effects and consequences of either witnessing or being the target of violence in the home.

Researchers have studied the impact of two different types of domestic violence: "ordinary" family violence, such as "minor" spouse abuse or physical punishment, and "deviant" family violence, such as severe spouse abuse, intimate rape, and child abuse. We begin with the first.

ORDINARY FAMILY VIOLENCE AND ITS CONSEQUENCES

Physical Punishment

Chapter 7 discussed the possibility that one consequence of corporal punishment of children may be an increase in the child's tendency to behave aggressively or violently. Apart from this tendency, does "ordinary" physical punishment result in any negative psychological consequences for its recipient? Certainly we are justified in calling physical punishment, or spanking, "ordinary"; as we have seen, it is used by almost 100% of American parents (Straus, 1991).

One possible side effect of spanking as a child may be an increased risk of becoming a child or spouse abuser as an adult. Straus (1991) found that the more parents believe in the use of corporal punishment and the more extensively they were physically punished themselves as children, the more likely they were to abuse either their spouses or their children.

A second possible consequence of physical punishment is depression. Greven (1991) theorized that being hit or hurt by a loved and trusted adult causes intense childhood anger, which does not simply go away, but rather is transformed into adult depression. Straus (1992) tested Greven's theory on a study of representative American families who physically punish their adolescent children. Straus and his colleagues interviewed more than 6,000 American families for the 1985 National Family Violence Resurvey (Straus & Gelles, 1990). Physically punishing teenagers is common in America but still much less frequent than physically punishing younger children. Straus and Gelles studied the effects of physical punishment by mothers and by fathers separately. He found that when mothers physically punish teenage boys, depressive symptoms seem to increase as the frequency of the physical punishment increases. For example, boys who were spanked once a year by their mothers had an average depression score of 46, whereas boys who were spanked 11 to 20 times a year by their mothers had an average depression score of approximately 52.

Girls who were spanked by their mothers may also tend to be more depressed than girls who were not spanked, although ironically the girls in the study who were spanked the most often (11 to 20 or more times per year) had lower depression scores than those who were spanked a moderate amount (3 to 10 times per year). Nevertheless, the lowest depression scores were among those girls whose mothers never spanked them. The relationship between the father's use of physical punishment and depression was similar to the relationship between the mother's use of physical punishment and depression.

It was true, furthermore, that both boys and girls had more suicidal thoughts if their parents had used physical punishment while they were teenagers (Straus, 1992). These findings suggest that depression as an adult may be related to physical punishment as a teenager. Unfortunately, they do not give us information about the relationship (if any) between physical punishment as a younger child and depression as an adult. Also, the study did not control for confounding factors: inasmuch as spanking teenagers is not near-universal (the way spanking small children is), perhaps the parents who spanked their adolescents were deficient in other ways and it was these deficiencies that led to increased depression in their children.

Finally, McCord (1988) studied the general personality differences between people who were physically punished as children and those people who were not. What she found was that children whose parents were "generally aggressive" became aggressive adults. In contrast, those who had been reared by generally nonaggressive parents who nevertheless used physical punishment tended to be self-centered; that is, they took pride in their own accomplishments and were unlikely to volunteer their services to other people.

In summary, some research has suggested that physical punishment does have a negative psychological effect on children. In general, though, the evidence is too weak for definitive conclusions and no research on any possible *positive* effects has been conducted.

Minor Spouse Abuse

Although marital violence occurs in more than 16% of American couples, most incidents are relatively minor; that is, they involve pushing, slapping, shoving, or throwing things, rather than kicking, punching, biting, or assault with a weapon. Almost two thirds of the violent couples (10% of the married population) report engaging in "minor" spouse assaults only (Straus & Gelles, 1990). Approximately 8.2% of American couples experienced minor husband-on-wife assaults; 7.6%, minor wife-on-husband assaults. It is clear that minor violence between spouses is much more normative and acceptable than severe violence; nevertheless, it seems probable that there are consequences. What are they?

Psychological injury resulting from minor spousal violence seems to be similar to, although less severe than, psychological injury resulting from severe spousal violence. In *nonviolent* marriages, 27% of women and 16% of men reported experiencing a "high" level of psychosomatic illness at one point or another. In contrast, in marriages characterized by minor violence, 33% of women and 22.4% of men experienced high levels of psychosomatic illness (Stets & Straus, 1990a). Minor violence also appears to exacerbate the level of stress a respondent reports feeling; the percentage of women in minor-violence marriages who reported feeling a "high" level of stress was almost 13% higher than that of women in nonviolent marriages. Similarly, the male rate of self-reported high stress doubled from 15% to 30% when men in nonviolent marriages were compared to those in minor-violence marriages (Stets & Straus, 1990a). Finally, the rate of depression in married couples also appeared to be affected by even minor violence. A high level of depression was reported by 33.4% of women and 29.5% of men in minor-violence marriages, versus only 21% of women and 14% of men in nonviolent marriages.

What these data make clear is that marital violence does worsen psychological distress, even when it is minor. Severe violence results in even more psychological distress, but minor violence by itself does have an impact on the psychological health of the persons involved.

DEVIANT FAMILY VIOLENCE AND ITS CONSEQUENCES

Child Sexual Abuse

Sexual abuse puts a child's psychological well-being at serious risk and thus has potentially major mental health effects. Much more specific information is needed, however, if we are to understand its impact precisely. For example, what symptoms do victims of child sexual abuse demonstrate? Are there common symptoms, or do individual victims have different patterns? In general, studies indicate that children who are sexually abused show at least certain symptoms more frequently than children who are not sexually abused (Kendall-Tackett, Williams, & Finkelhor, 1993). Individual symptoms include fears, nightmares, withdrawn behavior, cruelty, delinquency, sexually inappropriate behaviors, regressive behaviors (reverting to an earlier stage of development), running away, self-injury, and poor self-esteem. In addition, such children are more often clinically diagnosed with posttraumatic stress disorder, neuroses, and a variety of general behavior problems. This is clearly a long and varied list and no one symptom is manifested by all, or even the majority of, sexually abused children. Researchers have reported that "only" about 20% to 30% of sexually abused children exhibited any given symptom. However, they were different from nonabused children in that their *total* number of symptoms was significantly greater.

Another difficulty in studying the effects of child sexual abuse is that many of the symptoms listed can have a wide variety of causes. Are there any symptoms that seem to occur in children who are sexually abused, but not in children with other psychological problems? In fact, one study suggests that posttraumatic stress disorder and sexualized behaviors seem to be more frequently associated with prior sexual abuse than with other difficulties in a child's life (Kendall-Tackett et al., 1993). Other symptoms may be caused by sexual abuse, but they may also be caused by other factors in a child's life. Nevertheless, it is important to reiterate that sexually abused children do show all of the symptoms listed more frequently than "normal" children.

When studying the impact of any event on children, it is important to remember that children of different ages are apt to react very differently. That is, the symptoms a younger child shows are likely to be different from those an older child shows, although some symptoms appear across all age groups. For example, depression in reaction to sexual abuse has been noted across a wide variety of age groups (Beitchman, Zucker, Hood, DaCosta & Akman, 1991). In addition, Kendall-Tackett and her colleagues (1993) pointed out that difficulties in school are also common among childhood sexual abuse victims of all ages.

In contrast, anxiety appears to be a symptom that is much more common in the preschool years and becomes less common as older children are studied. Nightmares, sexualized behavior, hyperactivity, and regression similarly appear to be dominant in preschool- and school-aged children, but are less commonly found in adolescents (Kendall-Tackett et al., 1993). In contrast, sexually abused adolescents are more likely than their younger counterparts to display poor self-esteem, or to be withdrawn or suicidal as a result of the abuse. They also may be more likely to engage in self-destructive behavior, run away, or get into trouble with the law.

Interestingly, a substantial proportion of children who are sexually abused apparently have *no* psychological symptoms after the abuse. The percentage who are symptom-free ranges from about one fifth (Conte & Schuerman, 1987), to one third (Mannarino & Cohen, 1986; Tong, Oates & McDowell, 1987), to about one half (Caffaro-Rouget, Lang, & vanSanten, 1989), depending on the study. It has been pointed out that the children who seem to be symptom-free may in fact have symptoms that they are not asked about or that may manifest themselves later (Kendall-Tackett et al., 1993). Alternatively, it is also possible that some children are *resilient*: that is, traumatic as the abuse is, it may not (in a minority of children) lead to significant psychological distress.

Some types of sexual abuse seem to place children at higher risk of developing symptoms than other types. For example, molestation by a perpetrator who is close to the child may result in more trauma. Similarly, if the abuse is chronic and ongoing (not a one-time event), a child is more likely to be affected. If the perpetrator uses force (rather than manipulation) or if the perpetrator attempts or succeeds in physically penetrating the child (engaging in some type of intercourse), the psychological damage may be greater. In any case, however, many symptoms of child sexual abuse abate, or lessen, as time goes on. In 50% to 70% of sexually abused children, symptoms will lessen within 18 months of the child's disclosing the attack. However, in a minority of children (10% to 24%), symptoms will actually worsen. Whether or not a child's symptoms abate or worsen is related to the supportiveness of the child's family. As with many childhood traumas, the more loving and supportive the child's family is, the better the sexually abused child will recover.

Child Physical Abuse

Apart from the physical damage caused by physical abuse, what are the psychological consequences? Certainly children who are physically abused tend to have low self-esteem (Coster, Gersten, Beeghly & Cicchetti, 1989). They may even blame themselves for the abuse, because young children tend to believe that they are responsible for all events in their lives, both positive and negative (Sroufe, Cooper, & DeHart, 1996). Physical abuse can disrupt a child's ability to form relationships (Cicchetti & Olson, 1990), and may blunt general feelings and expressions of emotions (Schneider-Rosen & Cicchetti, 1984). In addition, abused children may see themselves as capable of handling interpersonal relationships only in violent and abusive ways (Gardner & Timmons-Mitchell, 1990). Because the child is unable to control the abuse and may be unable to predict when it will happen, learned helplessness may also result: In other words, he or she may learn that attempts to avoid distress or pain have no impact on how he or she is ultimately treated (Goldstein, Keller, & Erne, 1985). Not surprisingly, children who are physically abused tend to be more aggressive than other children; it may be that living in an abusive family teaches these children that violence is a normal part of relationships with other people, especially relationships with other family members (Gardner & Timmons-Mitchell, 1990). Like sexual abuse, therefore, physical abuse is likely to leave a child with one or several of a myriad of possible psychological symptoms.

Well-intentioned adults are sometimes frustrated by children who do not defend themselves against parental abuse and further, do not report the abuse to parties who might be willing to protect them (e.g., police, teachers). Why would children resist the help of adults who are concerned by their victimization? Clearly, children cannot defend themselves against an abusive adult, but why would they choose to remain abused when they are offered a chance to escape their families?

Some authors have pointed out that children in abusive families lack the experience of normality and thus tend to assume that abuse is a typical state of affairs (Bakan, 1971). After all, children know only the families in which they have lived; therefore, it is logical that they may assume that there are no situations in which they would not be abused. As a child grows, or possibly experiences other families (such as in foster care), this assumption becomes less plausible; however, in a younger child, it may be a strong incentive to remain with parents.

A second reason may be apparent to anyone. Children are completely dependent on their caregivers, abusive or loving. That dependency is both financial and deeply emotional. Children may clearly see that turning in a parent to authorities is a betrayal that will rob them of their only perceived resource for survival. Abusive parents may even remind a child that if anyone knows about the "secret" (i.e., the abuse), the child will be homeless and will have to live on the street. A child's profound fear of losing parents may make it impossible for them to reveal abuse or to support an investigation of abuse.

Third, it is not unusual for abused children to blame themselves for the abuse (Ney, 1992). Developmentally, it is appropriate for young children to believe themselves responsible for most of what happens to them—good or bad (Sroufe et al., 1996). Furthermore, abusive parents frequently assure their victimized children that the abuse is a punishment for their "badness." Given these circumstances, it is not unusual for children to hold themselves responsible for their parents' violence and to seek the answers to that violence in their own behavior.

Finally, abused children, like abused spouses, may be fearful of punishment or retribution. Their chronic poor self-esteem may lead them to believe that they are apt to be punished for reporting, or the abuser himself or herself may emphasize that the child will be punished if the abuse is discovered. Children may fear that the abuser will "come back to get them" and that any respite from the abuse will only be temporary. It is certainly true that abused children, like other victims of domestic violence, may be threatened with retribution and assured by the abuser that he or she will not be imprisoned long, if at all.

Intimate Sexual Assault

What are the effects of sexual assault upon the victim when the perpetrator is someone the victim is intimately acquainted with, such as a husband or boyfriend? In general, female rape victims tend to demonstrate a cluster of symptoms. Fears and anxiety following the assault are probably most commonly noted (Resick, 1993); researchers have found that they are much more common among victims of sexual assault than they are among nonvictims. However, when victims of sexual assault are compared to victims of robbery, the only difference is that the former have more sexual fears (Resick, Jordan, Girelli, Hutter, & Marhoefer-Dvorak, 1988). Posttraumatic stress disorder appears to be almost universal among rape victims immediately following the assault, and may persist in those victims who report the most severe distress immediately following the attack (Rothbaum, Foa, Murdock, Riggs, & Walsh, 1992). Depression is not universal but is still quite common among rape victims (Resick et al., 1988; Rothbaum et al., 1992). Problems adjusting to work may often surface following a sexual assault, although marital and family adjustment problems were not necessarily noted (Resick, Calhoun, Atkeson, & Ellis, 1981). Finally, sexual problems are among the longest lasting of the symptoms following the rape; one study (Ellis, Calhoun, & Atkeson, 1980) found that almost two thirds had reduced or eliminated sexual activity at 2 weeks following the rape and almost half were still not sexually active a month after the assault. For women with a regular sexual partner, sexual activity returned to normal levels within one year postassault.

Given that these are all common reactions to the trauma of sexual assault, are there differences in recovery between women who are raped by an intimate and women who are raped by strangers? It is commonly believed that rape by a stranger is much more traumatic than rape by an intimate. However, several researchers noted that there is little or no difference in symptoms between women who are raped by strangers and those who are raped by intimates (Resick, 1993). Other researchers actually found that victims of intimate rape suffer significantly more than victims of stranger rape, particularly in the areas of self-esteem and general maladjustment (Hassell, 1981; McCahill, Meyer, & Fishman, 1979). Thus, contrary to common beliefs, rape by an intimate is at least as traumatic as stranger rape, and in fact may be even more traumatic.

Severe Spouse Abuse

Severe spouse abuse (kicking, punching, using weapons, etc.) is less common than minor spouse abuse, but still far too common in the United States. The rates of reported severe spouse abuse tend to differ, depending on whether men or women are questioned. Men report that they severely abuse their wives in 1.3% of marriages, whereas women report that they are the victims of severe abuse by their husbands in approximately 5% of marriages.[1] Both men and

---

[1] As discussed in Chapter 6, research suggests that men may underreport their rates of abusive behavior, which may account for the discrepancy between men's and women's reported rates of severe husband-on-wife abuse.

women report that women severely abuse their husbands in approximately 5% of American marriages. What are the effects of severe marital violence?

Physical injury is a very real danger in severe spouse abuse. Of those women reporting severe spouse abuse, 7.3% needed to see a doctor for their injuries. Probably because of their typically larger size and strength, men were much less likely to sustain injuries severe enough to require medical attention: Only 1% of male victims of severe spouse abuse needed to see a doctor (Stets & Straus, 1990b).

Sometimes injuries prevent victims from going to work. In fact, this problem was very common: 19% of female victims and 10% of male victims of severe spouse assault reported that they needed to take time off from their jobs (Stets & Straus, 1990b). In keeping with this trend, female victims are more likely to need a day in bed to recover from their injuries than are male victims of severe spouse assault: 23% of women versus 14% of men reported needed time in bed.

Physical injury aside, there are serious psychological costs to severe spouse abuse as well. Levels of psychosomatic illness, stress, and depression all rise precipitously when individuals are involved in severely violent marriages. For example, whereas only 21% of women in nonviolent marriages and 33.4% of women in minor-violent marriages report problems with depression, almost 60% of women in severely violent marriages have depressive difficulties. Similarly, approximately 60% of women in severely violent marriages report problems with stress, with about one third of men in severely violent marriages reporting high levels of stress and depression (Stets & Straus, 1990).

Why Does She Stay?   To outsiders, to those who have never known domestic abuse, and even to some victims, perhaps the most confusing aspect of family violence is the senselessness of the crime and the apparent futility of the relationships. Why on earth would any woman choose to live with a man who beats her? If such behavior appears "crazy" to laypeople, it has seemed that way to experts as well.

In the past, psychologists suggested that women who "willingly" endured an abusive relationship did so because they had a masochistic personality disorder. Masochism, which is defined as excessively self-defeating behavior, has been associated with women in the psychiatric and psychological literature. Masochists are thought of as those who are excessively self-sacrificing and are too willing to please others, and masochistic women have been characterized as likely to choose cold and unloving mates (Glickauf-Hughes & Wells, 1991). *Masochistic personality disorder* is a clinical disorder in which women might remain in an abusive relationship because they enjoyed the abuse or it met some psychological need or desire (Pizzy, 1974). Many psychologists have protested the association of masochistic personality disorder and being a battered woman (Ritchie, 1989), and research does not support that hypothesis; it is now known that abused women are no more likely to be masochistic than any other segment of the population (Pizzy, 1974; Skodol, Oldham, Gallaher, & Bezirganian, 1994).

Of course, this does not mean that there are not women who choose to stay with men who are abusive. More recent research has provided explanations of why abused women stay in abusive relationships, and sometimes even defend their mate and their relationship when it is threatened by agencies seeking to protect the woman (such as the police). One reason that women stay is that they may believe that their husbands or boyfriends have the right to beat them, inasmuch as they "belong" to their mates (Straus, 1976). As was pointed out in chapter 1, husbands did indeed have that right until relatively recently.

Poor self-esteem frequently characterizes women who endure abusive relationships. The sense that one is worthless and unlovable makes abuse seem more logical and less a violation of rights. Believing that you deserve to be treated badly facilitates tolerating bad treatment. One typical study of violence in dating relationships found that low self-esteem predicted sustained abuse, particularly sexual abuse (Pirog-Good, 1992). In fact, this study found that a small decrease in a subject's self-esteem score disporportionately increased her chance of multiple victimizations. Other studies also noted low self-esteem in abused women (Follingstad, 1980), but all these studies found that it is difficult to know whether the low self-esteem anteceded the abuse or resulted from it. If women with poor self-esteem tend to become entangled in abusive relationships that they choose to endure, then poor self-esteem may be a central risk factor for victimization. If, conversely, women begin to suffer from poor self-esteem following the onset of abuse, then poor self-esteem may not be a preexisting risk factor but a consequence of which the abuser takes advantage to keep the woman in the relationship.

Other cognitive characteristics may increase the chance that a victim remains in an abusive relationship. Beliefs and thought patterns and habits may operate to keep women from leaving abusive partners. One study of college students found that some students in violent relationships consider the violence to be an indication of love (Cate, Henton, Koval, Christopher, & Lloyd, 1982). This attitude was more prevalent in couples who remained together even after the violent episodes had begun. Earlier researchers pointed out that the beliefs of an abused woman may be part of the reason she accepts the violence and stays in the relationship (Gelles, 1985; Walker, 1979). For example, Owens and Straus (1975) found that witnessing physical abuse during one's childhood may predispose some women to believe that it is tolerable in adulthood. Forsstrom-Cohen and Rosenbaum (1985) found that women who witnessed parental abuse as children tend to be more depressed, which may put them at greater risk for tolerating abuse. Davis and Carlson (1987) noted specifically that such women tended to react passively to their parents' violence, which may teach them that a passive response is the best. Finally, Adler (1991) found that 54% of women in persistently abusive relationships had witnessed parental abuse. Although these studies indicate that a woman's cognitive and psychological development may be affected by parental abuse in such a way as to place her at increased risk of victimization, they do not point to what may be the most important reason why women stay: their attempt to promote their own safety.

For many women, the ultimate reason they cannot leave an abusive relationship is fear. It is common for abusive husbands to warn wives against entertaining any ideas of leaving, and to insist that if they attempt to flee they will be tracked down and beaten or killed (Browne, 1987). The threat of retaliation, made by an individual who clearly has the capacity to be violent, can be serious enough to deter even the most severely beaten wife from attempting to leave an abuser. Certainly it deters many women from pressing assault or other charges against their abusers; many believe that any jail time would be temporary and the subsequent consequences even worse.

All these factors make it logical, rather than illogical, that most women choose to stay in abusive relationships. Staying means abuse and violence, but leaving may mean death. A bureaucracy may promise safety, but cannot ensure it. For many battered women, this is a risk they cannot take.

Effects on the Children. Serious spouse abuse has effects beyond those on the participants, however. Although women in severely violent marriages are usually the most seriously injured victims, their children suffer as well (Forsstrom-Cohen & Rosenbaum, 1985). It is often difficult to tease apart the effects of witnessing parental violence from the effects of having been abused oneself as a child. However, some research has excluded all abused individuals and subsequently compared individuals who had witnessed parental violence with those whose parents had nonviolent discord and those whose parents were satisfactorily married (Forsstrom-Cohen & Rosenbaum, 1985). The results indicated clearly that having witnessed severe spouse abuse has a psychological impact on the children involved; specifically, children who witnessed violence between their parents were much more likely, as young adults, to have difficulties with anxiety, depression, and aggression. Other studies noted similarly that spouse abuse tends to cause depression and anxiety in the witnessing children (Levine, 1975).

CONCLUSION

In summary, even when it is not severe, domestic violence appears to have a detrimental effect on both the victim and the family. The more severe the violence is, the more serious the psychological symptoms that result. Some victims appear resilient, but many have serious difficulties.

Among those who work to help victims of abuse, perhaps the most frustrating aspect of an abusive situation is a victim's refusal to press criminal charges against the violent abuser. This refusal may, and almost certainly will, hurt the victim; it also tends to feed the public's perception that domestic abuse is not a serious criminal offense. If abuse were serious, the reasoning goes, victims would be eager to press charges and would not repeatedly return to the abuser.

Although in some cases the minimal nature of the violence may be the reason that victims of abuse refuse to press charges, in the majority of cases it is not. Victims may in fact abhor the abuse, may see it correctly as very violent, and may even fear for their lives. If, despite all this, they refuse to press charges, it is simply because doing so appears even more dangerous to their welfare than remaining with the abuser. Victims may believe that whereas their abusers may kill them if they stay, they will certainly kill them if they leave and press charges. The victim's lack of faith in the protection offered by the criminal justice system may compel him or her to accept what appears to be the lesser of two evils. This lack of faith in the criminal justice system, moreover, may not be mistaken; most experts in that system agree that if an estranged spouse is determined to wreak revenge, he (or, less often, she) will probably do so despite restraining orders and other legal niceties.

Further, family members may or may not be happy at the prospect of punishment or incarceration for the perpetrator of the abuse. Although they may desire immediate safety from the violence, they may fear the effect of punishment on the abuser, and lifetime imprisonment is generally not a possibility. Furthermore, victims of abuse may undergo a process similar to that undergone by drug and alcohol abusers, in which they need to "hit bottom" before they are really ready to release their desire to have both an intact family and no abuse. Generally these two goals are incompatible, but victims of abuse must accept that if they are to escape their abusers, they may have to relinquish their dream of a happy, intact family. Because hope springs eternal, and victims of abuse (like other people) would generally prefer to solve problems rather than escape them, it can be difficult for a victim who has not "hit bottom" to accept that escape is the only logical alternative.

Victims of abuse require support to escape the abuser (Sullivan et al., 1991). This support must assure them of physical safety and help them meet basic needs, including emotional needs. If the support is inadequate on either of these counts, which it generally is, it is not surprising that abuse may be seen as the lesser of two evils, for which the victim must settle.

Chapter 14

Epilogue:
Preventing and Controlling Violence

On September 11, 2001, terrorists hijacked and flew two commercial airplanes into the World Trade Center towers in New York City. In one fell swoop, they killed nearly 3,000 innocent people. The violence and death following this terrible attack has dwarfed much of the interest and research into "ordinary" street and family violence. Despite this, research on violence and its causes is not irrelevant to an understanding of what causes terrorism. Although much is motivated by extreme political or social views, some individuals are undoubtedly drawn to radical terrorist groups by their potential to offer opportunities to behave very violently.

Some of the questions that frequently arise are: How can basic research help us understand people, and what do we do with it? Investigations of the causes of violence may be very interesting intellectually, but what can the results do for us today? How can we apply our knowledge to increase our safety and sense of security? How can we reduce violence in our society? These are more complicated questions than they appear to be.

During the 1990s, we learned a great deal about policies that might help reduce violence and violent crime. A police force and a judiciary that take domestic violence seriously have gone far to help victims trapped in violent households. Community policing is one of the policies that have helped reduce violent crime in the streets. And yet some lessons remain unlearned.

Many people can recognize situations in which "an ounce of prevention is worth a pound of cure." Wearing seatbelts has become a habit for many Americans, and tobacco use is at an all-time low. These are circumstances where, clearly, prevention can reduce tragedy. But the lesson may not be learned in the case of violence.

Reading newspapers or listening to congressional debates, I do not get a clear message that Americans want to prevent criminal violence. They seem to want, rather, to punish it. Perhaps it is merely that punishment is perceived as the most effective way to prevent violence. Perhaps "prevention" programs simply are not effective enough, and punishment is a swifter and surer route.

Or is it? Psychologists have long studied punishment and its potential effectiveness in changing human behavior. Although they do not have all the answers, researchers have clearly delineated the necessary components of an effective punishment. Even a casual glance at the criminal justice system reveals several ways in which it does not punish effectively. For example, we know that for a punishment to be effective, it must follow the undesirable behavior closely in time. That is, it must be swift, or the violent individual will fail to connect the punishment to the violent behavior. America's frustration with the slow and lengthy justice procedure is often reflected in the media. It seems ridiculous that it can take years to prosecute someone for a violent crime, and many have called for a shortening of the criminal justice process. However, those who seek to implement the knowledge that effective punishment follows swiftly on the heels of a crime encounter an obstacle called *due process.* The U.S. Constitution has been interpreted to mean that all persons accused of a violent crime are entitled to a trial by their peers, and so on. Due process takes time. The choice may, in fact, be between a lawful, more violent society and a less violent society that abandons due process. Although I have spent my career to date studying behavior I personally abhor, I would never opt to abandon the judicial system as it is set out in the U.S. Constitution, which I see as a critical process protecting individuals from a lawless government. Destructive as individuals are, I still believe that a government can be much more destructive.

Given the necessary time lapse between crime and punishment, can punishment work? Perhaps, to a limited extent. Can it work for people who have both a biological and learned propensity to be violent? Anecdotal evidence suggests not, although it should be pointed out that most violent felons do not commit violent crimes again: Studies on recidivism again and again find that the majority of violent felons are one-time offenders (Mednick & Kandel, 1988). This fact actually suggests that the criminal justice system is sufficiently punishing to deter most violent individuals from repeating their offenses. On the other hand, perhaps most violent individuals do not have stable behavioral tendencies to be violent. Because we run a country and not an experiment with controlled conditions, we can never know the answer to this question precisely. Does punishment work? Well, most convicted violent felons do not commit further violent felonies —for whatever reasons.

In trying to figure out ways to reduce crime, one is repeatedly drawn to the problem of recidivism. After all, it is the chronic recidivists who commit most of the violent crime we fear. What characterizes people who re-offend, who beat their wives and their children, who rape and strangle and shoot strangers, seemingly without the ability or the desire to stop? Even though they constitute only a small proportion of criminals, they commit the lion's share of crimes (Piper, 1985). Even if we could separate out the potential recidivists from the likely one-timers early in their criminal careers, could we abandon the legal principle that we cannot imprison people for crimes they may commit in the future? Some states have already begun to acknowledge that some offenders are very likely to offend again. For example, New Jersey lawmakers, in reaction to the killing of 7-year-old Megan Kanka by a convicted sex criminal, enacted "Megan's Law," which requires notification to communities when sex offenders are released into their area (Barron, 1994). Washington State went further; it enacted a law permitting authorities to indefinitely confine "habitual" sex offenders (Geyelin, 1993). These solutions are popular but not without legal problems, and judicial rulings have deemed some of them unconstitutional (Hanley, 1995). It has also proved difficult to enforce notification laws (Gladwell, 1995).

Perhaps, however, there are other ways to seek to control those individuals who are identified as stably aggressive. The best cure is prevention. Reexamining some of the research reported in this book, particularly the research on characteristics of recidivistically violent individuals, might yield some clues as to possible preventative measures.

Biological influences certainly seem stronger in such persons. They have experienced disorders prenatally and during birth; they have more health problems, more head injuries, more learning disorders, more intellectual problems, and so on. The difficulty is that biology is commonly seen as immutable. Nothing could be further from the truth. Every day, medical science proves its mutability. Unfortunately, the United States does not furnish universal access to health care. Such access—at a minimum, during pregnancy and childhood—might help alleviate many of the relevant problems, like prenatal disorders and malnutrition and childhood head injuries. Could better health care reduce recidivistic violence? Research suggests that the answer may be yes.

There seems little doubt that violent recidivists are more likely to be domestic than street offenders are. Violence in the family arena is easier and more convenient to perpetrate, more acceptable, and less likely to land the perpetrator in serious trouble. The most straightforward way to approach this issue, it seems to me, is to reduce the social and legal acceptability of domestic violence. There are several ways society might do this. Helping families in day-to-day living might reduce the stress levels that predispose the vulnerable to violence. In addition, public education campaigns can be important. Information should be widely disseminated. Excellent models to follow are the very successful campaigns to inform the public about the dangers of driving while intoxicated.

Furthermore, despite claims that government can't regulate morality, government can, in fact, take the lead in changing social mores. For example, in Sweden it is currently illegal to spank children. When this law was first enacted, most Swedish parents practiced, and believed in, physical punishment. Today, more than two decades after the enactment, most Swedish parents do not believe in spanking children. The important issue here is not the question of whether or not people should spank their children, but rather the point that government legislation can help bring about changes in peoples' thinking about appropriate behavior. The Swedish legislation may not have regulated morality, but it clearly nudged it in a different direction. Stronger laws about domestic violence might have a similar effect in this country.

Finally, we cannot ignore the role that larger social problems play in at least some types of recidivistic violence: poverty and drug abuse (especially alcohol abuse), for example. Policy discussions of poverty and drug abuse are too often divorced from those of crime and violence. There are no simple solutions to the problems of poverty and drug abuse, which in turn are not simply related to the problem of violence. Nevertheless, to ignore them is to enormously reduce our chances of passing on to our children a safe, relatively harmonious society in which they can work and love.

References

Abbey, A., & Harnish, R. (1995). Perception of sexual intent: the role of gender, alcohol consumption, and rape supportive attitudes. *Sex Roles: A Journal of Research, 32*(5–6), 297–314.

Adams, D., Barnett, S., Bechtereva, N., Carter, B., Delgado, J., Diaz, J., Eliasz, A., & Genoves, S. (1990). The Seville statement on violence. *American Psychologist, 45*(10), 1167–1168.

Adessky, R. (1997). *The relationship of group and family experiences to peer-rated aggression and popularity in middle class kindergarten children.* Unpublished doctoral dissertation, Concordia University, Austin, TX.

Adler, T. (1991, December). Abuse within families emerging from closet. *APA Monitor,* pp. 16–17.

Ageton, S. S. (1983). The dynamics of female delinquency, 1976–1980. *Criminology, 21*(4), 555–584.

Akers, R. L. (1985). *Deviant behavior: A social learning approach.* Belmont, CA: Wadsworth.

Akins, K. A., & Windham, M. E. (1992). Just science? *Behavioral and Brain Sciences, 15*(2), 376–378.

Allen, M., Emmers, T., & Giery, M. (1995). Exposure to pornography and acceptance of rape myths. *Journal of Communication, 45*(1), 5–27.

Allgeier, E. R., & Wiederman, M. W. (1992). Evidence for an evolved adaptation to rape? Not yet. *Behavioral and Brain Sciences, 15*(2), 377–380.

American Humane Association. (1998). *Answers to common questions about child abuse and neglect.* Englewood, CO: Author.

Anderson, C., & Dill, K. (2000). Video games and aggressive thoughts, feelings, and behavior in the laboratory and in life. *Journal of Personality & Social Psychology, 78*(4), 772–790.

Anderson, C. A. (1987). Temperature and aggression: Effects of quarterly, yearly, and city rates of violent and nonviolent crime. *Journal of Personality and Social Psychology, 52,* 1161–1173.

Anderson, C. A. (2000). Violence and aggression. In A. E. Kazdin (Ed.), *Encyclopedia of psychology* (pp. 162–169). New York, NY: Oxford University Press.

Anderson, C. A., & Anderson, D. C. (1984). Ambient temperature and violent crime: Tests of the linear and curvilinear hypothesis. *Journal of Personality and Social Psychology, 46,* 91–97.

Anderson, C. A., Deuser, W., & DeNeve, K. (1995). Hot temperatures, hostile affect, hostile cognition, and arousal: Tests of a general model of affective aggression. *Personality & Social Psychology Bulletin, 21*(5), 434–449.

Anderson, J. E. (1972). *The young child in the home: A survey of three thousand families.* White House Conference on Child Health and Protection: Report of the Committee on the Infant and Preschool Child.

Anderson, K., & Anderson, D. (1976). Psychologists and spanking. *Journal of Clinical Child Psychology, Fall,* 46–49.

Andrews, T., Rose, F., & Johnson, D. (1998). Social and behavioural effects of traumatic brain injury in children. *Brain Injury, 12*(2), 133–138.

Arends, L. (1996, February 24). Concern about crime overflows. *The Bakersfield Californian,* pp. 1–2.

Arseneault, L., Tremblay, R., Boulerice, B., Seguin, J., & Saucier, J. (2000). Minor physical anomalies and family adversity as risk factors for violent delinquency in adolescence. *American Journal of Psychiatry, 157*(6), 917–923.

Arsenio, W. F., & Cooperman, S. (2000). Affective predictors of preschoolers' aggression and peer acceptance: Direct and indirect effects. *Developmental Psychology, 36*(4), 438–449.

Arsenio, W. F., & Lemerise, E. A. (2001). Varieties of childhood bullying: Values, emotion processes, and social competence. *Social Development, 10*(1), 59–74.

Ascher, C. (1991). School programs for African American males. *ERIC Digest, 72,* 1–3.

Ashley, L. (1999). *An integrated model of understanding adolescent females' pathways into violent offending.* Unpublished doctoral dissertation. California School of Professional Psychology, San Diego.

Associated Press. (1995, May 25). Suspect in death of woman freed. *The Boston Globe,* p. 14.

Associated Press. (1995, July 10). Increase in gun use in violent crime reported. *The Boston Globe,* p. 7.

Associated Press. (1995, August 1). Father convicted in twins' death. *The Boston Globe,* p. 53.

Associated Press. (1995, August 8). Man gets 10 years for beating baby. *The Boston Globe,* p. 11.

Associated Press. (1995, October 17). Trial opens in I-95 killing with crossbow. *The Boston Globe,* p. 1.

Associated Press. (1995, October 17). Youth's lawyer blames abuse for murder of Rochester family. *The Boston Globe,* p. 3.

Associated Press. (1995, October 26). Federal death-penalty jury hears slain girl's 911 tape. *The Boston Globe,* p. 11.

Associated Press. (1995, November 6). Graf beat his daughter, says associate of family. *The Boston Globe,* p. 25.

Associated Press. (1995, November 11). Sauce jar used in assault, police say. *The Boston Globe,* p. 24.

Associated Press. (1995, November 21). Bid to steal baby is linked to gruesome Illinois deaths. *The Boston Globe,* p. 11.

Associated Press. (1995, December 1). Son, 20, charged with killing father. *The Boston Globe,* p. 56.

Associated Press. (1995, December 10). Salesman attacks Texas woman, 88. *The Boston Globe,* p. 16.

Associated Press, & Seattle Times Staff. (1998, May 21). Here's a look at shootings in U.S. schools. *Seattle Times,* p. 3.

Atkin, C. K. (1983). Effects of realistic TV violence versus fictional violence on aggression. *Journalism Quarterly, 60,* 615–621.

Atkins, M. S., Stoff, D. M., Osborne, M. L., & Brown, K. (1993). Distinguishing instrumental and hostile aggression: Does it make a difference? *Journal of Abnormal Child Psychology, 21*(4), 355–366.

August, G., Stewart, M., & Holmes, C. (1983). A four-year follow-up of hyperactive boys with and without conduct disorder. *British Journal of Psychiatry, 143,* 192–198.

Babinszki, A., Kerenyi, T., Torok, O., Grazi, V., Lapinski, R., & Berkowitz, R. (1999). Perinatal outcome in grand and great-grand multiparity: Effects of parity of obstetric risk factors. *American Journal of Obstetrics and Gynecology, 181*(3), 669–675.

Bachman, R. (1994). *Violence against women: A national crime victimization survey report.* Washington, DC: U.S. Department of Justice.

Bakan, D. (1971). *Slaughter of the innocents: A study of the battered child phenomenon.* Boston: Beacon Press.

Bandura, A. (1989). Human agency in social congitive theory. *American Psychologist, 44,* 1175–1184.

Bandura, A., & Huston, A. (1961). Identification as a process of incidental learning. *Journal of Abnormal and Social Psychology, 63,* 311–318.

Bandura, A., Ross, D., & Ross, S. (1963). Vicarious reinforcement and imitative learning. *Journal of Abnormal and Social Psychology, 67,* 601–607.

Banks, T., & Dabbs, J. (1996). Salivary testosterone and cortisol on delinquent and violent urban subculture. *Journal of Social Psychology, 136*(1), 49–56.

Barber, B. K., Olsen, J. E., & Shagle, S. C. (1994). Associations between parental psychological and behavioral control and youth internalized and externalized behaviors. *Child Development, 65*(4), 1120–1137.

Barkley, R. (2000). Attention-deficit hyperactivity disorder; combined modality therapy; child psychology. *Journal of Abnormal Child Psychology, 28*(6), 595.

Barrett, P. (1991, March 25). Killing of 15-year-old is part of escalation of murder by juveniles. *The Wall Street Journal,* pp. A1–A5.

Barron, J. (1994, August 3). Vigil for slain girl, 7, backs a law on offenders; a convicted sex criminal has confessed. *The New York Times,* p. B4.

Bartol, C. (1991). *Criminal behavior: A psychosocial approach* (3rd ed.). Englewood Cliffs, NJ: Prentice-Hall.

Bartol, C. (1995). *Criminal behavior: A psychosocial approach* (4th ed.). Englewood Cliffs, NJ: Prentice-Hall.

Bassuk, E., Schoonover, S., & Gelenberg, A. (1983). *The practitioner's guide to psychoactive drugs* (2nd ed.). New York: Plenum.

Bastian, L. D., & Taylor, B. M. (1991). *School crime: A national crime victimization survey report* (NCJ-131645). Washington, DC: U.S. Department of Justice.

Baumrind, D. (1994). The social context of child maltreatment. *Family Relations, 43*(4), 360–369.

Beck, A. J., & Shipley, B. E. (1989). *Recidivism of prisoners released in 1983* (Special report). Washington, DC: U.S. Department of Justice.

Becker, W., Peterson, D., Luria, Z., Shoemaker, D., & Hellmer, L. (1962). Relations of factors derived from parent-interview ratings to behavior problems of five-year-olds. *Child Development, 33,* 509–535.

Beitchman, J. H., Zucker, K. J., Hood, J. E., DaCosta, G. A., & Akman, D. (1991). A review of the short-term effects of child sexual abuse. *Child Abuse & Neglect, 14,* 537–556.

Belfrage, H. (1998). A ten-year follow-up of criminality in Stockholm mental patients: new evidence for relation between mental disorder and crime. *British Journal of Criminology, 38*(1), 145–155.

Bell, R. Q. (1979). Parent, child, and reciprocal influences. *American Psychologist, 34*(10), 821–826.

Belsky, J. (1988). Child maltreatment and the emergent family system. In K. Browne, C. Davies, & P. Strattan (Eds.), *Early prediction and prevention of child abuse* (pp. 291–302). New York: Wiley.

Bender, L. (1959). Children and adolescents who have killed. *American Journal of Psychiatry, 12*(3), 34–40.

Berenbaum, S., & Resnick, S. (1997). Early androgen effects on aggression in children and adults with congenital adrenal hyperplasia. *Psychoneuroendocrinology, 22*(7), 505–515.

Berenbaum, S. A., & Hines, M. (1992). Early androgens are related to childhood sex-typed toy preferences. *Psychological Science, 3*(3), 203–206.

Berkow, R. (Ed.). (1987). *The Merck manual of diagnosis and therapy.* Rahway, NJ: Merck, Sharp, and Dohme, Inc.

Berliner, L. (1988). Corporal punishment: Institutionalized assault or justifiable discipline? *Journal of Interpersonal Violence,* June, 222–223.

Berman, M., & Coccaro, E. F. (1998). Neurobiologic correlates of violence: Relevance to criminal responsibility. *Behavioral Sciences & Law, 16*(3), 303–318.

Berman, S. L., Silverman, W. K., & Kurtines, W. M. (2000). Childrens' and adolescents' exposure to community violence, post-traumatic stress reactions, and treatment implications. *The Australasian Journal of Disaster and Trauma Studies, 1*(1174-4707), 1–10.

Bernard, F. (1975). An inquiry among a group of pedophiles. *Journal of Sex Research, 11*, 242–255.

Bernhardt, P. (1997). Influences of serotonin and testosterone in aggression and dominance: Convergence with social psychology. *Current Directions in Psychological Science, 6*(2), 44–48.

Bichard, K. (1999). Irish studies show abuse of parents is rising. *Lancet, 353*(9160), 1251–1254.

Biden, J. (1998). Attacking youth violence. *Criminal Justice Ethics, 17*(1), 2–4.

Bjorkqvist, K. (1994). Sex differences in physical, verbal, and indirect aggression: A review of recent research. *Sex Roles: A Journal of Research, 30*(3–4), 177–189.

Block, R. (1977). *Violent crime.* Lexington, MA: Lexington Books.

Blum, N. J. (1999, July 1). Trouble making friends. *Contemporary Pediatrics, 16*(10), 39.

Bonafina, M., Newcorn, J., McKay, K., Koda, V., & Halperin, J. (2000). ADHD and reading disabilities: A cluster analytic approach for distinguishing subgroups. *Journal of Learning Disabilities, 33*(3), 297.

Bonfante, J. (1995, February 27). Entrepreneurs of crack: An L.A. street gang transforms itself into a cross-country cocaine empire—until the FBI busts it all over. *Time, 145,* 22–24.

Bower, B. (1994). Monkeys defy crowding-aggression link. *Science News, 146*(2), 20–21.

Boxley, J., Lawrance, L., & Gruchow, H. (1995). A preliminary study of eigth grade students' attitudes toward rape mythes and women's roles. *Journal of School Health, 65*(3), 96–101.

Boyajian, A., DuPaul, G., Handler, M., Eckert, T., & McGoey, K. (2001). The use of classroom-based brief functional analyses with preschoolers at-risk for attention deficit hyperactivity disorder. *School Psychology Review, 30*(2), 278.

Braithwaite, J. (1981). The myth of social class and criminality reconsidered. *American Sociological Review, 46,* 36–57.

Brantley, A. C., & DiRosa, A. (1994). Gangs: A national perspective. *The FBI Law Enforcement Bulletin, 63*(5), 1(6).

Brennan, P. A. (1999). Biosocial risk factors and juvenile violence. *Federal Probation, 58*(2), 58–60.

Brezina, T. (1999). Teenage violence toward parents as an adaptation to family strain. *Youth & Society, 30*(4), 416–455.

Briggs, J., Martin, H., & Cuza, B. (2000, August 14). An ominous upturn in L.A. gang violence raises the question anew: Why? *Los Angeles Times,* p. 1.

Brown, G. (1990). CSF Serotonin metabolite (5-HIAA) studies in depression, impulsivity and violence. *Journal of Clinical Psychiatry, 51*(4), 31.

Browne, A. (1984). *Assault and homicide at home: When battered women kill.* Paper presented at the Second National Conference for Family Violence Researchers, University of New Hampshire, Durham.

Browne, A. (1987). *When battered women kill.* New York: The Free Press.

Bryan, J., & Freed, F. (1982). Corporal punishment: Normative data and sociological and psychological correlates in a community college population. *Journal of Youth and Adolescence, 11*(2), 77–87.

Buchholz, E. S., & Korn-Bursztyn, C. (1993). Children of adolescent mothers: Are they at risk for abuse? *Adolescence, 28*(110), 361–383.

Burne, J. (1993). When the medium's message is violent. *New Scientist, 138*(1875), 12–14.

Burrell, B. (1990). *The relationship between child abuse potential and the presence of a family member with a handicap.* Paper presented at the National Council on Family Relations, Seattle, Washington.

Busch, K., Zagar, R., Hughes, J. R., Arbit, J., & Bussell, R. B. (1990). Adolescents who kill. *Journal of Clinical Psychology, 46,* 472–485.

Cadoret, R. J., Leve, L. D., & Devor, E. (1997). Genetics of aggressive and violent behavior. *Psychiatric Clinics of North America, 20*(2), 301–322.

Caesar, P. (1988). Exposure to violence in the families-of-origin among wife-abusers and maritally nonviolent men. *Violence and Victims, 3*(1), 49–64.

Caffaro-Rouget, A., Lang, R., & vanSanten, V. (1989). The impact of child sexual abuse. *Annals of Sex Research, 2*, 29–47.

Calabrese, K. R. (2000). Interpersonal conflict and sarcasm in the workplace. *Genetic, Social & General Psychology Monographs, 126*(4), 459–494.

Calhoun, J. B. (1961). Phenomena associated with population density. *Proceedings of the National Academy of Sciences, 47*, 428–429.

Campbell, S. B. (1994). Hard to manage pre-school boys: Externalizing behavior, social competence, and family context: A two-year followup. *Journal of Abnormal Psychology, 22*(2), 147–167.

Carroll, J. (1977). The intergenerational transmission of family violence: The long-term effects of aggressive behavior. *Aggressive Behavior, 3*, 289–299.

Caspi, A., & Silva, P. (1995). Temperamental qualities at age three predict personality traits in young adulthood: Longitudinal evidence from a birth cohort. *Child Development, 66*(2), 486–498.

Catalano, R. F., Loeber, R., & McKinney, K. C. (1999). *School and community interventions to prevent serious and violent offending.* Juvenile Justice Bulletin (NCJ-177624). Washington, DC: U.S. Department of Justice.

Cate, R. M., Henton, J., Koval, J., Christopher, F. S., & Lloyd, S. (1982). Premarital abuse: A social psychological perspective. *Journal of Family Issues, 3*, 79–90.

Caudill, B., Hoffman, J., Hubbard, R., Flynn, P., & Luckey, J. (1994). Parental history of substance abuse as a risk factor in predicting crack smokers' substance use, illegal activities, and psychiatric status. *American Journal of Drug and Alcohol Abuse, 20*(3), 341–355.

Cazenave, N. A., & Zahn, M. A. (1992). Women, murder, and male domination: Police reports of domestic violence in Chicago and Philadelphia. In E. C. Viano (Ed.), *Intimate violence: Interdisciplinary perspectives* (pp. 83–97). Washington, DC: Hemisphere Publishing Corporation.

Centerwall, B. (1992). Television and violence: The scale of the problem and where to go from here. *Journal of the American Medical Association, 267*(22), 3059–3064.

Cervi, D. (1991). *Wife and child abuse and non-family violence.* Durham, NH: University of New Hampshire Press.

Cherek, D. R., & Lane, S. D. (1999). Effects of dl-fenfluramine on aggressive and impulsive responding in adult males with a history of conduct disorder. *Psychopharmacology, 146*(4), 473–482.

Cherkes-Julkowski, M. (1998). Learning disability, attention-deficit disorder, and language impairment as outcomes of prematurity: A longitudinal descriptive study. *Journal of Learning Disabilities, 31*(3), 294–306.

Cicchetti, D. (1990). A historical perspective on the discipline of developmental psychopathology. In J. Rolf & A. Masten & D. Cicchetti & K. Neuchterlein & S. Weintraub (Eds.), *Risk and protective factors in the development of psychopathology* (pp. 2–28). New York: Cambridge University Press.

Cicchetti, D., & Olson, K. (1990). The developmental psychopathology of child maltreatment. In M. Lewis & S. Miller (Eds.), *Handbook of developmental psychopathology.* New York: Plenum Press.

Clay, D., & Aquila, F. (1994). Gangs and America's schools. *Phi Delta Kappan, 76*, 65–68.

Cleare, A., & Bond, A. (1997). Does central serotonergic function correlate inversely with aggression? A study using D-fenfluramine in healthy subjects. *Psychiatry Research, 69*, 87–95.

Clelland, D., & Carter, T. (1980). The new myth of class and crime. *Criminology, 18*, 319–336.

Clinton, W. (1994). Proclamation 6717—National gang violence prevention week. *Weekly Complication of Presidential Documents, 30*(37), 1750–1752.

Cohen, D., & Strayer, J. (1996). Empathy in conduct-disordered and comparison youth. *Developmental Psychology, 32*(6), 988–998.

Cohen, D. L. (1992, May 20). Children in Boston exposed early to violence. *Education Week,* pp. 11–12.

Cohen, J. M., & Cohen, M. J. (1993). *New Penguin dictionary of quotations.* New York: Penguin Books.

Coleman, J., & Kardash, C. (1999). Encoding and retrieval of ambiguous information by aggressive and nonaggressive elementary boys. *Child Study Journal, 29*(2), 133–150.

Comings, D. (1997). Genetic aspects of childhood behavioral disorders. *Child Psychiatry and Human Development, 27*(3), 139–150.

Conklin, J. (1986). *Criminology* (2nd ed.). New York: Macmillan.

Conte, J., & Schuerman, J. (1987). The effects of sexual abuse on children: A multidimensional view. *Journal of Interpersonal Violence, 2,* 380–390.

Convit, A., Isay, D., Otis, D., & Volavka, J. (1990). Characteristics of repeatedly asaultive psychiatric inpatients. *Hospital and Community Psychiatry, 41*(10), 1112–1115.

Coolidge, F. L., Thede, L., & Jang, K. (1999). *Genetic contributions to personality disorders in childhood.* Paper presented at the 29th annual meeting of the Behavior Genetics Association, Vancouver, B.C., Canada.

Cornwall, A., & Bawden, H. (1992). Reading disabilities and aggression: A critical review. *Journal of Learning Disabilities, 25*(5), 281–288.

Coster, W., Gersten, M., Beeghly, M., & Cicchetti, D. (1989). Communicative functioning in maltreated toddlers. *Developmental Psychology, 25,* 1020–1029.

Crick, N., & Dodge, K. (1996). Social information-processing mechanisms in reactive and proactive aggression. *Child Development, 67*(3), 993–1003.

Curtis, G. C. (1963). Violence breeds violence. *American Journal of Psychiatry, 120,* 386–387.

Dabbs, J. (1995). Testosterone, crime, and misbehavior among 692 male prison immates. *Personality and Individual Differences, 18*(5), 34–40.

Dabbs, J., & Morris, R. (1990). Testosterone, social class, and antisocial behavior in a sample of 4,462 men. *Psychological Science, 1,* 209–211.

Davidson, R., & Putman, K. (2000). Dysfunction in the neural circuitry of emotion regulation—Possible prelude to violence. *Science, 289*(5479), 591–594.

Davis, L. V., & Carlson, B. E. (1987). Observation of spouse abuse: What happens to the children? *Journal of Interpersonal Violence, 2*(3), 278–291.

Davis, R. H. (1995). Cruising for trouble: Gang-related drive-by shootings. *The FBI Law Enforcement Bulletin, 64*(1), 16–23.

Davis, S., & Mares, M.-L. (1998). Effects of talk show viewing on adolescents. *Journal of Communication, 48*(3), 69–87.

Deckel, A., Hesselbrock, V., & Bauer, L. (1996). Antisocial personality disorder, childhood delinquency, and frontal brain-functioning: EEG and neuropsychological findings. *Journal of Clinical Psychology, 52*(6), 639–650.

Dee, J. (1999, January 17). Ax attacker using Lyme disease as defense case intensifies debate over ailment's effects on the brain. *Hartford Courant,* p. 3.

DeFrances, C. J., & Smith, S. (1994). *Crime and neighborhoods* (NCJ-147005). Washington, DC: U.S. Department of Justice.

Deley, W. (1988). Physical punishment of children: Sweden and the USA. *Journal of Comparative Family Studies, 19*(3), 419–431.

Denham, S. A. (1994). Mother–child emotional communication and preschoolers' security of attachment and dependency. *Journal of Genetic Psychology, 155*(1), 119–122.

Denno, D. (1990). *Biology and violence: From birth to adulthood.* New York: Cambridge University Press.

Dhossche, D. M. (1999). Aggression and recent substance abuse: Absence of association in psychiatric emergency room patients. *Comprehensive Psychiatry, 40*(5), 343–346.

DiLalla, L., Mitchell, C., Arthur, M., & Pagliocca, P. (1988). Aggression and delinquency: Family and environmental factors. *Journal of Youth and Adolescence, 17*(3), 233–246.

Dilillo, D., Giuffre, D., Tremblay, G. C., & Peterson, L. (2001). A closer look at the nature of intimate partner violence reported by women with a history of child sexual abuse. *Journal of Interpersonal Violence, 16*(2), 116–133.

Dill, K. (1999). *Violent video game and trait aggression effects on aggressive behavior, thoughts, and feelings, delinquency, and world.* Unpublished doctoral dissertation, University of Missouri, Columbia.

Dillingham, S. D. (1992, April 1). President Bush calls for "renewed investment in fighting violent street crime." In *Bureau of Justice Statistics National Update.* Washington, DC: Bureau of Justice Statistics.

Divoky, D. (1989). Ritalin: Education's fix-it drug? *Phi Delta Kappan, 70*(8), 599–606.

Dodge, K. (1993). Attributional bias in aggressive children. In P. Kendall (Ed.), *Advances in cognitive-behavioral research and therapy* (pp. 73–110). New York: Academic.

Dodge, K., Bates, J., & Pettit, G. (1990). Mechanisms in the cycle of violence. *Science, 250,* 1678–1683.

Dodge, K. A., Price, J. M., Bachorowski, J., & Newman, J. P. (1990). Hostile attributional biases in severely aggressive adolescents. *Journal of Abnormal Psychology, 99*(4), 385–392.

Downey, G., & Walker, E. (1989). Social cognition and adjustment in children at risk for psychopathology. *Developmental Psychology, 25*(5), 835–845.

Draijer, N., & Langeland, W. (1999). Childhood trauma and perceived parental dysfunction in the etiology of dissociative symptoms. *American Journal of Psychiatry, 156*(3), 379–386.

Dumas, J. E., & Neese, D. E. (1996). Short-term stability of aggression, peer rejection, and depressive symptoms in middle childhood. *Journal of Abnormal Child Psychology, 24*(1), 105–120.

Duncan, R. D. (1999). Peer and sibling aggression: An investigation of intra- and extra-familial bullying. *Journal of Interpersonal Violence, 14*(8), 871.

Eberly, M. B., & Montemayor, R. (1999). Adolescent affection and helpfulness toward parents: A 2-year follow-up. *Journal of Early Adolescence, 19*(2), 226–249.

Egeland, B., Jacobvitz, D., & Sroufe, L. A. (1988). Breaking the cycle of abuse: Relationship predictions. *Child Development, 59,* 1080–1088.

Eley, T., Lichtenstein, P., & Stenvenson, J. (1999). Sex differences in the etiology of aggressive and nonaggressive antisocial behavior: Results from two twin studies. *Child Developement, 70*(1), 155–168.

Ellement, J. (1995, November 1). Dedham man arraigned in rape, murder of friends' disabled sister. *The Boston Globe,* p. 18.

Elliot, D., & Ageton, S. (1980). Reconciling race and class differences in self-reported and official estimates of delinquency. *American Soiological Review, 45,* 95–110.

Elliott, F. A. (1978). Neurological aspects of antisocial behavior. In W. H. Reid (Ed.), *The psychopath* (pp. 146–189). New York: Bruner/Mazel.

Ellis, E. M., Calhoun, K. S., & Atkeson, B. M. (1980). Sexual dysfunctions in victims of rape: Victims may experience a loss of sexual arousal and frightening flashbacks even one year after the assault. *Women and Health, 5,* 39–47.

Ellis, L. (1990). Left- and mixed-handedness and criminality: Explanations for a probable relationship. In S. Coren (Ed.), *Left-handedness: Behavioral implications and anomalies* (pp. 485–505). North Holland: Elsevier Science Publishers B.V.

Ellis, L. (1991). Monoamine oxidase and criminality: Identifying an apparent biological marker for antisocial behavior. *Journal of Research in Crime and Delinquency, 28*(2), 227–251.

Emotion and temperament. (2001). *Developmental Science, 4*(3), 313–330.

Engfer, A., & Schneewind, K. (1982). Causes and consequences of harsh parental punishment: An empirical investigation in a representative sample of 570 German families. *Child Abuse & Neglect, 6*(2), 129–139.

Englander, E. (1997). *Understanding violence.* Mahwah, NJ: Lawrence Erlbaum Associates.

Entner Wright, B. R., & Caspi, A. (1999). Reconsidering the relationship between SES and delinquency: Causation but not correlation. *Criminology, 37*(1), 175.

Eron, L. (1982). Parent–child interaction, television violence, and aggression of children. *American Psychologist, 37*(2), 197–211.

Eron, L. D. (1987). The development of aggressive behavior from the perspective of a developing behaviorism. *American Psychologist, 42*, 435–442.

Escovar, L., & Escovar, P. (1985). Retrospective perception of child-rearing practices in three culturally different college groups. *International Journal of Intercultural Relations, 9*(1), 31–49.

Evans, G., & Lepore, S. (1993). Household crowding and social support: A quasiexperimental analysis. *Journal of Personality and Social Psychology, 65*(2), 308–317.

Evans, G., Lepore, S., Shejwal, B., & Palsane, M. (1998). Chronic residential crowding and children's well-being: An ecological perspective. *Child Development, 69*(6), 1514–1515.

Fagan, J., & Chin, K. (1989). Initiation into crack and cocaine: A tale of two epidemics. *Contemporary Drug Problems, 16*(4), 579–617.

Fagan, J., & Wexler, S. (1987). Crime at home and in the streets: The relationship between family and stranger violence. *Violence and Victims, 2*(1), 5–23.

Fagan, J. A., Stewart, D. K., & Hansen, K. V. (1983). Violent men or violent husbands: Background factors and situational correlates. In D. Finkelhor (Ed.), *The dark side of families: Current family violence research.* Beverly Hills, CA: Sage Publications.

Farnham-Diggory, S. (1978). *Learning disabilities.* Cambridge, MA: Harvard University Press.

Farrington, D. P. (1978). The family backgrounds of aggressive youths. In L. A. Hersov & M. Berger & D. Schaffer (Eds.), *Aggression and anti-social behavior in childhood and adolescence* (pp. 73–93). Oxford: Pergamon.

Faulk, M. (1974). Men who assault their wives. *Medicine, Science and the Law, 14*(18), 1–13.

Federal Bureau of Investigation. (189). *Uniform crime reports.* Washington, DC: Author.

Fergusson, D., & Horwood, L. J. (1995). Early disruptive behavior, IQ, and later school achievement and delinquent behavior. *Journal of Abnormal Child Psychology, 23*(2), 183–200.

Ferrari, J., & Parker, J. (1992). High school achievement, self-efficacy, and locus of control as predictors of freshman academic performance. *Psychological Reports, 71*(2), 515–519.

Feshbach, N. (1980). Tomorrow is here today in Sweden. *Journal of Child Clinical Psychology, 9*(2), 109–112.

Finkelhor, D. (1988). An epidemiologic approach to the study of child molestation. In R. Prentky & V. Quinsey (Eds.), *Human sexual aggression: Current perspectives* (pp. 136–142). New York: Annals of the New York Academy of Sciences.

Finkelhor, D., & Yllo, K. (1985). *License to rape.* New York: Hold, Rinehart & Winston.

Fischer, M., & Newby, R. F. (1991). Assessment of stimulant response in ADHD children using a refined multimethod clinical protocol (Attention Deficit Hyperactivity Disorder) (Special issue on child psychopharmacology). *Journal of Clinical Child Psychology, 20*(3), 232–245.

Fishbein, D. H. (1992). The psychology of female aggression. *Criminal Justice and Behavior, 19*(2), 99–126.

Fisher, L., & Blair, R. (1998). Cognitive impairment and its relationships to psychopathic tendencies in children with emotional and behavioral difficulties. *Journal of Abnormal Child Psychology, 26*(6), 511–520.

Fitzpatrick, K. (1999). Violent victimization among America's school children. *Journal of Interpersonal Violence, 14*(10), 1055–1068.

Flynn, J. D. (1977). Recents finds related to wife abuse. *Social Casework, 58,* 17–18.

Fogel, C. A., Mednick, S. A., & Michelsen, N. (1985). Hyperactive behavior and minor physical anomalies. *Acta Psychiatrica Scandinavia, 75*, 551–556.

Follingstad, D. (1980). A reconceptualization of issues in the treatment of abused women: A case study. *Psychotherapy: Theory, Research and Practice, 17*, 294–303.

Foote, J. (1997). *Expert panel issues report on serious and violent juvenile offenders.* Washington, DC: U.S. Department of Justice.

Forsstrom-Cohen, B., & Rosenbaum, A. (1985). The effects of parental marital violence on young adults: An exploratory investigation. *Journal of Marriage and the Family, May,* 467–472.

Foshee, V. A., Bauman, K. E., & Linder, G. F. (1999). Family violence and the perpetration of adolescent dating violence: Examining social learning and social control processes. *Journal of Marriage & the Family, 61*(2), 331–343.

Fox, J. A., & Zawitz, M. W. (1999). *Homicide trends in the United States.* Washington, DC: U.S. Department of Justice.

Francis, C., Hughes, H., & Hitz, L. (1992). Physically abusive parents and the 16-PF: A preliminary psychological typology. *Child Abuse & Neglect, 16*(5), 673–692.

Frankel, M. (1992). Suicide highest in wide-open spaces. *American Demographics, 14*(4), 9(1).

Freedman, J. L. (1975). *Crowding and behavior.* San Francisco: W.H. Freeman.

Freedman, J. L., Levy, A., Buchanan, R. W., & Price, J. (1972). Crowding and human aggressiveness. *Journal of Experimental Social Psychology, 8,* 528–548.

Freeh, L. J. (1995). *Uniform crime report press release.* Washington, DC: U.S. Department of Justice.

Freyne, A., & O'Connor, A. (1992). XYY genotype and crime. *Medicine, Science and the Law, 32*(3), 261.

Friedrich, L., & Stein, A. H. (1973). Aggressive and prosocial television programs and the natural behavior of preschool children. *Monographs of the Society for Research in Child Development, 38,* 151.

Friedt, L., & Gouvier, W. (1989). Bender Gestalt screening for brain dysfunction in a forensic population. *Criminal Justice & Behavior, 16*(4), 455.

Frieze, I. H., & Browne, A. (1989). Violence in marriage. In L. Ohlin & M. Tonry (Eds.), *Family violence* (Vol. 11, pp. 163–218). Chicago: University of Chicago Press.

Futterman, A., & Zirkel, S. (1992). Men are not born to rape. *Behavioral and Brain Sciences, 15*(2), 385–387.

Gaes, G. (1994). Prison crowding research reexamined. *Prison Journal, 74*(3), 329–364.

Gainetdinov, R. R., & Wetsel, W. C. (1999). Role of serotonin in the paradoxical calming effect of psychostimulants on hyperactivity. *Science, 283*(5400), 397.

Gallagher, W. (1994, September). How we become what we are. *The Atlantic Monthly, 274,* 38(12).

Garbarino, J. (1999). How we can save violent boys. *Education Digest, 65*(4), 28–33.

Gardner, S., & Timmons-Mitchell, J. (1990). Facilitating capable parenting among Black single mothers in violent families. In E. C. Viano (Ed.), *The victimology handbook* (pp. 275–284). New York: Garland Publishing.

Garrett, D. (1997). Co-victimization among African-American adolescents. *Adolescence, 32*(127), 635–639.

Garrison, W. T., & Earls, F. J. (1987). *Temperament and child psychopathology* (Vol. 12). Newbury Park, CA: Sage Publications.

Gaustad, J. (1990). Gangs. *ERIC Digest, 52,* 1–4.

Gaustad, J. (1991). Schools attack the root of violence. *ERIC Digest, 63,* 1–4.

Gayford, J. J. (1975). Ten types of battered wives. *Welfare Officer, 25,* 5–9.

Gayford, J. J. (1983). Battered wives. In R. J. Gelles & C. Pedrick Cornell (Eds.), *International perspectives on family violence* (pp. 234–257). Lexington, MA: Lexington Books.

Gelles, R. (1974). *The violent home: A study of physical aggression between husbands and wives.* Beverly Hills, CA: Sage Publications.

Gelles, R. (1978). Violence towards children in the United States. *American Journal of Orthopsychiatry, 48*(4), 580–592.

Gelles, R. (1985). Family violence. *Annual Review of Sociology, 11,* 347–367.

Gelles, R. J., & Pedrick Cornell, C. (Eds.). (1983). *International perspectives on family violence.* Lexington, MA: Lexington Books.

George, D., Hibbeln, J., Ragan, P., Umhau, J., Phillips, M., Doty, L., Hommer, D., & Rawling, R. (2000). Lactate-induced rage and panic in a select group of subjects who perpetrate acts of domestic violence. *Biological Psychiatry, 47,* 804–812.

Gerbner, G. (1990). Stories that hurt: Tobacco, alcohol, and other drugs in the mass media. In H. Resnik (Ed.), *Youth and drugs: Society's mixed messages* (pp. 174). Rockville, MD: U.S. Department of Health and Human Services.

Gerstein, L. (2000). In India, poverty and lack of education are associated with men's physical and sexual abuse of their wives. *International Family Planning Perspectives, 26*(1), 44.

Geschwind, N., & Galaburda, A. M. (1987). *Cerebral lateralization: Biological mechanisms, associations, and pathology.* Cambridge, MA: MIT Press.

Geyelin, M. (1993, August 11). Sex-predator law upheld. *The Wall Street Journal,* p. B2.

Giancola, P., & Zeichner, A. (1994). Neuropsychological performance on tests of frontal-lobe functioning and aggressive behavior in men. *Journal of Abnormal Psychology, 103*(4), 832–836.

Giannini, A. J., Miller, N., Loiselle, R., & Turner, C. (1993). Cocaine-associated violence and relationship to route of administration. *Journal of Substance Abuse Treatment, 10*(1), 67–70.

Gibby-Smith, B. M. (1995). Correlations of grade point averages at a rural college with reports of abuse in rural families. *Psychological Reports, 77*(2), 619–621.

Gidycz, C. A., Coble, C. N., Latham, L., & Layman, M. J. (1993). Sexual assault experience in adulthood and prior victimization experiences: A prospective analysis. *Psychology of Women Quarterly, 17*(2), 151–169.

Gidycz, C. A., Hanson, K., & Layman, M. (1995). A prospective analysis of the relationships among sexual assault experiences: An extension of previous findings. *Psychology of Women Quarterly, 19*(1), 5–30.

Gil, D. (1971). Violence against children. *Journal of Marriage and the Family, 33,* 637–648.

Gladwell, M. (1995, January 16). N.J. law on released sex offenders proves problematic; ex-inmates must report addresses, but enforcement is burdensome; some are harassed. *The Washington Post,* p. A6.

Glickauf-Hughes, C., & Wells, M. (1991). Current conceptualizations on masochism: Genesis and object relations. *American Journal of Psychotherapy, 45*(1), 53(16).

Goldman, H. (1977). The limits of clockwork: The neurobiology of violent behavior. In J. P. Conrad & S. Dinitz (Eds.), *In fear of each other* (pp. 226–237). Lexington, MA: Lexington Books.

Goldstein, A. P., Keller, H., & Erne, D. (1985). *Changing the abusive parent.* Champaign, IL: Research Press.

Goldstein, P., Bellucci, P., Spunt, B., & Miller, T. (1991). Volume of cocaine use and violence: A comparision between men and women. *Journal of Drug Issues, 21*(2), 345–368.

Gortmaker, S., Salter, C., Walker, D., & Dietz, W. (1990). The impact of television viewing on mental aptitude and achievement: A longitudinal study. *Public Opinion Quarterly, 54*(4), 594–605.

Gottfredson, M., & Hirschi, T. (1995). National crime control policies. *Society, 32*(2), 30–37.

Gove, W. R., Hughes, M., & Galle, O. R. (1979). Overcrowding in the home: An empirical investigation of its possible pathological consequences. *American Sociological Review, 44*(February), 59–80.

Grace, J. (1994, September 12). There are no children here. *Time, 144,* 44–45.

Graff, T. T. (1979). *Personality characteristics of battered women.* Unpublished doctoral thesis, Brigham Young University, Provo, UT.

Greenfeld, L. A. (1992). *Prisons and prisoners in the United States* (NCJ-137002). Washington, DC: U.S. Department of Justice.

Greenfeld, L. A. (1996). *Child victimizers: Violent offenders and their victims* (153258). Washington, DC: U.S. Department of Justice.

Greenwood, P. (1995). Juvenile crime and juvenile justice. In J. Q. Wilson & J. Petersilia (Eds.), *Crime* (pp. 91–117). San Francisco, CA: ICS Press.

Greven, P. (1991). *Spare the child: The religious roots of physical punishment and the psychological impact of physical abuse.* New York: Knopf.

Griffiths, M. (1999). Violent video games and aggression: A review of the literature. *Aggression & Violent Behavior, 4*(2), 203–212.

Grimes, P., & Rogers, K. E. (1999). Truth-in-sentencing, law enforcement, and inmate population growth. *Journal of Socio-Economics, 28*(6), pp. 745–800.

Grof, P. (2001). Mood and temperament. *Canadian Journal of Psychiatry, 46*(1), 84–86.

Groth, A. N. (1979). *Men who rape: The psychology of the offender.* New York: Plenum.

Grusec, J. E., & Goodnow, J. J. (1994). Impact of parental discipline methods on the child's internalization of values: A reconceptualization of current points of view. *Developmental Psychology, 30*(1), 4(16).

Guillette, E., Meza, M., Aquilar, M., Soto, A., & Garcia, I. (1998). An anthropological approach to the evaluation of preschool children exposed to pesticides in Mexico. *Environmental Health, 106*(6), 347–353.

Guns, lies, and videotape. (1999). *Lancet, 354*(9178), 525.

Haddad, J. D., Barocas, R., & Hollenbeck, A. R. (1991). Family organization and parent attitudes of children with conduct disorder. *Journal of Clinical Child Psychology, 20*(2), 152–162.

Hagedorn, J. M. (1994). Homeboys, dope friends, legits, and new jacks (gang members and drug dealing). *Criminology, 32*(2), 197–219.

Halford, W. K., Sanders, M. R., & Behrens, B. C. (2000). Repeating the errors of our parents? Family-of-origin spouse violence and observed conflict. *Family Process, 39*(2), 219–236.

Halperin, J. M., & Newcorn, J. H. (1997). Serotonin, aggression, and parental psychopathology in children with attention-deficit. *Journal of the American Academy of Child & Adolescent Psychiatry, 36*(10), 1391–1399.

Hamberger, L. K., & Hastings, J. E. (1990). Recidivism following spouse abuse abatement counseling: Treatment program implications. *Violence and Victims, 5*, 157–169.

Hanley, R. (1995, March 1). Decision by judge in New Jersey deals setback to "Megan's Law." *The New York Times*, p. A1.

Hannon, L. D., & Defronzo, J. (1998). The truly disadvantaged, public assistance, and crime. *Social Problems, 45*(3), 383–392.

Hare, R. (1996). Psychopathy: A clinical construct whose time has come. *Criminal Justice and Behavior, 23*(1), 24–54.

Harnish, J. (1998). *The influence of socioeconomic status and neighborhood crime level on child externalizing behavior problems: The compensatory, protective, and mediational roles of parenting practices.* Unpublished doctoral thesis, Vanderbilt University, Nashville, TN.

Harris, M. (1992). Television viewing, aggression, and ethnicity. *Psychological Reports, 70*(1), 137–139.

Hart, J. (1995, November 19). Teacher, 78, punched as classmates cheer. *The Boston Globe*, pp. 37–41.

Haskett, M., Johnson, C., & Miller, J. (1994). Individual differences in risk of child abuse by adolescent mothers: Assessment in the perinatal period. *Journal of Child Psychology and Psychiatry and Allied Disciplines, 35*(3), 461–477.

Hassell, R. A. (1981). *The impact of stranger versus nonstranger rape: A longitudinal study.* Paper presented at the eighth annual conference of the Association for Women in Psychology, Boston, MA.

Hay, D. F., & Castle, J. (2000). Toddlers' Use of Force against Familiar Peers: A Precursor of Serious Aggression? *Child Development, 71*(2), 457–468.

Hazzard, A., Celano, M., Gould, J., Lawry, S., & Webb, C. (1995). Predicting symptomatology and self-blame among child sex abuse victims. *Child Abuse and Neglect, 19*(6), 707–708.

Hegar, R. L., Zuravin, S., & Orme, J. (1994). Factors predicting severity of physical child abuse injury. *Journal of Interpersonal Violence, 9*(2), 170–184.

Heimer, K. (1997). Socioeconomic status, subcultural definitions, and violent delinquency. *Social Forces, 75*(3), 799–833.

Heimer, K., & Matsueda, R. (1994). Role-taking, role committment, and delinquency: A theory of differential social control. *American Sociological Review, 59*(3), 365–391.

Henderson, M. (1983). An empirical classification of non-violent offenders using the MMPI. *Personality and Individual Differences, 4*, 671–677.

Herrenkohl, T., Huang, B., Kosterman, R., Hawkins, J. D., Catalano, R. F., & Smith, B. H. (2001). A comparison of social development processes leading to violent behavior in late adolescence for childhood initiators and adolescent initiators of violence. *Journal of Research in Crime & Delinquency, 38*(1), 45–64.

Herrera, V. M., & McCloskey, L. A. (2001). Gender differences in the risk for delinquency among youth exposed to family violence. *Child Abuse & Neglect, 25*(8), 1037–1053.

Herschel, M. (1978). Dyslexia revisited. *Human genetics, 40,* 115–134.

Hewitt, J. D. (1988). The victim–offender relationship in convicted homicide cases: 1960–1984. *Journal of Criminal Justice, 16,* 25–33.

Himelein, M. J., Vogel, R. E., & Wachowiak, D. G. (1994). Nonconsensual sexual experiences in precollege women: Prevalence and risk factors. *Journal of Counseling and Development, 72*(4), 411–416.

Hinshaw, S., & Owens, E. (2000). Family processes and treatment outcome in the MTA: negative/ ineffective parenting practices. *Journal of Abnormal Child Psychology, 28*(6), 555.

Hirschi, T. (1969). *Causes of delinquency.* Berkeley: University of California Press.

Hirschi, T. (1990). Control: Society's central notion. *The American Journal of Sociology, 96*(3), 750–753.

Hobbes, T. (1651). *The Leviathan* (Chapter XIII).

Horan, S. (1992). The XYY supermale and the criminal justice system: A square peg in a round hole. *Loyola of Los Angeles Law Review, 24*(4), 1343.

Hotaling, G. T., Straus, M. A., & Lincoln, A. J. (1989). Intrafamily violence, and crime and violence outside the family. In L. Ohlin & M. Tonry (Eds.), *Family Violence* (pp. 315–375). Chicago: University of Chicago Press.

Hotaling, G. T., & Sugarman, D. B. (1986). An analysis of risk markers in husband-to-wife violence: The current state of knowledge. *Violence and Victims, 1*(2), 101–124.

Houston, R., & Stanford, M. (2001). Mid-latency evoked potentials in self-reported impulsive aggression. *International Journal of Psychophysiology, 40,* 1–15.

Hubbard, J. A., & Newcomb, A. F. (1991). Initial dyadic peer interaction of attention deficit-hyperactivity disorder and normal boys. *Journal of Abnormal Child Psychology, 19*(2), 179–197.

Hudziak, J., Rudiger, L., Neale, M., Heath, A., & Todd, R. (2000). A twin study of inattentive, aggressive, and anxious/depressed behaviors. *Journal of the American Academy of Child and Adolescent Psychiatry, 39,* 469–476.

Huesmann, L., Eron, L., Lefkowitz, M., & Walder, L. (1984). Stability of aggression of time and generations. *Developmental Psychology, 20*(6), 1120–1134.

Huesmann, L. R., & Eron, L. D. (1986). *Television and the aggressive child: A cross national comparison.* Hillsdale, NJ: Lawrence Erlbaum Associates.

Hughes, J., Zagar, R., Sylvies, R. B., Arbit, J., Busch, K. G., & Bowers, N. D. (1991). Medical, family, and scholastic conditions in urban delinquents. *Journal of Clinical Psychology, 47*(3), 448–464.

Hull, J. D. (1993, February 8). The knife in the book bag. *Time,* p. 37.

Humphrey, J. A., & Palmer, S. (1987). Race, sex, and criminal homicide offender–victim relationships. *Journal of Black Studies, 18,* 45–57.

Hunt, G., & Joe-Laidler, K. (2001). Situations of violence in the lives of girl gang members. *Health Care for Women International, 22*(4), 123–127.

Huston, A., Watkins, B., & Kunkel, D. (1989). Public policy and children's television. *American Psychology, 44,* 424–433.

Huston, A., Wright, J., Rice, M., Kerkman, D., & St.Peters, M. (1990). Development of television viewing patterns in early childhood: A longitudinal investigation. *Developmental Psychology, 26*(3), 409–421.

Inciardi, J., & Pottieger, A. (1994). Crack-cocaine use and street crime. *Journal of Drug Issues, 24*(1–2), 273–293.

Irwin, A. R., & Gross, A. (1995). Cognitive tempo, violent video games, and aggressive behavior in young boys. *Journal of Family Violence, 10*(3), 337–350.

Jackson, J. K. (1958). Alcoholism and the family. *Annals of the American Academy of Political and Social Science, 315,* 90–98.

Jackson, K. L. (1997). Differences in the background and criminal justice characteristics of young Black, White and Hispanic male federal prison inmates. *Journal of Black Studies, 27*(4), 494–509.

Jacobvitz, D., & Sroufe, L. A. (1987). The early caregiver–child relationship and attention deficit disorder with hyperactivity in kindergarten. *Child Development, 58,* 1488–1495.

Janokowski, G. (1985, September 30). Direct causal relationship between TV and undesirable behavior yet to be proven. *Television-Radio Age, 33,* 65.

Jellinek, M., Murphy, J. M., Poitrast, F., Quinn, D., Bishop, S. J., & Goshko, M. (1992). Serious child mistreatment in Massachusetts: The course of 206 children through the courts. *Child Abuse & Neglect, 16,* 179–185.

Jennings, P. (1999, May 20). School shooting in Conyers, Georgia. New York: ABC News, *World News Tonight with Peter Jennings.*

Johannesson, I. (1974). Aggressive behavior among school children related to maternal practices in early childhood. In J. de Wit & W. W. Hartup (Eds.), *Determinants and origins of aggressive behavior* (pp. 413–425). The Hague: Mouton.

Johnson, J. (1991). The oldest DNA in the world. *New Scientist, 130*(1768), 44–49.

Jones, D. (1995). Editorial: Parental empathy, emotionality, and the potential for child abuse. *Child Abuse & Neglect, 19*(6), 765–767.

Jones, E. (1955). *The life and work of Sigmund Freud* (Vol. 2). New York: Basic Books.

Jones, J. (1990, October). Violent statistics. *APA Monitor,* p. 3.

Jouriles, E. N., & Norwood, W. D. (1995). Physical aggression toward boys and girls in families characterized by the battering of women. *Journal of Family Psychology, 9*(1), 69–78.

Juss, S. (1997). Modest link between mental illness and violence. *Lancet, 349*(9047), 263–264.

Kagan, J. (1988). The meanings of personality predicates. *American Psychologist, 438,* 614–620.

Kahn, A. S., Mathie, V. A., & Torgler, C. (1994). Rape scripts and rape acknowledgement. *Psychology of Women Quarterly, 18*(1), 53(14).

Kalof, L. (1993). Rape-supportive attitudes and sexual victimization experiences of sorority and nonsorority women. *Sex Roles: A Journal of Research, 29*(11–12), 767–781.

Kandel, E. (1987). *IQ as a protective factor for subjects at high risk for anti-social behavior.* Paper presented at the Western Psychological Association Convention, Long Beach, CA.

Kandel, E. (1988). *Minor physical anomalies and parental modeling of aggression predict violent criminal behavior.* Paper presented at the American Association for the Advancement of Science, Boston, MA.

Kandel, E. (1989). Genetic and perinatal factors in anti-social personality in a birth cohort. *Journal of Crime and Justice, 12*(2), 61–78.

Kandel, E., Brennan, P., & Mednick, S. A. (1989). Minor physical anomalies and recidivistic adult violent offending: Evidence from a birth cohort. *Acta Psychiatrica Scandinavia, 79,* 103–107.

Kandel, E., & Freed, D. (1989). Frontal lobe dysfunction and antisocial behavior: A review. *Journal of Clinical Psychology, 45*(3), 404–413.

Kandel, E., & Mednick, S. A. (1989). *The relationship between perinatal factors, hyperactivity, and violent offending.* Paper presented at the National Institute of Justice Conference on Violence, Palm Springs, CA.

Kandel, E., & Mednick, S. A. (1991). Perinatal factors predict violent offending. *Criminology, 29*(3), 101–111.

Kandel, E., Mednick, S. A., Sorensen, L. K., Hutchings, B., Knop, J., Rosenberg, R., & Schulsinger, F. (1988). High IQ as a protective factor for subjects at high risk for anti-social behavior. *Journal of Consulting and Clinical Psychology, 56*(2), 224–226.

Kandel-Englander, E. (1992). Wife-battering and violence outside the family. *Journal of Interpersonal Violence, 7*(4), 462–470.

Kang, S., Magura, S., & Shapiro, J. L. (1994). Correlates of cocaine/crack use among inner-city incarcerated adolescents. *American Journal of Drug and Alcohol Abuse, 20*(4), 413–430.

Kaufman Kantor, G., & Straus, M. (1987). The "drunken bum" theory of wife beating. *Social Problems, 34*(3), 213–231.

Kelleher, K., Chaffin, M., Hollenberg, J., & Fischer, E. (1994). Alcohol and drug disorders among physically abusive and neglectful parents in a community-based sample. *The American Journal of Public Health, 84*(10), 1586–1591.

Kelley, B. T., Thornberry, T. P., & Smith, C. A. (1997). *In the wake of childhood maltreatment.* Washington, DC: U.S. Department of Justice, Office of Justice Programs, Office of Juvenile Justice and Delinquency Prevention.

Kelley, S. (1992). Parenting stress and child maltreatment in drug-exposed children. *Child Abuse & Neglect, 16*(3), 317–330.

Kempe, C. H., Silverman, F. N., & Steele, B. F. (1962). The battered child syndrome. *Journal of the American Medical Association, 181*(17), 39–42.

Kemper, T., & Reichler, M. (1976). Marital satisfaction and conjugal power as determinants of intensity and frequency of rewards and punishments administered by parents. *Journal of Genetic Psychology, 129*(2), 221–234.

Kendall-Tackett, K. A., Williams, L., & Finkelhor, D. (1993). Impact of sexual abuse on children: A review and synthesis of recent empirical studies. *Psychological Bulletin, 113*(1), 164–180.

Killory, J. F. (1974). In defense of corporal punishment. *Psychological Reports, 35,* 575–581.

Kilpatrick, D. G. (1993). Rape and other forms of sexual assault. *Journal of Interpersonal Violence, 8*(2), 193–198.

Kim, J., & Rubin, A. (1997). The variable influence of audience activity on media effects. *Communication, 24,* 107–135.

Kingston, L., & Prior, M. (1995). The development of patterns of stable, transient, and school-age onset aggressive behavior in young children. *Journal of the American Academy of Child & Adolescent Psychiatry, 34*(3), 348–358.

Kirkegaard-Sorenson, L., & Mednick, S. A. (1977). A prospective study of predictors of criminality: 4. School behavior. In S. A. Mednick & K. O. Christiansen (Eds.), *Biosocial bases of criminal behavior* (pp. 255–266). New York: Gardner Press.

Klaus, K. (1994). Crime statistics. *Congressional Digest, 73*(6–7), 167–170.

Knox, M., King, C., Hanna, G., Logan, D., & Ghaziuddin, N. (2000). Aggressive behavior in clinically depressed adolescents. *Journal of the American Academy of Child and Adolescent Psychiatry, 39*(5), 611–618.

Kohn, A. (1989, November). Suffer the restless children: Though nearly a million children are regularly given drugs to control "hyperactivity," we know little about what the disorder is, or whether it is really a disorder at all. *The Atlantic, 264,* 90–98.

Koppel, T. (1998, August 6). Crime and punishment, Part I. New York: ABC News, *Nightline Special Report.*

Kosky, R. (1983). Childhood suicidal behavior. *Journal of Child Psychology & Psychiatry & Allied Disciplines, 24*(3), 457–468.

Koss, M., Gidycz, C., & Wisniewski, N. (1987). The scope of rape: Incidence and prevalence of sexual aggression and victimization in a national sample of higher education students. *Journal of Consulting & Clinical Psychology, 55,* 162–170.

Koss, M. P., & Gaines, J. A. (1993). The prediction of sexual aggression by alcohol use, athletic participation, and fraternity affiliation. *Journal of Interpersonal Violence, 8*(1), 94–108.

Kroeker, M., & Haut, F. (1995). A tale of two cities: The street gangs of Paris and Los Angeles. *The Police Chief, 62*(5), 32–38.

Kruesi, M. J., & Jacobsen, T. (1997). Serotonin and human violence: Do environmental mediators exist? In A. Raine & P. Brennan (Eds.), *Biosocial bases of violence* (Vol. 292, pp. 189–205). New York: Plenum Press.

Krynicki, V. E. (1978). Cerebral dysfunction in repetitively assaultive adolescents. *Journal of Nervous and Mental Disease, 166,* 59–67.

Kunitz, S. J., & Levy, J. E. (1998). Alcohol dependence and domestic violence as sequelae of abuse and conduct disorder in childhood. *Child Abuse & Neglect, 22*(11), 1079–1092.

Kyriacou, D. N., Anglin, D., Taliaferro, E., Stone, S., Tubb, T., Linden, J. A., Muelleman, R., Barton, E., & Kraus, J. F. (1999). Risk factors for injury to women from domestic violence. *New England Journal of Medicine, 341*(25), 1892–1898.

Lance, L. M., & Ross, C. E. (2000). Views of violence in American sports: A study of college students. *College Student Journal, 34*(2), 191–200.

Landrigan, P., Claudio, L., Markowitz, S., Berkowitz, G., Brenner, B., Romero, H., Wetmur, J., Matte, T., Gore, A., Godbold, J., & Wolff, M. (1999). Pesticides and inner-city children: Exposures, risks, and preventions. *Environmental Health Perspectives, 107*(3), 431–437.

Lane, K., & Gwartney-Gibbs, P. (1985). Violence in the context of dating and sex. *Journal of Family Issues, 6,* 45–59.

Langan, P. A., & Innes, C. A. (1986). *Preventing domestic violence against women.* Washington, DC: U.S. Department of Justice.

Langhinrichsen-Rohling, J., Neidig, P., & Thorn, G. (1995). Violent marriages: Gender differences in levels of current violence and past abuse. *Journal of Family Violence, 10*(2), 159–175.

Lanier, C. A., & Elliott, M. N. (1998). Evaluation of an intervention to change attitudes. *College Teaching, 46*(2), 76–79.

LaPierre, D., Claude, M., Braun, J., & Hodgins, S. (1995). Recognition of emotion in facial psychopathy: Neuropsychological test findings. *Neuropsychologia, 33*(2), 5–9.

Larkin, M. (2000). Violent video games increase aggression. *Lancet, 355*(9214), 1525.

Larsen, J. (2001). *Bad boys, bad men.* London: Oxford University Press.

Larzelere, R. (1986). Moderate spanking: Model or deterrent of children's aggression in the family? *Journal of Family Violence, 1*(1), 27–36.

Lau, M., Pihl, R., & Peterson, J. (1995). Provocation, acute alcohol intoxication, cognitive performance, and aggression. *Journal of Abnormal Psychology, 104*(1), 150–156.

Lee, M. R. (2000). Concentrated poverty, race and homicide. *Sociological Quarterly, 41*(2), 189.

Lee, N. (1995). Culture conflict and crime in Alaskan native villages. *Journal of Criminal Justice, 23*(2), 177–189.

Lefkowitz, M., Eron, L., Walder, L., & Huesmann, L. (1977). *Growing up to be violent: A longitudinal study of the development of aggression.* New York: Pergamon.

Lefkowitz, M., Walder, L., & Eron, L. (1963). Punishment, identification, and aggression. *Merrill Palmer Quarterly, 9,* 159–174.

Lesnik-Oberstein, M., Koers, A. J., & Cohen, L. (1995). Parental hostility and its sources in psychologically abusive mothers: A test of the three factor theory. *Child Abuse & Neglect, 19*(1), 33–50.

Levine, M. (1975). Interparental violence and its effects on the children: A study of 50 families in general practice. *Medicine, Science and Law, 15,* 172–176.

Leviton, H. (1976). The individualization of discipline for behavior disorder pupils. *Psychology in the Schools, 13*(4), 445–448.

Lewis, D., Moy, E., Jackson, L. D., Aaronson, R., Ritvo, U., Settu, S., & Simons, A. (1985). Biopsychosocial characteristics of children who later murder: A prospective study. *American Journal of Psychiatry, 142,* 1161–1166.

Lewis, D., Shanok, S., & Balla, D. (1979). Perinatal difficulties, head and face trauma, and child abuse in the medical histories of seriously delinquent children. *American Journal of Psychiatry, 136,* 419–423.

Lewis, D. O., Pincus, J. H., Bard, B., Richardson, E., Prichep, L. S., Feldman, M., & Yeager, C. (1988). Neuropsychiatric, psychoeducational, and family characteristics of 14 juveniles condemned to death in the United States. *American Journal of Psychiatry, 145*(5), 584–589.

Lewis, D. O., Pincus, J. H., Feldman, M., Jackson, L., & Bard, B. (1986). Psychiatric, neurological, and psychoeducational characteristics of 15 death row inmates in the United States. *American Journal of Psychiatry, 143*(7), 838–845.

Lindgren, C. (1990). *Justice expenditure and employment.* Washington, DC: U.S. Department of Justice.

Linz, D., Donnerstein, E., & Adams, S. (1989). Physiological desensitization and judgement about female victims of violence. *Human Communications Research, 15*(4), 509–523.

Lockwood, D. (1997). *Violence among middle school and high school students: Analysis and implications for prevention* (Report Number 81[5]). Washington, DC: National Institute of Justice.

Loeber, R., & Hay, D. (1997). Key issues in the development of aggression and violence from childhood to early adulthood. *Annual Review of Psychology, 48*, 371–411.

Lonsway, K. A., & Fitzgerald, L. F. (1994). Rape myths: In review. *Psychology of Women Quarterly, 18*(2), 133–165.

Loosen, P., Purdon, S., & Pavlou, S. (1994). Effects on behavior of modulation of gonadal function in men with gonadaltropin-releasing antagonists. *American Journal of Psychiatry, 151*(2).

Los Solidos Nation. (1995). Family values: The gangster version. *Harper's Magazine, 290*(1739), 18–21.

Lowenstein, L. (1977). The value of corporal punishment. *News and Views, 3*(4), 14–15.

Loza, W., & Loza-Fanous, A. (1999). Anger and prediction of violent and nonviolent offender's recidivism. *Journal of Interpersonal Violence, 14*(10), 1014–1029.

Lykken, D. T. (1998). The case for parental licensure. In T. S. Millon (Ed.), *Psychopathy: Antisocial, criminal, and violent behavior* (pp. 122–143). New York: Guilford Press.

Lynam, D. (1996). Early identification of chronic offenders: Who is fledgling psychopath? *Psychological Bulletin, 120*(2), 209–234.

Lyons-Ruth, K., Alpern, L., & Repacholi, B. (1993). Disorganized infant attachment classification and maternal psychosocial problems as predictors of hostile-aggressive behavior in the preschool classroom. *Child Development, 64*(2), 572–586.

Magaw, J. (1995). *ATF's role in a GREAT program (Gang Resistance Education Training).* Washington, DC: Bureau of Alcohol, Tobacco and Firearms.

Magmer, E., & Ipfling, H. (1973). On the problem of specific social class punishments. *Scientia Paedagogica Experimentalis, 10*(2), 170–192.

Makepeace, J. M. (1981). Courtship violence among college students. *Family Relations, 30*(1), 97–102.

Malamuth, N. (1992). Evolution and laboratory research on men's sexual arousal: What do the data show and how can we explain them? *Behavioral and Brain Sciences, 15*(2), 394–397.

Malamuth, N., & Brown, L. (1994). Sexually aggressive men's perceptions of women's communications: Testing three explanations. *Journal of Personality and Social Psychology, 67*(4), 699–713.

Mann, C. R. (1992). Female murderers and their motives: A tale of two cities. In E. C. Viano (Ed.), *Intimate violence: Interdisciplinary perspectives* (pp. 73–81). Washington, DC: Hemisphere.

Mannarino, A., & Cohen, J. (1986). A clinical-demographic study of sexually abused children. *Child Abuse & Neglect, 10*, 17–23.

Manuck, S., Flory, J., McCaffrey, J., Matthews, K., Mann, J., & Muldoon, M. (1998). Aggression, impulsivity, and central nervous system serotonergic responsivity in a nonpatient sample. *Neuropsychopharmacology, 19*(4), 287–299.

Mark, V. H., & Ervin, F. R. (1970). *Violence and the brain.* Hagerstown, MD: Harper & Row.

Marks, A. (1999). Violence at home vs. on the street: A link? *Christian Science Monitor, 91*(212), 3.

Marks, C., Glaser, B., Glass, J. B., & Home, A. M. (2001). Effects of witnessing severe marital discord on children's social competence and behavioral problems. *Family Journal, 9*(2), 94–102.

Marshall, W. L., & Barbaree, H. E. (1988). An outpatient treatment program for child molesters. In R. A. Prentky & V. L. Quinsey (Eds.), *Human sexual aggression: Current perspectives* (pp. 205–215). New York: New York Academy of Sciences.

Matthys, W., Cohen-Kettenis, P., & Berkhout, J. (1994). Boys' and girls' perceptions of peers in middle childhood: Differences and similarities. *Journal of Genetic Psychology, 155*(1), 15–25.

Maurer, A. (1974). Corporal punishment. *American Psychologist, 29,* 614–626.

Mawson, A. R. (1999). Reinterpreting physical violence: Outcome of intense stimulation-seeking behavior. *Academic Emergency Medicine, 6*(8), 863–865.

Maxwell, S. R. (2001). A focus on familial strain: Antisocial behavior and delinquency in Filipino society. *Sociological Inquiry, 71*(3), 265–293.

McBurnett, K., Lahey, B., Rathouz, P., & Loeber, R. (2000). Low salivary cortisol and persistent aggression in boys referred for disruptive behavior. *Archives of General Psychiatry, 57*(1), 38–43.

McCahill, T., Meyer, L. C., & Fishman, A. M. (1979). *The aftermath of rape.* Lexington, MA: D.C. Heath.

McCord, J. (1979). Some child-rearing antecedents of criminal behavior in adult men. *Journal of Personality and Social Psychology, 37*(9), 1477–1486.

McCord, J. (1988). Parental aggressiveness and physical punishment in long-term perspective. In G. T. Hotaling, D. Finkelhor, J. T. Kirkpatrick, & M. A. Straus (Eds.), *Family abuse and its consequences: New directions in research* (pp. 91–98). Newbury Park, CA: Sage Publications.

McEvoy, A., & Welker, R. (2000). Antisocial behavior, academic failure, and school climate: A critical review. *Journal of Emotional and Behavioral Disorders, 8*(3), 130–141.

McGuffin, P., & Thapar, A. (1997). Genetic basis of bad behavior in adolescents. *The Lancet, 350,* 411–412.

McKinney, K. C. (1988). Juvenile gangs: Crime and drug trafficking. *Juvenile Justice Bulletin, September,* 1–8.

McNulty, C., Cahil, K., & Tom, M. (1999). Attempted child-stealing: Post-ictal psychosis and psychological distress. *Medicine, Science and the Law, 39*(2), 146–152.

Mednick, S. A., Gabrielli, W., & Hutchings, B. (1984). Genetic influences in criminal convictions: Evidence from an adoption cohort. *Science, 234,* 891–894.

Mednick, S. A., Harway, M., Mednick, B., & Moffitt, T. (1981). Longitudinal research: North American data sets. In T. E. Jordan (Ed.), *Child development, information and formation of public policy* (pp. 14–25). St. Louis: University of Missouri Press.

Mednick, S. A., & Hutchings, B. (1978). Genetic and psychophysiological factors in asocial behavior. *Journal of the American Academy of Child and Adolescent Psychiatry, 17,* 209–223.

Mednick, S. A., & Kandel, E. (1988). Genetic and perinatal factors in violence. In T. E. Moffitt & S. A. Mednick (Eds.), *Biological contributions to crime causation* (pp. 121–134). Dordecht, The Netherlands: Martinus Nijhoff.

Mednick, S. A., Mura, E., Schulsinger, F., & Mednick, B. (1971). Perinatal conditions and infant development in the children of schizophrenic parents. *Social Biology, 18*(Supplement), S103–S113.

Megargee, E. I. (1966). Undercontrolled and overcontrolled personality types in extreme antisocial aggression. *Psychological Monographs, 80*(3), 149–210.

Megargee, E. I. (1982). Psychological determinants and correlates of criminal violence. In M. E. Wolfgang & N. A. Weinder (Eds.), *Criminal violence* (pp. 81–171). Beverly Hills, CA: Sage.

Meredith, W. H., Abbott, D. A., & Adams, S. L. (1986). Family violence: Its relation to marital and parental satisfaction and family strengths. *Journal of Family Violence, 1,* 299–305.

Mestel, R. (1994). What triggers the violence within? *New Scientist, 141*(1914), 30–35.

Miller, D., & Challas, G. (1981). *Abused children as parents: A twenty-five year longitudinal study.* Paper presented at the National Conference on Family Violence Research, University of New Hampshire, Durham.

Miller, E. (1998). Evidence from the opposite-sex twins for the effect if prenatal sex hormones. In L. Ellis & L. Ebertz (Eds.), *Males, females and behavior: Toward biological understanding* (pp. 27–57). New York: Academic Press.

Miller, G. E., & Prinz, R. J. (1990). Enhancement of social learning family interventions for childhood conduct disorder. *Psychological Bulletin, 108*(2), 291–308.

Milne, J. (1995, November 16). Girl, 11, testifies father watched, urged on rapist. *The Boston Globe,* p. 30.

Milner, J., Halsey, L., & Fultz, J. (1995). Empathic responsiveness and affective reactivity to infant stimuli in high- and low-risk for physical child abuse mothers. *Child Abuse & Neglect, 19*(6), 767–781.

Mind and murder. (1994, February 26). *The Economist,* pp. 86–87.

Modestin, J., Hug, A., & Ammann, R. (1997). Criminal behavior in males with affective disorders. *Journal of Effective Disorders, 42,* 29–38.

Moeller, F. G., Dougherty, D., Rustin, T., Swann, A., Allen, T., Shah, N., & Cherek, D. (1997). Antisocial personality disorder and aggression in recently abstinent cocaine dependent subjects. *Drug & Alcohol Dependence, 44*(2–3), 175–182.

Moeller, T. G. (1994). What research says about self-esteem and academic performance. *Education Digest, 59*(5), 34–38.

Moffitt, T. E., Brammer, G. L., Caspi, A., Fawcett, J. P., Raleigh, M., Yuwiler, A., & Silva, P. (1998). Whole blood serotonin relates to violence in an epidemiological study. *Biological Psychiatry, 43*(6), 446–457.

Monahan, J. (1992). Mental disorder and violent behavior. *American Psychologist, 47*(4), 511–521.

Moon, M. (2000). Mild concussion triggered kleptomania. *Clinical Psychiatry News, 28*(2), 30.

Moore, J., Vigil, J. D., & Levy, J. (1995). Huisas of the street: Chicana gang members. *Latino Studies Journal, 6*(1), 27–49.

Morell, V. (1993). Evidence found for a possible "aggression" gene. *Science, 260*(5115), 1722–1724.

Moss, H., Mezzick, A., Yao, J., Gavaler, J., & Martin, C. (1995). Aggressivity among sons of substance-abusing fathers: association with psychiatric disorder in the father and son, paternal personality, pubertal development, and socioeconomic status. *American Journal of Drug and Alcohol Abuse, 21*(2), 195–209.

Mpofu, E., & Crystal, R. (2001). Conduct disorder in children: Challenges, and prospective cognitive behavioural treatments. *Counselling Psychology Quarterly, 14*(1), 21–34.

Mueller, C. W. (1983). Environmental stressors and aggressive behavior. In R. G. Geen & E. I. Donnerstein (Eds.), *Aggression: Theoretical and empirical reviews* (Vol. 2, pp. 213–245). New York: Academic Press.

Mueller, M. M., Wilczynski, S. M., Moore, J. W., Fusilier, I., & Trahant, D. (2001). Antecedent manipulations in a tangible condition: Effects of stimulus preference on aggression. *Journal of Applied Behavior Analysis, 34*(2), 237–239.

Muhajarine, N., & D'Arcy, C. (1999). Physical abuse during pregnancy: prevalence and risk factors. *Canadian Medical Association Journal, 160*(7), 1007–1012.

Mydans, S. (1995, March 18). Gangs reach a new frontier: Reservations. *The New York Times,* p. 44.

Nada Raja, S., McGee, R., & Stanton, W. R. (1992). Perceived attachments to parents and peers and psychological well-being in adolescence. *Journal of Youth and Adolescence, 21*(4), 471–485.

Nagaraja, J. (1984). Non-compliance: A behavior disorder. *Child Psychiatry Quarterly, 17*(4), 127–132.

Nagin, D., & Paternoster, R. (1994). Personal capital and social control: The deterrence implications of a theory of individual differences in criminal offending. *Criminology, 32*(4), 581–606.

National Archive of Criminal Justice Data. (1991). *The national crime surveys.* Washington, DC: Bureau of Justice Statistics.

National Institute on Alcohol Abuse and Alcoholism. (1994). *Studies of alcohol-related impairment* (Report No. 25 PH 351). Washington, DC: National Institutes of Health.

National Research Council. (1993). *Understanding child abuse and neglect.* Washington, DC: National Academy Press.

Nettles, S., Mucherah, W., & Jones, D. S. (2000). Understanding resilience: The role of social resources. *Journal of Education for Students Placed at Risk, 5*(1/2), 47–61.

New, A., Trestman, R., Mitropoulou, V., Benishay, D., Coccaro, E., Silverman, J., & Siever, L. (1997). Serotonergic function and self-injurious behavior in personality disorder patients. *Psychiatry Research, 69,* 17–26.

Ney, P. (1992). Causes of child abuse and neglect. *Canadian Journal of Psychiatry, 37*(6), 401–405.

Nichols, K., Gergely, G., & Fonagy, P. (2001). Experimental protocols for investigating relationships among mother–infant interaction, affect regulation, physiological markers of stress responsiveness, and attachment. *Bulletin of the Menninger Clinic, 65*(3), 371–380.

Nichols, P. (1987). Minimal brain dysfunction and soft signs: The collaborative perinatal project. In D. Tupper (Ed.), *Soft neurological signs* (pp. 179–200). New York: Grune & Stratton, Inc.

Nickerson, C. (1995, June 4). "Stuff of nightmares" marks Canadian trial. *The Boston Globe,* p. 2.

Nolan, E., & Gadow, K. (1997). Children with ADHD and tic disorder and their classmates. *Journal of the American Academy of Child Adolescent Psychiatry, 36*(5), 597.

O'Leary, K. D., Barling, J., Arias, I., Rosenbaum, A., Malone, J., & Tyree, A. (1989). Prevalence and stability of physical aggression between spouses: A longitudinal analysis. *Journal of Consulting and Clinical Psychology, 57,* 263–268.

Olweus, D. (1979). Stability of aggressive reaction patterns in males: A review. *Psychological Bulletin, 86,* 852–875.

Ommaya, A., Salazar, A., Dannenberg, A., Chervinsky, A., & Schwab, K. (1996). Outcome after traumatic brain injury in the US military medical system. *Journal of Trauma, 41*(6), 972–975.

Orengo, C., Kunik, M., Ghusn, H., & Yudofsky, S. (1997). Correlation of testosterone with aggression in demented elderly men. *Journal of Nervous and Mental Disorders, 185*(5), 349–351.

Ornduff, S. R., & Kelsey, R. M. (2001). Childhood physical abuse, personality, and adult relationship violence: A model of vulnerability. *American Journal of Orthopsychiatry, 71*(3), 322–332.

Owens, D., & Straus, M. (1975). The social structure of violence in childhood and approval of violence as an adult. *Aggressive Behavior, 1,* 193–211.

Pagelow, M. D. (1993). Response to Hamberger's comments. *Journal of Interpersonal Violence, 8*(1), 137–139.

Pajer, K., Gardner, W., Rubin, R., Perel, J., & Neal, S. (2001). Decreased cortisol levels in adolescent girls with conduct disorder. *Archives of General Psychiatry, 58*(3), 297–302.

Parke, R., & Collmer, C. (1975). Child abuse: An interdisciplinary analysis. In E. M. Hetherington (Ed.), *Review of child development research* (pp. 509–590). Chicago: University of Chicago Press.

Parke, R., & Slaby, R. (1983). The development of aggression. In P. Mussen (Ed.), *Handbook of child psychology* (Vol. 4, pp. 547–621). New York: Wiley & Sons.

Parker, K., & Pruitt, M. (2000). Poverty, poverty concentration, and homicide. *Social Science Quarterly, 81*(2), 555–570.

Pasamanick, B., Rodgers, M. E., & Lilienfield, A. M. (1956). Pregnancy experiences and the development of behavior disorders in children. *American Journal of Psychiatry, 112,* 613–618.

Paterson, E. J. (1979). How the legal system responds to battered women. In D. M. Moore (Ed.), *Battered women* (pp. 79–99). Beverly Hills, CA: Sage.

Patrick, C. (1994). Emotion and psychopathy: Startling new insights. *Psychophysiology, 31,* 319–330.

Patrick, C., Cuthbert, B., & Lang, P. (1994). Emotion in the criminal pychopath: fear image processing. *Journal of Abnormal Psychology, 103*(3), 9–13.

Patterson, G. R. (1986). Performance models for antisocial boys. *American Psychologist, 4*(4), 432–444.

Payne, R. (1997). The V-chip—Victory or vendetta? *Contemporary Education, 68*(2), 114–118.

Peele, S. (1984). The cultural context of psychological approaches to alcoholism. *American Psychologist, 39,* 1337–1351.

Perse, E. (1994). Uses of erotica and acceptance of rape myths. *Communication Research, 21*(4), 488–516.

Peterson, R., & Baily, W. (1992). Rape and dimensions of gender socioeconomic inequality in U.S. metropolitan areas. *Journal of Research in Crime and Delinquency, 29*(2), 162–178.

Pierce, C. (1984). Television and violence: Social psychiatric perspectives. *American Journal of Social Psychiatry, 3,* 41–44.

Pillemer, K., & Finkelhor, D. (1988). The prevalence of elder abuse: A random sample survey. *The Gerontologist, 28*(2), 51–57.

Pillmann, F., Rohde, A., Ullrich, S., Draba, S., Sannemueller, U., & Marneros, A. (1999). Violence, criminal behavior, and the EEG: Signifigance of left hemisheric focal abnormalties. *Journal of Neuropsychiatry & Clinical Neurosciences, 11*(4), 454–457.

Piper, E. S. (1985). Violent recidivism and chronicity in the 1958 Philadelphia cohort. *Journal of Quantitative Criminology, 1*(4), 319–344.

Pirog-Good, M. (1992). Sexual abuse in dating relationships. In E. C. Viano (Ed.), *Intimate violence: Interdisciplinary perspectives* (pp. 101–110). Washington: Hemisphere Publishing Corporation.

Pisecco, S., Baker, D. B., Silva, P. A., & Brooke, M. (2001). Boys with reading disabilities and/or ADHD: Distinctions in early childhood. *Journal of Learning Disabilities, 34*(2), 98–108.

Pittman, D. J., & Handy, W. (1964). Patterns in criminal aggravated assault. *Journal of Criminal Law, Criminology and Police Science, 55*(4), 462–470.

Pizzy, E. (1974). *Scream quietly or the neighbors will hear.* London: Penguin.

Pliszka, S., Sherman, J., Barrow, M., & Irick, S. (2000). Affective disorder in juvenile offenders: A preliminary study. *American Journal of Psychiatry, 157*(1), 130–132.

Pliszka, S. R. (1991). Attention-deficit hyperactivity disorder: A clinical review. *American Family Physician, 43*(4), 1267–1276.

Pope, A. W., Bierman, K. L., & Mumma, G. H. (1991). Aggression, hyperactivity, and inattention-immaturity: Behavior dimensions associated with peer rejection in elementary school. *Developmental Psychology, 27*(4), 663–672.

Porter, S., Yuille, J., & Bent, A. (1995). A comparison of the eyewitness accounts of deaf and hearing children. *Child Abuse & Neglect, 19*(1), 51–62.

Potter, W. J., & Smith, S. (2000). The context of graphic portrayals of television violence. *Journal of Broadcasting & Electronic Media, 44*(2), 301–324.

Puzzanchera, C. M. (1998). *The youngest offenders, 1996.* Washington, DC: U.S. Department of Justice.

Radecki, T. (1989). On picking good television and film entertainment. *NCTV News, 10*(1–2), 5.

Raine, A. (1997). Antisocial behavior and psychophysiology. In D. M. Stoff & J. Breiling (Eds.), *Handbook of antisocial behavior* (pp. 289–304). New York: John Wiley & Sons.

Raine, A., Lencz, T., Bihrle, S., LaCasse, L., & Colletti, P. (2000). Reduced prefrontal grey matter volume and reduced autonomic activity in antisocial personality disorder. *Archives of General Psychiatry, 57*(2), 119–127.

Raine, A., Meloy, J. R., Bihrle, S., Stoddard, J., LaCasse, L., & Buchsbaum, M. (1998). Reduced prefrontal and increased subcortical brain functioning assessed using Positron Emission Tomography in predatory and affective murderers. *Behavioral Sciences and the Law, 16,* 319–332.

Raine, A., Reynolds, C., Venables, P. H., Mednick, S. A., & Farrington, D. P. (1998). Fearlessness, stimulation-seeking, and large body size at age 3 years as early predispositions to childhood aggression at age 11 years. *Archives of General Psychiatry, 55*(8), 745–751.

Rand, M. R. (1991). *Crime and the nation's households, 1990.* Washington, DC: U.S. Department of Justice, Bureau of Justice Statistics.

Rapaport, K., & Burkhart, B. (1984). Personality and attitudinal characteristics of sexually coercive college males. *Journal of Abnormal Psychology, 93,* 216–221.

Raphael, J., & Tolman, R. M. (1997). *Trapped by poverty, trapped by abuse: New evidence documenting the relationship between domestic violence and welfare* (773-342-5510). Taylor Institute and University of Michigan School of Social Work.

Reed, J. (1989). Mechanical Man: John Broadus Watson and the beginnings of behaviorism. *Science, 244*(4910), 1386–1388.

Reel violence [editorial]. (1994). *The Lancet, 343,* 127–129.

Reiss, A. (1975). Inappropriate theories and inadequate methods as policy plagues: self-reported delinquency and the law. In N. Demerath & O. Larsen & K. Schulessler (Eds.), *Social policy and sociology* (pp. 163–174). New York: Academic Press.

Rennison, C. M. (1999). *Criminal victimization 1998.* Washington, DC: U.S. Department of Justice, Bureau of Justice Statistics.

Resick, P. A. (1993). The psychological impact of rape. *Journal of Interpersonal Violence, 8*(2), 223–255.

Resick, P. A., Calhoun, K. S., Atkeson, B. M., & Ellis, E. M. (1981). Social adjustment in victims of sexual assault. *Journal of Consulting and Clinical Psychology, 49,* 705–712.

Resick, P. A., Jordan, C. G., Girelli, S. A., Hutter, C. K., & Marhoefer-Dvorak, S. (1988). A comparative outcome study of behavior group therapy for sexual assault victims. *Behavior Therapy, 19,* 385–401.

Reuters. (1995, November 21). Boy, 9, is charged in sister's killing. *The Boston Globe,* p. 11.

Reuters. (1995, November 27). NY police allege copycat subway blast. *The Boston Globe,* p. 3.

Rice, M., Chaplin, T. C., Harris, G. T., & Coutts, J. (1994). Empathy for the victim and sexual arousal among rapists and nonrapists. *Journal of Interpersonal Violence, 9*(4), 435–450.

Rigdon, J., & Tapia, F. (1977). Children who are cruel to animals: A follow-up study. *Journal of Operational Psychology, 8,* 27–36.

Ritalin study could enhance ADHD diagnosis, treatment. (2001). *Mental Health Weekly, 11*(4), 6.

Ritchie, K. (1989). The little woman meets son of DSM-III. *Journal of Medicine and Philosophy, 14*(6), 695–709.

Rivera, B., & Spatz Widom, C. (1990). Childhood victimization and violent offending. *Violence and Victims, 5*(1), 19–35.

Rizzuto, A. (1991). Sigmund Freud: The secrets of nature and the nature of secrets. *International Review of Psychoanalysis, 18*(2), 143.

Roberts, J. (1995). Sexual assault is a crime of violence. *Canadian Journal of Criminology, 37*(1), 88–93.

Robinson, M., & Kelley, T. (1998, August). *The use of neurological cues by probation officers to assess brain dysfunction in offenders.* Paper presented at the annual meeting of the Academy of Criminal Justice Sciences, Albuquerque, NM.

Rosenbaum, A., & Hoge, S. (1989). Head injury and marital aggression. *American Journal of Psychiatry, 146*(8), 1048–1051.

Rossow, I., Pape, H., & Wichstrom, L. (1999). Young, wet & wild? Associations between alcohol intoxication and violent behavior in adolescence. *Addiction, 94*(7), 1017–1035.

Rothbart, M. K., Calkins, S. D., Gunnar, M., Kalin, N., Panksepp, J., & Reiman, E. (2001). Emotion and temperament. *Developmental Science, 4*(3), 313–330.

Rothbaum, B. O., Foa, E. B., Murdock, T., Riggs, D., & Walsh, W. (1992). A prospective examination of post-traumatic stress disorder in rape victims. *Journal of Traumatic Stress, 5,* 455–475.

Rotton, J. (1993). Ubiquitous errors: A reanalysis of Anderson's (1987) "Temperature and aggression" (geophysical variables and behavior, part 73). *Psychological Reports, 73*(1), 259–272.

Rounsaville, B. J. (1978). Theories in marital violence: Evidence from a study of battered women. *Victimology, 3*(1), 11–31.

Rousseau, F., & Standing, L. (1995). Zero effect of crowding on arousal and performance: On "proving" the null hypothesis. *Perceptual and Motor Skills, 81*(1), 72–75.

Ruback, R. B., & Riad, J. K. (1994). The more (men), the less merry: social density, social burden, and social support. *Sex Roles: A Journal of Research, 30*(11–12), 743–764.

Russell, D. (1983). *Rape in marriage.* New York: Collier.

Rust, J., & Kinnard, K. (1983). Personality characteristics of the users of corporal punishment in schools. *Journal of School Psychology, 21*(2), 91–98.

Salzer Burks, V., Laird, R., Dodge, K., Pettit, G., & Bates, J. (1999). Knowledge structures, social information processing, and children's aggressive behavior. *Social Development, 8*(2), 220–237.

Sanchez-Martin, J., Fano, E., Ahedo, L., Cardas, J., Brain, P., & Azpiroz, A. (2000). Relating testosterone levels and free play social behavior in male and female preschool children. *Psychoneuroendocrinology, 25*(8), 773–783.

Sanson, A., Oberklaid, F., Pedlow, R., & Prior, M. (1991). Risk indicators: Assessment of infancy predictors of pre-school behavioural maladjustment. *Journal of Child Psychology & Psychiatry, 32*(4), 609–626.

Sargeant, G. (1994). Children with disabilities found more apt to be abused. *Trial, 30*(2), 87–89.

Saunders, B. (1999). Prevalence, case characteristics, and long-term psychological correlates of child rape among women: A national survey. *Child Maltreatment, 4*(3), 187.

Saunders, D. G. (1992). A typology of men who batter: Three types derived from cluster analysis. *American Journal of Orthopsychiatry, 62*(2), 264–275.

Saunders, D. G., & Size, P. B. (1986). Attitudes about woman abuse among police officers, victims, and victim advocates. *Journal of Interpersonal Violence, 1*(1), 25–42.

Scahill, L., & Schwab-Stone, M. (1999). ADHD is caused by families: Psychosocial and clinical correlates of ADHD in a community sample of school-age children. *Journal of the American Academy of Child & Adolescent Psychiatry, 38*(8), 976.

Sccente, D. D. (1993). RAP to street gang activity. *The Police Chief, 60*(2), 28–30.

Schafer, J., & Caetano, R. (1998). Rates of intimate partner violence in the United States. *American Journal of Public Health, 88*(11), 1702–1705.

Schneider-Rosen, K., & Cicchetti, K. (1984). The relationship between affect and cognition in maltreated infants: Quality of attachment and the development of visual self-recognition. *Child Development, 55*, 648–658.

Schonfeld, I., Shaffer, D., O'Connor, P., & Portnoy, S. (1988). Conduct disorder and cognitive functioning: Testing three causal hypotheses. *Child Development, 59*(4), 993–1007.

Schuck, J. R. (1974). The use of causal nonexperimental models in aggression research. In J. de Wit & W. W. Hartup (Eds.), *Determinants and origins of aggressive behavior* (pp. 381–389). The Hague: New Babylon.

Scott, C. S., Lefley, H. P., & Hicks, D. (1993). Potential risk factors for rape in three ethnic groups. *Community Mental Health Journal, 29*(2), 133–142.

Scott, D. (1995). The effect of video games on feelings of aggression. *Journal of Psychology Interdisciplinary & Applied, 129*(2), 121–133.

Scott, P. D. (1974). Battered wives. *British Journal of Psychiatry, 125*(Nov.), 433–441.

Sears, R. (1961). Relation of early socialization experiences to aggression in middle childhood. *Journal of Abnormal and Social Psychology, 63*(3), 466–492.

Sears, R., Maccoby, E., & Levin, H. (1957). *Patterns of child rearing.* New York: Harper & Row.

Sears, R., Whiting, J., Nowlis, V., & Sears, P. (1953). Some childrearing antecedents of aggression and dependency in young children. *Genetic Psychology Monograms, 47*, 135–234.

Sechrest, D. K. (1991). The effects of density on jail assaults. *Journal of Criminal Justice, 19*(3), 211–223.

Shalev, R. S. (2001). Developmental dyscalculia is a familial learning disability. *Journal of Learning Disabilities, 34*(1), 59–67.

Shanok, S. S., & Lewis, D. O. (1981). Medical histories of female delinquents. *Archives of General Psychiatry, 38*, 211–213.

Shaw, J., Appleby, L., Amos, T., McDonnell, R., Harris, C., McCann, K., Kiernan, K., Davies, S., Bickley, H., & Parsons, R. (1999). Mental disorder and clinical care in people convicted of homicide: National clinical survey. *British Medical Journal, 318*(7193), 1240–1244.

Sheley, J., Zhang, J., Brody, C., & Wright, J. (1995). Gang organization, gang criminal activity and individual gang members' criminal behavior. *Social Science Quarterly, 76*(1), 53–69.

Sheremata, D. (1997, May 12). Free to repeat the crime. *Alberta Report Newsmagazine,* 22–24.

Sheridan, M. (1995). A proposed intergenerational model of substance abuse, family functioning, and abuse/neglect. *Child Abuse & Neglect, 19*(5), 519–531.

Sherman, C. (2000). Brain changes appear early in ADHD children. *Clinical Psychiatry News, 28*(4), 15.

Sherman, D. (1997). Attention-deficit hyperactivity disorder dimensions: A twin study of inattention and impulsivity-hyperactivity. *Journal of the American Academy and Adolescent Psychiatry, 36*(6), 745–753.

Shields, N. M., McCall, G. J., & Hanneke, C. R. (1988). Patterns of family and nonfamily violence: Violent husbands and violent men. *Violence and Victims, 3*(2), 83–97.

Shihadeh, E., & Ousey, G. C. (1998). Industrial restructuring and violence: The link between entry-level jobs, economic deprivation, and Black and White homicide. *Social Forces, 77*(1), 185–206.

Singer, J., Singer, D., & Rapaczynski, W. (1984). Family patterns and television viewing as predictors of children's beliefs and aggression. *Journal of Communication,* Spring, 73–89.

Sink, C., Barnett, J., & Pool, B. (1993). Perceptions of scholastic competence in relation to middle-school achievement. *Perceptual and Motor Skills, 76*(2), 471–479.

Skodol, A. E., Oldham, J., Gallaher, P., & Bezirganian, S. (1994). Validity of self-defeating personality disorder. *American Journal of Psychiatry, 151*(4), 560–568.

Skrabanek, P. (1988). Cervical cancer in nuns and prostitutes. *Journal of Clinical Epidemiology, 41*(6), 577–582.

Slutske, W., Heath, A., Dinwiddie, S., Madden, P., Bucholz, K., Dunne, M., Statham, D., & Martin, N. (1997). Modeling genetic and environmental influences in the etiology of conduct disorder: A study of 2,682 adult twin pairs. *Journal of Abnormal Psychology, 106*(2), 266–279.

Smedley, M. (2000, December 7). *Equinox.* London, England: Channel 4.

Snell, R. L. (1992). *Women in jail 1989.* Washington, DC: U.S. Department of Justice.

Snyder, H. N., & Sickmund, M. (1995). *Juvenile offenders and victims: A focus on violence.* Washington, DC: National Center for Juvenile Justice.

Soler, H., Vinayak, P., & Quadagno, D. (2000). Biosocial aspects of domestic violence. *Psychoendocrinology, 25*(7), 721–739.

Solomon, C. R., & Serres, F. (1999). Effects of parental verbal aggression on children's self-esteem and school marks. *Child Abuse & Neglect: The International Journal, 23*(4), 339–351.

Sorenson, S., & Siegel, J. (1992). Gender, ethnicity, and sexual assaults: Findings from a Los Angeles study. *Journal of Social Issues, 48*(1), 93–105.

Sorenson, S., & White, J. (1992). Adult sexual assault: Overview of research. *Journal of Social Issues, 48*(1), 1–9.

Spatz Widom, C. (1989a). Child abuse, neglect, and violent criminal behavior. *Criminology, 272,* 251–271.

Spatz Widom, C. (1989b). Does violence beget violence? A critical examination of the literature. *Psychological Bulletin, 106*(1), 3–28.

Spellacy, F. (1977). Neuropsychological differences between violent and nonviolent adolescents. *Journal of Clinical Psychology, 334,* 966–969.

Spellacy, F. (1978). Neuropsychological discrimination between violent and nonviolent men. *Journal of Clinical Psychology, 341,* 49–52.

Spergel, I. A. (1986). A newer threat than ever. *American School Board Journal, 173*(8), 19–24.

Spodak, M., Falck, A., & Rappeport, J. (1978). The hormonal treatment of paraphiliacs with Depo-provera. *Criminal Justice & Behavior, 5*(4), 304–314.

Sprich, S., Biederman, J., Crawford, M., Mundy, E., & Faraone, S. (2000). Adoptive and biological families of children and adolescents with ADHD. *Journal of American Academy of Child and Adolescent Psychiatry, 39*(11), 1432–1437.

Sroufe, L., Cooper, R., & DeHart, G. (1996). *Child development: Its nature and course* (3rd ed.). New York: McGraw-Hill.

Stacey, W. A., & Shupe, A. (1983). *The family secret: Domestic violence in America.* Boston: Beacon.

Stanley, B., Molcho, A., Stanley, M., Winchel, R., Gameroff, M., B., P., & Mann, J. (2000). Association of aggressive behavior with altered serotonergic function in patients who are not suicidal. *American Journal of Psychiatry, 157,* 609–614.

Steinmetz, S. (1979). Disciplinary techniques and their relationship to aggressiveness, dependency, and conscience. In W. Burr, R. Hill, F. Nye, & I. Reiss (Eds.), *Contemporary theories about the family* (pp. 405–438). London: The Free Press.

Stephan, J. J., & Jankowski, L. W. (1991). *Jail Inmates, 1990.* Washington, DC: U.S. Department of Justice.

Stephens, R. D. (1994, January 1). Gangs, guns, and school violence (the young desperadoes) (Cover Story). *USA Today, 122*(2584), 29–33.

Stephenson, F. (1996). The algebra of aggression (research in review), [online]. *http://www.research.fsu.edu/ResearchR/spring96/features/algebra.html,* University of Florida [May, 2000].

Stets, J. E., & Straus, M. A. (1990a). Gender differences in reporting marital violence and its medical and psychological consequences. In M. A. Straus & R. J. Gelles (Eds.), *Physical violence in American families* (pp. 151–166). New Brunswick, NJ: Transaction.

Stets, J., & Straus, M. A. (1990b). The marriage license as a hitting license: A comparison of assaults in dating, cohabiting and married couples. In M. A. Straus & R. J. Gelles (Eds.), *Physical violence in American families* (pp. 227–241). New Brunswick, NJ: Transaction.

Stevens, D., Charman, T., & Blair, R. J. R. (2001). Recognition of emotion in facial expressions and vocal tones in children with psychopathic tendencies. *Journal of Genetic Psychology, 162*(2), 201–212.

Stover, D. (1986). A newer threat than ever. *American School Board Journal, 173*(8), 19–24.

Strasburger, V. (1985). When parents ask about the influence of TV on their kids. *Contemporary Pediatrics, May,* 18–30.

Straus, M. (1983). Ordinary violence, child abuse, and wife-beating: What do they have in common? In D. Finkelhor, R. Gelles, G. Hotaling, & M. Straus (Eds.), *The dark side of families: Current family violence research* (pp. 213–234). Beverly Hills, CA: Sage.

Straus, M. (1985). Family training in crime and violence. In A. J. Lincoln & M. A. Straus (Eds.), *Crime and the family* (pp. 164–185). Springfield, IL: Thomas.

Straus, M. A. (1976). Sexual inequality, cultural norms, and wife-beating. *Victimology, 1*(Spring), 54–76.

Straus, M. A. (1991). *Bibliography of the conflicts tactics scale.* Durham, NH: University of New Hampshire Press.

Straus, M. A. (1992). Family violence. In E. F. Borgatta & M. L. Borgatta (Eds.), *Encyclopedia of sociology* (Vol. 3, pp. 682–689). New York: Macmillan.

Straus, M. A., & Gelles, R. J. (1986). Societal change and change in family violence from 1975 to 1985 as revealed by two national surveys. *Journal of Marriage and the Family, 48,* 465–479.

Straus, M. A., & Gelles, R. J. (1988). How violent are American families? Estimates from the National Family Violence Resurvey and other studies. In G. T. Hotaling, D. Finkelhor, J. T. Kirkpatrick, & M. A. Straus (Eds.), *Family abuse and its consequences: New directions in research* (pp. 14–37). Newbury Park: Sage Publications.

Straus, M. A., & Gelles, R. J. (1990). *Physical violence in American families.* New Brunswick, NJ: Transaction.

Straus, M. A., Gelles, R. J., & Steinmetz, S. K. (1980). *Behind closed doors: Violence in the American family.* New York: Doubleday.

Straus, M. A., & Hotaling, G. (1980). Culture, social organization, and irony in the study of family violence. In M. A. Straus (Ed.), *The social causes of husband–wife violence* (pp. 3–22). Minneapolis: University of Minnesota Press.

Stringer, S. J., Morton, R. C., & Bonikowski, M. H. (1999). Learning disabled students: Using process writing to build autonomy and self esteem. *Journal of Instructional Psychology, 26*(3), 196–201.

Struckman-Johnson, C., & Struckman-Johnson, D. (1992). Acceptance of male rape myths among college men and women. *Sex Roles: A Journal of Research, 27*(3/4), 85–101.

Sullivan, C. M., Davidson, W. S., Basta, J., Rumptz, M., Tan, C., & Geml, G. (1991). *Women escaping abuse: Their changing needs over time.* Paper presented at the American Psychological Association Convention, San Francisco, CA.

Sutherland, E. H. (1947). *Principles of criminology* (4th ed.). Philadelphia: Lippincott.

Swagerty, D., Takahashi, P., & Evans, J. (1999). Elder mistreatment. *American Family Physician, 59*(10), 2804–2808.

Swedo, S., Leonard, H., Garvey, M., Mittleman, B., Allen, A., Perlmutter, S., Dow, S., Zamkoff, J., Dubbert, B., & Lougee, L. (1998). Strep throat bacteria linked to hyperactivity. *American Journal of Psychiatry, 155*(2), 264–271.

Tanner, D. E. (2001). The learning disabled: A distinct population of students. *Education, 121*(4), 795–799.

Tardiff, K., & Marzuk, P. M. (1996). Violence by patients admitted to a private psychiatric hospital. *American Journal of Psychiatry, 154*(1), 88–94.

Tauber, E., Meda, C., & Vitro, V. (1977). Child ill-treatment as considered by the Italian criminal and civil codes. *Child Abuse and Neglect, 1*(1), 149–152.

Taus, M. (1995, November 30). Twenty years later, man admits to 2 murders. *The Boston Globe,* p. B3.

Taylor, E., Chadwick, O., Heptinstall, E., & Danckaerts, M. (1996). Hyperactive kids: Growing up is no cure. *Journal of the American Academy of Child and Adolescent Psychiatry, 35*(9), 67–91.

Taylor, S. P., Schmutte, G. T., Leonard, K. E., & Cranston, J. (1979). The effects of alcohol and extreme provocation on the use of highly noxious shock. *Motivation and Emotion, 3,* 73–81.

Taylor, S. P., & Sears, J. D. (1988). The effects of alcohol and persuasive social pressure on human physical aggression. *Aggressive Behavior, 14,* 237–244.

Thomas, J. D., Garrision, C., Slawecki, C., Elhers, C., & Riely, E. (2000). Nicotine exposure during the neonatal brain growth spurt produces hyperactivity in preweaning rats. *Neurotoxicology and Teratology, 22*(5), 695–701.

Thornberry, T., & Farnworth, M. (1982). Social correlates of criminal involvement: Further evidence on the relationship between social status and criminal behavior. *American Sociological Review, 47,* 505–518.

Thornhill, R., & Thornhill, N. W. (1992). The evolutionary psychology of men's coercive sexuality. *Behavioral and Brain Sciences, 15*(2), 363–376.

Tittle, C., Villemez, W., & Smith, D. (1978). The myth of social class and criminality: An empirical assessment of the empirical evidence. *American Sociological Review, 43,* 643–656.

Tong, L., Oates, K., & McDowell, M. (1987). Personality development following sexual abuse. *Child Abuse & Neglect, 11,* 371–383.

Treuting, J., & Hinshaw, S. (2001). Depression and self-esteem in boys with attention-deficit/hyperactivity disorder. *Journal of Abnormal Child Psychology, 29*(1), 23.

Triplett, R., & Jarjoura, G. R. (1997). Specifying the gender-class-delinquency relationship: Exploring the effects of educational experiences. *Sociological Perspectives, 40*(2), 287–317.

Troy, M., & Sroufe, L. A. (1987). Victimization among preschoolers: Role of attachment relationship history. *Journal of the American Academy of Child and Adolescent Psychiatry, 26,* 166–172.

Tschann, J., Kaiser, P., Chesney, M., & Alkon, A. (1996). Resilience and vulnerability among pre-school children: Family functioning, temperament, and behavior problems. *Journal of the American Academy of Child & Adolescent Psychiatry, 35*(2), 184–192.

Tuckman, B. W. (1965). Developmental sequences in small groups. *Psychological Bulletin, 63*, 384–399.

Turner, C. W., Hesse, B. W., & Peterson-Lewis, S. (1986). Naturalistic studies of the long-term effects of television violence. *Journal of Social Issues, 42*(3), 7–28.

U.S. Department of Health and Human Services. (2000). *Child maltreatment 1998: Reports from the states to the National Child Abuse and Neglect Data System.* Washington, DC: Government Printing Office.

U.S. Department of Justice. (1988). *Report to the nation on crime and justice: The data* (2nd ed.). Washington DC: Author.

U.S. Department of Justice. (1990). *Drugs and crime facts, 1990.* Washington, DC: Author.

U.S. Department of Justice. (1991). *Tracking offenders, 1988.* Washington, DC: Author.

U.S. Department of Justice. (1992a). *Expenditure and employment statistics* (NCJ 148821). Washington, DC: Author.

U.S. Department of Justice. (1992b). *National update* (Annual Volume 1, Number 3). Washington, DC: Author.

U.S. Department of Justice. (1994). *Elderly crime victims* (NCJ-147002). Washington, DC: Author.

U.S. Department of Justice. (2000). *Criminal victimization in United States, 1998.* Washington, DC: Author.

Ullman, S., Karabatsos, G., & Koss, M. (1999). Alcohol and sexual assault in a national sample of college women. *Journal of Interpersonal Violence, 14*(6), 603–626.

Unis, A. S., Cook, E. H., Vincent, J. G., Gjerde, D. K., Perry, B. D., Mason, C., & Mitchell, J. (1997). Platelet serotonin measures in adolescents with conduct disorder. *Biological Psychiatry, 42*(7), 553–559.

United Press. (1988, October 21). Father of dead girl says beatings only "tough discipline." *The Fayetteville Observer,* p. 22.

Valas, H. (2001). Learned helplessness and psychological adjustment, Part II: Effects of learning disabilities and low achievement. *Scandinavian Journal of Educational Research, 45*(2), 32–37.

Van De Vliert, E., Schwartz, S. H., Huismans, S. E., Hofstede, G., & Daan, S. (1999). Temperature, cultural masculinity, and domestic political violence. *Journal of Cross-Cultural Psychology, 30*(3), 291–295.

van den Oord, E., Boomsma, D., & Verhulst, F. (1994). A study of problem behaviors in 10-to 15-year-old biologically related and unrelated international adoptees. *Behavior Genetics, 24*(3), 193–205.

van Goozen, S. H. M., & van den Ban, E. (2000). Increased adrenal androgen functioning in children with oppositional defiant disorder: A comparison with psychiatric and normal controls. *Journal of the American Academy of Child & Adolescent Psychiatry, 39*(11), 1446–1452.

Vaughn, S., Hogan, A., Lancelotta, G., Shapiro, S., & Walker, J. (1992). Subgroups of children with severe and mild behavior problems: Social competence and reading achievement. *Child Psychology, 21*(2), 98–107.

Vernberg, E. M. (1990). Psychological adjustment and experiences with peers during early adolescence: reciprocal, incidental, or undirectional relationships? *Journal of Abnormal Child Psychology, 18*(2), 187–199.

Viewing violent sports not a trigger. (1997). *USA Today Magazine, 126*, 3–5.

Vince, C. (1989). *Assaultive injuries.* (Report from the National Committee for Injury Prevention & Control). New York: Oxford University Press.

Violence and aggression in psychiatric patients [news]. (1999). *Harvard Mental Health Letter, 15*(11), 6–7.

Virkkunen, M., & Linnoila, M. (1993). Brain serotonin, Type II alcoholism and impulsive violence. *Journal of Studies on Alcohol, 11*, 163–169.

Vissing, Y. M., Straus, M. A., Gelles, R. J., & Harrop, J. W. (1991). Verbal aggression by parents and psychosocial problems of children. *Child Abuse & Neglect, 15*, 223–238.

Vitaro, F., Gendreau, P., Tremblay, R., & Oligny, P. (1998). Reactive and proactive aggression differentially predict later conduct problems. *Journal of Child Psychology & Psychiatry & Allied Disciplines, 39*(3), 377–385.

Vitaro, F., Pelletier, D., & Coutu, S. (1989). Effects of a negative social experience on the emotional and social-cognitive responses of aggressive-rejected children. *Perceptual & Motor Skills, 69*(2), 371–382.

The wages of crack. (1994). *The Economist, 332*(7879), A29–A31.

Wagner, M., Schubert, H., & Schubert, D. (1985). Family size effects: A review. *Journal of Genetic Psychology, 146*(1), 65–78.

Waldrop, M. F., & Goering, J. D. (1971). Hyperactivity and minor physical anomalies in elementary school children. *American Journal of Orthopsychiatry, 41*, 602–607.

Walker, L. E. (1979). *The battered woman.* New York: Harper & Row.

Walker, L. E. (1989). *Terrifying love.* New York: Harper & Row.

Walker, M. (2000). Causes of violence in children [editorial]. *Journal of Child Psychotherapy, 26*(1), 1–3.

Wang, A. Y. (1994). Pride and prejudice in high school gang members. *Adolescence, 29*(114), 279–292.

Ware, H. S., Jouriles, E. N., Spiller, L. C., McDonald, R., Swank, P. R., & Norwood, W. D. (2001). Conduct problems among children at battered women's shelters: Prevalence and stability. *Journal of Family Violence, 16*(3), 291–309.

Wasserman, G. A., Pine, D. S., Workman, S. B., & Bruder, G. E. (1999). Dichotic listening deficits and the prediction of substance use in young boys. *Journal of the American Academy of Child and Adolescent Psychiatry, 38*(8), 1032.

Webster-Stratton, C. (2000). Oppositional-defiant and conduct-disordered children. In M. Hersen & R. Ammerman (Eds.), *Advanced abnormal child psychology* (2nd ed., pp. 387–412). Mahwah, NJ: Lawrence Erlbaum Associates.

Weiss, B., Dodge, K. A., Bates, J. E., & Pettit, G. S. (1992). Some consequences of early harsh discipline: Child aggression and a maladaptive social information processing style. *Child Development, 63*(6), 1321–1336.

Weiss, G. (1990). Hyperactivity in childhood. *The New England Journal of Medicine, 323*(20), 1413–1415.

Weisz, J. R., Martin, S. L., Walter, B. R., & Fernandez, G. A. (1991). Differential prediction of young adult arrests for property and personal crimes: Findings of a cohort follow-up study of violent boys from North Carolina's Willie M Program. *Journal of Child Psychology & Psychiatry, 32*(5), 783–792.

Welsh, R. (1976). Severe parental punishment and delinquency: A developmental theory. *Journal of Clinical Child Psychology, Spring,* 17–21.

Welsh, W. N., Stokes, R., & Greene, J. R. (2000). A macro-level model of school disorder. *Journal of Research in Crime & Delinquency, 37*(3), 243–284.

Werner, E. E., & Smith, R. S. (1982). *Vulnerable but invincible: A study of resilient children.* New York: McGraw-Hill.

Wesley, J. (1994). Effects of ability, high school achievement, and procrastinatory behavior on college performance. *Educational and Psychological Measurement, 54*(2), 404–409.

West, D. J. (1988). Psychological contributions to criminology. *British Journal of Criminology, 28*(2), 77–92.

West, J., & Templer, D. I. (1994). Child molestation, rape, and ethnicity. *Psychological Reports, 75*(3), 1326–1327.

Whalen, C. K. (2001). ADHD treatment in the 21st century: Pushing the envelope. *Journal of Clinical Child Psychology, 30*(1), 136–139.

Wickelgren, I. (1993). Can TV trigger violence? *Psychology Source: Current Science, 79*(7), 8–10.

Williams, F., & McShane, M. (1999). *Criminological theory* (3rd ed.). Englewood Cliffs, NJ: Prentice-Hall.

Williams, J. H. (1987). *Psychology of women: Behavior in a biosocial context* (3rd ed.). New York: W.W. Norton & Company.

Williams, J. W. (1992). Understanding how youth gangs operate. *Corrections Today, 54*(5), 86–88.

Wilson, J. (1995). What to do about crime: Blaming crime on root causes. *Vital Speeches, 61*(12), 373–377.

Winder, C. L., & Rau, L. (1962). Parental attitudes associated with social deviance in preadolescent boys. *Journal of Abnormal and Social Psychology, 64*(6), 418–424.

Wolfgang, M. E. (1958). *Patterns in criminal homicide.* Philadelphia: University of Pennsylvania Press.

Wolfgang, M. E. (1983). Delinquency in two birth cohorts. *American Behavioral Scientist, 27,* 75–86.

Wood, R., & Spear, L. (1998). Prenatal cocaine alters social competition of infant, adolescent, and adult rats. *Behavioral Neuroscience, 112*(2), 419–431.

Wood, W., Wong, F., & Chachere, J. (1991). Effects of media violence on viewers' aggression in unconstrained social interaction. *Psychological Bulletin, 109*(3), 371–384.

Woodward, S. A., Mcmanis, M. H., Kagan, J., Deldin, P., Snidman, N., Lewis, M., & Kahn, V. (2001). Infant temperament and the brainstem auditory evoked response in later childhood. *Developmental Psychology, 37*(4), 533–539.

Yanagida, E., & Ching, J. (1993). MMPI profiles of child abusers. *Journal of Child Psychology, 49*(4), 569–577.

Yarrow, M., Campbell, J. D., & Burton, R. V. (1968). *Child rearing: An inquiry into research and methods.* San Francisco: Jossey-Bass.

Yates, A. J. (1962). *Frustration and conflict.* New York: Wiley.

Yegidis, B. (1986). Date rape and other forced sexual encounters among college students. *Journal of Sex Education & Therapy, 12*(1), 51–54.

Yescavage, K. (1999). Teaching women a lesson: Sexually aggressive and sexually nonaggressive men's perceptions of acquaintance and date rape. *Violence Against Women, 5*(7), 796–813.

Yeudall, L. T., & Fromm-Auch, D. (1979). Neuropsychological impairments in various psychopathological populations. In J. Gruzelier & P. Flor-Henry (Eds.), *Hemisphere asymmetries of function and psychopathology* (pp. 79–110). New York: Elsevier/North Holland Biomedical Press.

Yeudall, L. T., Fromm-Auch, D., & Davies, P. (1982). Neuropsychological impairment of persistent delinquency. *The Journal of Nervous and Mental Disease, 170*(5), 257–265.

Young, S. (2000). ADHD children grown up: An empirical review. *Counselling Psychology Quarterly, 13*(2), 191.

Young, T. J. (1993). Unemployment and property crime: Not a simple relationship. *American Journal of Economics & Sociology, 52*(4), 413–416.

Zagar, R., Arbit, J., Hughes, J. R., Busell, R. E., & Busch, K. (1989). Developmental and disruptive behavior disorders among delinquents. *Journal of the American Academy of Child and Adolescent Psychiatry, 28*(3), 437–440.

Zagar, R., Arbit, J., Sylvies, R., Busch, K. G., & Hughes, J. R. (1990). Homicidal adolescents: A replication. *Psychological Reports, 67,* 1235–1242.

Zajonc, R. B., & Bargh, J. (1980). Birth order, family size, and decline of SAT scores. *American Psychologist, 357,* 662–668.

Zebrowitz, L. A., Kendall-Tackett, K., & Fafel, J. (1991). The influence of children's facial maturity on parental expectations and punishments. *Journal of Experimental Child Psychology, 52,* 221–238.

Zobeck, T. S., Stinson, F., Grant, B., & Bertolucci, D. (1993). *Trends in alcohol-related fatal traffic crashes, United States: 1979–91* (Report No. 26). Washington, DC: National Institute on Alcohol Abuse and Alcoholism.

Author Index

Subject Index